D1706524

Life Cycles, Money Cycles

Life Cycles, Money Cycles

Using Your Intuition for Personal Power & Financial Success

Patricia Lynch, CFP

John Wiley & Sons, Inc.
New York • Chichester • Brisbane • Toronto • Singapore

Credits

The author wishes to thank the following for permission to quote from the sources listed: Alfred A. Knopf, Inc., from *Boxcar in the Sand* by Laurence Hewes, copyright © 1957 by Laurence I. Hewes, Jr.; *Business Week*, from various articles mentioned; Edward Dewey, from *Cycles: Selected Writings*, Foundation for the Study of Cycles, copyright © 1970; Edward Robb Ellis, from *A Nation in Torment*, The Putman Publishing Group, copyright © 1970; Scott Erickson, from *Futurist*, copyright © 1985; Jonas Salk, from *Anatomy of Reality*, Columbia University Press, copyright © 1983; John Skow, from "When the Great Developer Became Extinct," reprinted from *The Saturday Evening Post*, copyright © 1966; *Time, The Weekly Newsmagazine*, from "New American Land Rush," copyright © Time Warner Inc., 1972.

In recognition of the importance of preserving what has been written, it is a policy of John Wiley & Sons, Inc., to have books of enduring value published in the United States printed on acid-free paper, and we exert our best efforts to that end.

Library of Congress Cataloging-in-Publication Data

Lynch, Patricia (Patricia Anne)
Life cycles, money cycles: using your intuition for personal power & financial success / Patricia Lynch.
p. cm.
Includes bibliographical references and index.
ISBN 0-471-53998-8 (alk. paper) :
1. Investments. 2. Business forecasting. I. Title.
HG4521.L863 1992
332.6—dc20 91-41266

Printed in the United States of America

10 9 8 7 6 5 4 3 2 1

Foreword

Patricia Lynch has written an extraordinary book. As former Chairman of the Board of the Foundation for the Study of Cycles, I have long been aware of the importance of cycles in all aspects of life, including, of course, business life. "Every growing organism grows to maturity, levels off and dies . . . unless there is new life, new book, new ideas, new activity." This I learned many years ago when I first read the book, *Cycles: The Science of Prediction* (1947) by Edward R. Dewey and Edwin F. Dankin. Recognizing this principle, I was able to move my business ahead swiftly during downward trends in either the industries in which I was involved or the general economy.

Recently, *Smithsonian* Magazine reported that "more and more evidence indicates now that plants, animals, people, storms, businesses and even wars seem to operate on a fairly predictable life cycle." Research at the Foundation for the Study of Cycles emphatically supports this view as we discover that cycles govern practically all aspects of everyday life.

Although many of the ideas presented in *Life Cycles, Money Cycles* are not new—Edward Dewey, founder of the Foundation for the Study of Cycles, discovered many of the principles in his pioneering work—what is new is the practical application of cycle laws to everyday investment decisions. In addition, Ms. Lynch shows us time and again how a positive mental attitude, visualization, and action combine to open the treasure chest of secrets to our own personal power.

Life Cycles, Money Cycles is a delightfully clear and concise explanation of research that has been going on for over 50 years. Ms. Lynch combines the knowledge of cycles and her own personal motivational style to give us a timeless book that will be read again and again. Welcome to the wonderful world of money making.

W. CLEMENT STONE
Chairman of the Board
Combined International Corporation

Acknowledgments

My deepest appreciation to the Foundation for the Study of Cycles. Its dedicated work as an international nonprofit research and educational institution is invaluable to us all. The Foundation, the only organization of its kind in the world, is dedicated to the collection, analysis, classification, and dissemination of information on multidisciplinary cycle research. It is located at 2600 Michelson Drive, Suite 1570, Irvine, California, 92715; telephone: 714-261-7261.

I also wish to thank Steve Ross for his support of this book through its evolution, and Terry Brown for editorial assistance of the highest quality. In addition, I send my grateful appreciation and love to my beautiful daughters, Amber and Tiffany, and to all my friends, especially Christy Hehr, Loretta Hill, Wanda Hodge, Charles Metzker, Kesler Stivers, and Nettie Van Alstine, who have given me love and support through the creation of this work.

PATRICIA LYNCH

Lexington, Kentucky
August 1992

Contents

Introduction

Early in July 1990, a friend approached me at a convention, eager to share a recent business success. He had quit the corporate world the preceding year and started his own consulting business. In the first year, he earned $350,000!

You would think a man in his position would feel fulfilled and at ease with his good fortune. Oddly enough, he was tentative and unsure—he didn't know what to do with the money! He had made several investments, but none of them "seemed right."

Some of his money was in the stock market. In casual conversation, he told me that the market had just dropped almost 100 points. His broker had called him at the convention, urging him to buy more stock: "It's always good to buy when prices are down." My friend asked me what I thought.

Without hesitation, I told him that it was "my feeling" that the market would be down by fall or certainly by the end of the year, and that, in any event, now was the time to sell, not buy. He agreed; to him, my opinion "felt" more correct than his broker's recommendations. Instead of buying more stock, he liquidated most of his holdings.

At this point, you may be thinking that a "feeling" isn't much to go on when making investment decisions. To the contrary, I think that your "feelings"—your intuition and insight—are a crucial, albeit often overlooked, element in making those decisions. If you rely on "insight" or "intuition," you have to be confident about them. In my case, *knowledge of CYCLES* had already alerted me that the strong phase of the stock market was most likely at an end. This, combined with the countless details that I had consciously and subconsciously picked up while monitoring the stock market, synthesized into a strong and immediate *feeling* that the stock market was going to go down. I felt *sure* of it.

I had no idea that some two weeks later, Saddam Hussein would invade Kuwait or that, by fall, the market would drop 500 points. I just knew that I could trust my own intuition and my knowledge of *cycles.* You can acquire the same skills and the same confidence in making your investments.

Each of us has the potential, the "power within," to make successful financial decisions. If you think about this statement for a moment, you'll realize that it's true. Have you ever *known* that a certain new restaurant was going to pack people in? Have you ever felt *sure* that it was the right time to buy real estate or stocks? When time and tide proved you right, didn't you say to yourself, "I KNEW IT!" Most people have had at least one, and usually many, such experiences.

Unfortunately, in most cases, these insights go by without being acted on. I have had such feelings throughout my career, and I've been fortunate to be able to act on many of them. But I don't think everything has hinged on my having good intuition. I think my knowledge of cycles acts as the touchstone, both stimulating insight and giving me the confidence to act on it. When I am faced with a financial decision, I simply analyze the problem in the context of cycle movements. There are no precise equations, no word formulas telling me exactly what to do or when. Cycles are well-researched charts that show regular rhythmic patterns. They act as a point of focus for my thought processes—my insights. The knowledge of cycles can help you connect to your own abilities as they have helped me connect to mine.

Cycles aren't a magic box containing the bases for every financial decision you face. Many short-term decisions require common-sense interpretations of whatever information is available. But even short-term decisions are stronger and clearer when we trust our instincts and intuition, which are real sources of power. Using cycles can give you confidence in the power of your mind; cycles can help you to trust yourself and make financial decisions with confidence.

Many of us have been programmed to believe that the investment world is for experts only, that it takes multiple university degrees and countless hours of study to understand the world of finance and make money with the knowledge gained. We are faced with numerous products, markets, and alternatives, with a barrage of advertisements "guaranteeing" this or "insuring" that. We may need to save for our children's education, and we must plan for our own retirement. It is easy for us to become intimidated and to lack confidence and resolve when we make investment decisions.

What does it take to be successful? An interest in financial affairs; a willingness and a desire to learn the rules; specific plans; and *action.* We have far more ability in all of these activities than we allow ourselves to believe. Knowledge and use of cycles can stimulate both your interest and your ability, increasing the prospects of your success.

You already know more about cycles than you may realize. Cycles are everywhere. From the motion of the planets to the oscillation of light waves, our universe is governed by cyclical behavior. The cycles you will read about in this book are a lot like the seasons of the year. The seasons vary in length and severity, but their cyclic pattern is regular—you know, in general, when to expect a certain type of climate.

Farmers use knowledge of the seasons when they plant crops. The more carefully they plan according to the seasons, the more successful are their crops. By knowing the investment seasons—when an investment market is strong or weak—you have a powerful filter for your thinking. There is no need to consider risking money in a market when you know it is in a period of weakness. There is no need to be timid when it is in a period of strength. When a broker suggests an investment, *you* can determine its soundness. You can evaluate the product using your own judgment and intuition in the context of your long-term financial plan. It may be a good investment in the future, but is it a good investment now?

This book will present predictable economic cycles that can help you forecast economic booms and busts throughout the 1990s and beyond. You will learn of cycles in many investment areas, including real estate activity, interest rates, the stock market, commodities markets, and more. You will learn why real estate is truly the foundation for wealth, and how the knowledge of future years of strength and weakness will enable you to time your buys and sells and increase your profits.

This is true whether you invest in rental property or just want to buy or sell your own home.

You will learn about future years of strength and weakness in stocks and bonds. Whether you invest a major portion of your assets in these markets or simply want to know how to handle the investment options within your company's benefit plan, cycles can help; they can be a guide that will allow you to trust your own judgment in the financial arena.

Money is a means for the exchange of goods and services; it does not guarantee happiness. However, money is a powerful financial resource, and you can use it to convert your dreams into reality. With money, you can "purchase" information, travel, education, food, shelter, and FREEDOM. With financial security, more choices are available in your life.

You have the ability to make successful financial decisions. The knowledge of cycles can be your guide, your sextant, your connection to your own intuitive abilities. Perhaps cycles are the one piece of the financial puzzle you have not yet found. If investment success has eluded you in the past, the investments may have been sound, but perhaps your timing was faulty. This need never happen again. With the knowledge and use of cycles, there WILL be success in your financial future.

Part 1

Cycles as a Tool for Personal Power and Prosperity

Chapter 1

The Search for the Money Cycle

It was a turning point, a significant moment that remains as vivid in my memory now as it was on the day it happened. The year was 1977. I was sitting on my redwood deck, reading the morning paper, and enjoying the life-style I had created for myself. I had started with a small sum of money after leaving a teaching career in 1969. I was now living in my custom-built dream home. I could enjoy mountains to the south, a valley of lights to the north at night, and the protective boughs of massive California oak trees through sunlit windows.

Every day was like being on vacation. On the Fourth of July, my friends and I could watch six or seven fireworks displays at once. By 1977, I had amassed what to me was a small fortune—a net worth of about half a million dollars. With a little effort on my part, my fortune would continue to increase.

Or would it? My sense of security and well-being was shattered by a small headline in the morning paper: "Depression due in the 1980s if cycle theory holds true." I wanted to know more! If this "Kondratieff Cycle" theory had any truth in it, my newly found financial independence might be at risk. I had worked hard for my success, and I didn't want to lose it. I knew what it meant to be without money.

My parents had lived through the Great Depression and had told me stories of the incredible poverty of those years. Men had worked at Conservation Corps camps for a dollar a day; my father had been one of them. Whole families had lived in automobiles or in shanty towns made of boxes and tin. Listening to my parents, I had learned that banks hadn't always been safe and that the massive bank failures in the 1930s had advanced the creation of the Federal Deposit Insurance Corporation (FDIC). I saw how my parents saved their money and were afraid to invest. They had seen times when investments had zero market value and absolutely no buyers.

Reflecting on my own life, I wondered what might be put at risk in a major recession or depression. I had accomplished a lot since my childhood, and I liked the affluence I had earned. I had designed and built my "mansion" on the hill, and I wanted to stay there. My home and my life-style were, quite literally, a childhood dream come true.

FORTUNES PONDERED OVER PEANUT BUTTER

My dreams of being an independent businesswoman began to turn into accomplishments when I was eight years old. On Saturday mornings, I sold flowers from my grandmother's garden. But the small sum she paid me for my efforts and the allowance my parents gave me for completing household chores didn't feel like real money. Real money was what you earned outside the family.

One afternoon, on the school playground, I overheard a group of boys talking about making money. After school, they were going to the newspaper office to pick up papers to sell. When I asked them how much they were paid to sell papers, they said it depended on how many they sold. I asked how much people paid for the papers. A nickel, they told me. I then asked the big question, "How do you make any money?" They all laughed and said they only paid 2 cents for the papers. It didn't take a professional money manager to figure out that was a 3 cent (or 60 percent) profit for each paper sold.

After school, the boys went to get their papers and I went home to wait for my mother to return at 4:00 P.M. from teaching school. I pondered my future fortune over a peanut-butter-and-jelly sandwich, mentally designing a marketing plan. Soon after my mother arrived, I eased into my first solicitation for venture capital.

After explaining the situation, I asked to borrow 20 cents on the next Thursday. I reasoned that if I could sell half-wilted flowers on Saturday—they always began to droop around 9:30 A.M.—I could certainly sell informative newspapers on Thursday. If I bought 10 newspapers for 20 cents and sold them all, I could repay my mother and have 30 cents left over. I did this every Thursday for almost a year. Then we moved.

We moved a lot while I was growing up. My father was a construction supervisor, and we went wherever he had work. He supervised the building of those large tracts of starter homes that were so much in demand in the 1950s. Each project lasted about a year; then we would move again. I went to a different school almost every year, up to and through junior high school.

In my next money-making venture, I became an independent entrepreneur, a baby-sitting tycoon with the motto, "Have books, will travel." It was an especially convenient way to make money: after the kids were in bed, I could do my homework. My biggest problem was staying awake during class the next day, and soon my mother made me refuse most midweek jobs. Still, weekend baby-sitting work provided me with money of my own.

Soon after I entered my teens, my brother got a job washing dishes at a drive-in restaurant near our house—burgers, hotdogs, shakes, and fries—a real classy menu. I was truly impressed with my brother's position. He had a real job and earned a real salary; he got a check once a week. One day, when I went to visit my brother, the manager of the restaurant noticed me. He asked my brother how old I was. Standing five feet nine, I looked a good deal older than my early teens.

My brother told him I was fourteen. The manager said I looked sixteen and that was good enough for him. He offered me a job working the lunch shift, two hours a day, four days a week. Who but a fourteen-year-old would take a job for only eight hours a week?

I loved it. Not only was I earning a real salary, but I got *tips*—cash-in-hand money that people gave me when I made sure their fast food was fast. I liked the money I earned from gratuities because it went home with me every day.

At the end of the second week, I received my first paycheck. I was very disappointed, not because of the size of the check—although it was small, to be sure—but because I hadn't received all of the money I earned. There were boxes on my check stub showing where money had been taken by people I didn't even know. (I set a goal to find out how to remedy that problem and became very good at it in later years, as you'll see in Chapter 7 where I discuss tax-saving strategies.) I decided I liked tips better. I kept what I earned, and there was a direct correlation between how hard I worked and how much money I made. (In those days, I didn't earn enough to even think about paying taxes on my tips.)

I worked a 40-hour week at the drive-in the next summer and at other restaurants every summer until I went off to college. It was my first taste of "real wealth," and I liked it. I had become quite experienced in the restaurant business and felt fortunate that I could always make a living. That knowledge provided an important sense of security. My parents had been unable to save for my college education; my mother had been ill for several years, and my father was no longer supervising construction. He had hurt his back working at one of the construction sites. My mother was working regularly again, but her salary as a teacher was just enough to pay the bills.

My high school grade-point average was 3.9, and I received a partial scholarship to Pepperdine University. Unfortunately, I couldn't swing the other expenses on my own, so, for one year, I went to Long Beach State University and lived at home. For my second year, I transferred to San Jose State University.

Many students think of their college years like a McDonald's ad: "Food, Folks, and Fun." For me, those years were: "Work, Study, and Sleep." Although my free time was scarce, I did manage some fun. I landed a part in a college variety show called "So This Is College?" Our troupe of 24 sang and danced its way through the seven western states. I won the Miss Greater San Jose Contest as part of the Miss America Pageant and competed for Miss California. That same year, I was San Jose State University's Homecoming Queen. My wardrobe for all these events consisted of borrowed clothes.

Supporting myself through college proved quite a challenge. My parents gave me some money during my second year, and I worked at three jobs to make up the difference. In one job, I read for a professor. I also worked in the university bookstore and in a drugstore on the weekends. Throughout my junior and senior years, I paid all my own expenses. I kept working and I obtained a student loan—and yes, I paid it all back.

After college, I did what all "sensible" women of that time did: took a job as a teacher, married, and planned a family. That takes my reminiscences to 1969, when I got involved in my first real estate deal. It was my first adventure with investment . . . and my first disaster. That story is reserved for another chapter.

Fortunately, I learned the lesson of my first investment "opportunity," and by 1977 I was on my way to financial independence. I had reflected long enough to know that I didn't want to start from scratch again. If Kondratieff's cycle theory could save me from financial disaster, I wanted to know *NOW*. I began the search to save my fortune—a search that led me to the study of cycles. Not only was I able to secure my personal wealth (when many people were losing a lot of money in the early 1980s), but I was able to increase my net worth. Because of my knowledge of cycles, even after I had to sacrifice considerable assets as part of a difficult divorce, I was able to send my two daughters to fine schools, treat myself to a three-year hiatus from work, pay the expenses of a severe illness, complete two separate master's degrees, and remain financially independent throughout. Thank goodness I hadn't missed that brief article.

DISCOVERING CYCLES

My local library was not exactly filled with books on cycles. Neither was the San Jose State University library nor the Stanford University library. There was ample information about the business cycle, but I was in search of the kind of cycles that forecast the next major depression.

Cycles are present in every aspect of existence, from the movements of galaxies to the functions of the human body.

Finally, I came across a book written by Edward R. Dewey and Og Mandino, *Cycles: The Mysterious Forces That Trigger*

Events. I was fascinated. I found that cycles are present in every aspect of existence, from the movements of galaxies to the functions of the human body. From astronomy to geology to biology, there is a rhythm, a pulse that ebbs and flows on a regular basis. In biology, there are cycles in tree rings, corn, cotton, rye, wheat, barley, peas, and pecans. The population of salmon in the Atlantic varies in cycles that predict three years of good fishing out of every nine. Even the suicidal lemming marches down the hills of Norway into the sea in a regular, though morbid, cycle.

There are also economic cycles. They are found in the stock market, real estate, interest rates, commodities, and the economy as a whole. I could see immediately that any cycle with a pattern that is repeated more than a few times couldn't simply be the result of chance. This was information I knew I could use.

AN EASILY UNDERSTOOD MYSTERY

Although Dewey was right when he called them "mysterious forces," cycles are easy to understand. Suppose you are at home, nursing a cold, and you turn on the radio. At 2:00 PM, the station broadcasts the news. Half an hour later, at 2:30 PM, you hear another newscast. At 3:00 PM, you hear another. Mentally you say to yourself, "Newscasts are transmitted on this station every 30 minutes." What you have observed is a recurring pattern, a cycle, in newscasts.

In this imaginary scenario, you can use your knowledge of the cycle for prediction, even if subconsciously. Assume your cold improves during the afternoon and you leave your room to get a snack. You miss the 3:30 PM newscast. You mentally note that if the cycle is continuing, the next newscast will be at 4:00 PM. The schedule may change; the station may only transmit one newscast an hour during commute time or may offer uninterrupted music during dinner time. Without advance knowledge of the schedule, you can't be entirely certain that the news will be broadcast at 4:00 PM. You can, however, predict the likelihood that the broadcast will occur, based on the number and pattern of past occurrences; that is, you can determine the *probability* of the event's occurring.

Cycles provide a concrete means to gauge the probability of future events.

Forecasting based on probabilities is essential to investment and financial success. Virtually every investor would agree that the time to invest is when as many of the odds as possible are working in your favor. As soon as you talk about *odds,* you're dealing in probabilities.

Probability is similar to rolling dice. If you have one die and six throws to roll a six, the odds are 1 to 1 that you'll succeed—you have a 50–50 chance of rolling at least one six. You may not roll any sixes, or you may roll more than one, but the probability of rolling at least one six is the same as that of getting heads when you flip a coin. If you have one die and 12 throws to roll one six, then your odds increase to 2 to 1 in favor of success; 18 throws, 3 to 1; 24 throws, 4 to 1; and so on. When you're investing, you should work *with* the odds, always attempting to keep them in your favor.

Many aspects of scientific study rely on knowledge of probabilities and odds. For example, when physicists predict the behavior of a given group of atoms, they determine the probable outcome based on the behavior of what the *average* atom would do. Physicist A. S. Eddington stated that, in analyzing the behavior of atoms, he "studies the art of the bookmaker, not the trainer." The goal for investments is to find a way to determine when the odds of success are highly in your favor.

The actual investment you are interested in may change very little—a house located at a street corner remains substantially the same for many years. Financial environments are different: they change significantly over time. Good investments can go bad because of events that are outside the investor's control. What you need is a method to identify the probability, *the odds,* that an investment environment is going to change. If you know the probable outcome of your investment environment in advance, you can increase the likelihood of succeeding with your financial strategy. That's where cycles come in, and you'll learn how to use cycles as you read this book.

THE DEVELOPMENT AND CREDIBILITY OF CYCLE THEORY

Although cycles of many kinds have been known for a long time, rigorous development of modern-day cycle theory began in 1931, when Edward R. Dewey, the young chief economic analyst of the Bureau of Foreign and Domestic Commerce, began looking for the cause of the Great Depression. He described his task with compassion:

> As a heartbroken President Hoover watched the country he loved falling apart before his eyes, I was assigned the task of discovering why a prosperous and growing nation had been reduced to a frightened mass of humanity selling apples on street corners and waiting in line for bowls of watery soup.
>
> I consulted with many economists and nearly everyone had a different theory to explain our economic sickness. It was almost as if you were ill and one doctor said you had gout, the next said you had cancer, a third diagnosed your troubles as leprosy, and a fourth said you had athlete's foot! If doctors disagreed about illness in this way, you would not have much faith in doctors. Economists disagreeing as radically as they did, I lost faith in economists, for none of them knew the answer.

For six years, Dewey studied cycles in search of an answer. In 1937, he joined forces with Charles Hoskins, former managing editor of *Forbes* magazine, who was advising industrial companies about cycles in business. Together, they formed a consulting company, and Dewey set out to sell their service. Because of their combined records and reputations, more work poured in than the two alone could handle. While researching cycles, Dewey discovered the work of Copley Amory, a wildlife expert and cycle enthusiast. They met, and together they established The Foundation for the Study of Cycles in 1941.

Dewey was a prolific writer. He wrote hundreds of articles and several books on cycles. In 1947, he completed a book with Edwin Dankin, *Cycles: The Science of Prediction.* It was on the *New York Times* best seller list for five weeks and sold well for many years. *Time* magazine called it "The latest and most understandable book on the cycle theory . . . Dewey was an accurate enough prophet to predict in 1943 that the boom would reach its peak in 1947." Arthur D. Gayer of the *New York Times* stated,

"Businessmen and students of economic dynamics alike will do well not to dismiss them [cycles] lightly."

As Dewey's research progressed, the focus of his work became more humanitarian than economic. He felt cycles would eventually answer some of the deeper problems facing humanity. For him, the purpose of cycle research was this:

> If these unknown (cycle) forces affect the behavior of human beings as they seem to, we find ourselves at the very core of the problem of wars and depressions. For if wars and depressions are not caused by generals, businessmen or politicians, as the mass of people believe, but are the results of—or at least are triggered by—natural physical forces in our environments, we are on the threshold of a completely different and extraordinary way of life for all mankind.

Whether cycle theorists will ever explain human behavior or allow us to avoid wars is not known, but the research goes on. Today, The Foundation for the Study of Cycles, through its world headquarters in Irvine, California, offers everything you ever wanted to know about cycles. The Foundation's library contains hundreds of books for examination and study; many others are offered for sale. (For membership, books, or other information, see the Acknowledgments.)

The Foundation has identified and studied thousands of cycles—everything from earthquakes in China to rainfall in Santa Barbara. Among the important economic cycles identified are a 6.3-year cycle in passenger car sales, a 33-month cycle in residential building construction, a 9.03-year cycle in insurance sales, and several cycles in the prices of common stocks.

Whether cycles represent a metaphysical key to understanding the universe or are simply observable phenomena doesn't really matter in the context of this book. What *does* matter is that you know that cycles exist, that they will continue to exist, that you can understand them, and, if you know what cycles to consider, that you can use them to your personal and financial advantage.

THE BASICS OF AN ECONOMIC CYCLE

One of the easiest ways to understand an economic cycle is to review the work of Joseph A. Schumpeter, who, in the words of one observer, was "one of the greatest economists of all time." Many economists feel Schumpeter's work failed to receive the acclaim it deserved because the U.S. intellectual community had already fallen in love with the work of the British economist, John Maynard Keynes.

Not only was Schumpeter a great scholar and an original thinker, but he also had a colorful personality and a superb sense of humor. Born in Austria in 1883, Schumpeter received a law degree from the University of Vienna in 1906. He held various important positions, including that of Minister of Finance of the Austrian Republic, before permanently relocating to the United States in 1932 to teach economics at Harvard.

His quick mind enabled him to read and absorb new ideas and facts with amazing speed, and he demonstrated a tremendous vocabulary in both German and English. His greatest work, the two-volume *Business Cycles,* was published in 1939. In addition to giving a complete historical account of three major economic cycle movements—the 54-year Kondratieff cycle, the 3½ year Kitchin cycle, and the 9- to 10-year Juglar cycle—this opus provides a historical account of developments in virtually every major manufacturing category.

In the course of his work, Schumpeter introduced the four-phase cycle model—prosperity, recession, depression, and recovery—to describe the recurrent pattern of economic activity (Figure 1.1). Based on extensive research of "business cycles," as he called them, he stated: "If our schema is to be trusted, recovery and prosperity phases should be more, and recession and depression phases less strongly marked during the next three decades, than they have been in the last two." As he predicted, compared to the past, economic recessions since 1939 have been relatively mild, while we have witnessed some of the most prolonged and

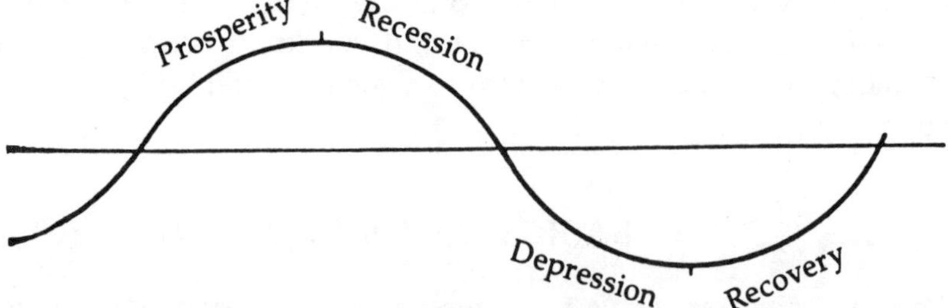

Figure 1.1 Schumpeter's Four-Phase Cycle

extensive periods of prosperity and economic growth in recorded history. Once again, cycle theory proved correct.

If you look at Schumpeter's four-phase cycle and substitute the words strength and weakness to indicate the basic trend for each cycle phase, then you have an idealized model that can be adapted to fit any valid economic cycle. This rhythm, this heartbeat-like pulse, can help you see probabilities in future economic trends. Knowing that economics was more than raw statistics, Schumpeter used to say that an economist who is not also a mathematician, a statistician, and, most of all, a historian, is not properly qualified for the profession. Luckily, you don't have to be an economist to understand and apply cycles.

PROFITS AND THE PRODUCT LIFE CYCLE

One very important cycle for business and investment alike is the life cycle of a product. Consider this example. Several years ago, Duncan Hines propelled the cookie market into chaos by introducing the new "soft cookie." Competitive companies couldn't get their soft cookie out fast enough, and litigation was rampant. Accusations of recipe stealing flew, and several companies filed huge lawsuits. Meanwhile, soft cookies overtook the market.

Today, soft cookies are still on grocery store shelves, but sales are nothing near what they once were. Soft cookie sales have long since peaked; the life cycle of the product is maturing.

Every product, whether it is a consumer item or an investment vehicle, goes through stages: introduction, growth, maturity, and decline.

Products, like people, pass through a series of stages—introduction, growth, maturity, and decline (Figure 1.2). During the introduction stage, a company spends a great deal of money. For soft cookies, the roll-out into the marketplace cost millions of promotion dollars, not to mention the expense for research and development. In the introduction stage, few companies make money, but the groundwork is being laid for future profits.

The growth stage is the time of action. Customers line up to purchase the new product as word-of-mouth induces people to "try something new." Other firms are quick to see the profit potential, and competitors emerge. It didn't take long for Duncan Hines's competitors to offer consumers alternate soft-cookie products on supermarket shelves.

As a product moves into the maturity phase of its life cycle, net sales proceeds begin to decline. The market becomes saturated with cloned products, and prices fall. Sales for each competitor eventually reach a lower plateau because so many companies are offering similar products. Profits decline as the competition intensifies. Eventually, supply exceeds demand and there is a product "shakeout." Only the strong companies survive.

Decline is the final stage. As new products and shifting consumer preferences reduce demand, sales fall off even further. Sooner or later, people decide to try a "new style, crisp cookie." The demand for soft cookies crumbles. New style, crisp cookies are introduced to take their place and a new product cycle begins.

It is easy to see the similarities between the life cycle of a product and the idealized economic cycle. What may not be easy to see is that investment vehicles are products. You buy a bag of cookies to satisfy your sweet tooth; you buy stocks in an attempt to satisfy your desire to make money. Like any other product, each investment vehicle goes through natural phases of growth

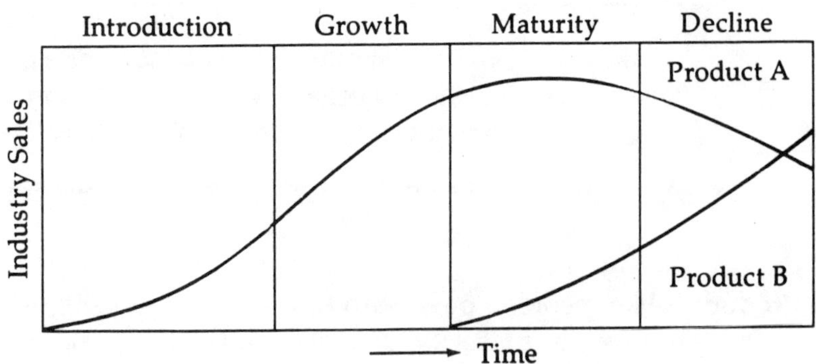

Figure 1.2 The Product Life Cycle

and decline and has areas of strength and weakness. That's why you hear so many brokerage houses say they carry a "full line of investment products."

Once you realize that investments are products, you can learn to time your purchases to optimize profits. Buying during the introductory or growth phase of the cycle will help you make more money. Buying during the maturity or decline phase will not.

There are hundreds of investment products to choose from, and making selections can be quite intimidating. The variety of choices reminds me of a scene from the movie *Moscow on the Hudson.* Robin Williams, playing the part of a newly arrived Soviet immigrant, has a nervous breakdown in a supermarket because he can't deal with all of the new and unfamiliar choices. Whereas he once had to beg, borrow, or steal to obtain the coarse, state-issued toilet paper of the Soviet Union, he now has to choose from dozens of brands. He just can't handle it.

I have found several easy-to-understand investment products that consistently make money. I don't always buy at the exact bottom and sell at the exact top—no one can do that—but by timing the purchase and sale of these investments, I receive maximum profits. Sometimes I choose not to be in the market at all, preferring to wait in the wings with cash until I *know* the time is right. That is good enough for me.

Cycles Are Not Perfect

The cycles I'll present to you in this book are well-researched. They all have occurred over and over again. The greater the number of waves in a cycle pattern, the greater the pattern's predictability. Some cycles have operated for centuries in spite of changing political, economic, and technological times. For example, the cycle of English wrought-iron prices has remained constant since before the industrial revolution, changelessly repeating itself through technological advancements like a trusted old clock.

Cycles are a tremendous resource. They give us perspective and help us to see where we're going. I'm reminded of the great lumbering station wagons we saw everywhere during the 1960s and 1970s, before the creation of the mini van. Early models of the "wagons" had an extra seat in the back that faced toward the rear window and the road behind the wagon. At first, the kids all fought over who got to ride in this rear seat, but before long these seats were empty. Everyone, even the kids, wanted to see where they were going.

Cycles also help us tap into our own unique selves. They offer us a visual aid, a rhythm, a beat to help us get in touch with that 90 percent of our brain we don't normally use. But they're not perfect. Sometimes the peaks and the troughs do not occur exactly on time. Some cycles move out of step with their own cadence. Any number of things can cause such a distortion: an especially severe winter or drought, an oil embargo, an international monetary crisis, or a war. *You can, however, count on true cycles to move back into their appointed rhythm as naturally as the seasons of the year.*

HOW CYCLES EXPAND MENTAL RESOURCES

You may already be aware of the concept that "thoughts are things." As Napoleon Hill says in *Think and Grow Rich,* "We are the masters of our fate, the captains of our souls because we have the power to control our thoughts—these magnets attract to us the forces, the people, the circumstances of life which harmonize with the nature of our dominating thoughts."

In a world filled with gloomy economic forecasts, currency fluctuations, rising and falling real estate prices, and a roller coaster stock market, it is easy to become pessimistic. Every day, we are hit with another wave of news that may contradict the news of the day before. I am convinced that our thoughts help shape our reality; specifically, my financial thoughts contribute to shaping my financial reality. Cycles give me the point of focus, the *optimism* to transform goals and dreams into actuality.

Knowledge of cycles can give you a point of focus, so you can use the power of optimism to transform dreams into reality.

Optimism is an important attitude for investment success: it attracts those situations, people, and opportunities that will be successful. This is true in all aspects of life, including financial life. I'm often asked "How can you remain optimistic and still be aware of the sometimes harsh elements of today's economic reality?"

Cycles can help. Because cycles show the natural rhythm of economic occurrences, we can always look forward to the up side—we can remain enthusiastic and hopeful. Even when the chances for future prosperity seem bleak, cycles show that eventually things *will* turn. Events are not linear, they are rhythmic. An awareness of this rhythm creates a mental environment that nurtures peace of mind. When you have this attitude, you are a participant, not a victim.

Cycles are an important aspect of my life. They nurture and sustain my own financial reality. I create a favorable environment with an optimistic attitude, which in turn becomes the fertile ground for the seeds that I plant with my thoughts. The events I create will "come into" my world in a matter of time. The clearer my perception of my goal and the more optimistic my environment, the shorter the amount of time I will need for creation of those events.

Cycles will not alter events, but they *will* connect you to the natural rhythm of financial affairs. With this connection, you will know that all events are taking place within a broader process of which you are a part. Being connected to this rhythm will allow your own creative processes—your own thoughts, your own intuition—to *realize* what you want. *You truly have the power within to make successful financial decisions.*

Chapter 2

Designing Your Financial Future

Planning for your future is important. It is where you will spend the rest of your life.

In 1922, Emily Post instructed that the proper mourning period for a mature widow was three years. Fifty years later, Amy Vanderbilt urged the bereaved to get back to the business of living within a week or so. Times *have* changed. Our view of time has been compressed because technological advances, which were supposed to provide us with more leisure time, have actually increased the pace of our lives. Beepers and car phones preclude a relaxing lunch. Fax machines eliminate the four-day respite that used to follow the mailing of a business letter. We are more productive and more *rushed* than ever before.

Digital clocks measure our lives with a steady hum, reminding us of deadlines in minutes and seconds. Television commercials sell us products in "sound bites," a new measure of time. Supercomputers operate at rates of one-trillionth of a second, a division so small it is beyond imagination. As we work harder to save time, the benefits returned to us seem to diminish.

The information age is accelerating the pulse of life. It is impossible to absorb, much less use, all of the new knowledge and events that occur each day. This is true in all phases of life, and especially in the world of business, economics, finance, and investments. A financial market is almost always open somewhere in the world, and the activity of one market affects all the others. No one, no matter what the level of his or her intellect or education, can keep up with it all!

As we grow older, our perception of time changes. Years seem like months to the fifty-year-old; months seem like years to the five-year-old. Scientists postulate that this difference in perception is due to an inverse relationship between metabolism and the evaluation of time. As metabolic rates diminish during the maturity and decline phases of the human life cycle, our perception of the passage of time seems to accelerate. When time seems to pass more quickly, it becomes more scarce and more precious.

With so much to do and so little time to do it, the problem of planning your financial future may seem overwhelming. I've been in that space myself, but then I found a way to evaluate problems and make decisions that allowed me to decompress time, to slow my life down, and to make each minute richer and fuller. *You* can apply this method to the process of planning *your* financial future.

CUTTING THROUGH INFORMATION OVERLOAD

If you find yourself constantly frustrated in your attempts to evaluate the overabundance of information available about planning a financial strategy, you are not alone. Millions of Americans ignore their financial future because they simply don't know where to begin. Since it is virtually impossible to gather and filter all available information on a potential investment, we must employ an alternative method that cuts through the problem of information overload.

***Intuitive financial planning* cuts through the problem of information overload.**

Intuitive financial planning is the method I use. It is a method that taps into personal power and engages at least a part of the 90 percent of brain power that is usually idle. It allows you to filter out unnecessary data and to select only the essential, important facts that are relevant to your financial future. It works without requiring days and nights of poring over prospectus after prospectus or hundreds of analysts' reports.

The method starts with motivating and developing your own intuitive perceptions so you can take advantage of them in your financial planning. What do I mean by "intuitive perceptions"? Your mind is a vast and powerful resource; for example, when you meet someone for the first time, you perceive literally thousands of characteristics and nuances of the person before you. In many cases, perhaps in *most* cases, you form an immediate impression, or "feeling." You may like the person or may feel uneasy. Quite often, as you get to know the person, you confirm that your initial impression was not only correct but was verified by events that later occurred. Mental events similar to first impressions are what I'm referring to with the expression "intuitive perceptions."

Saying that something is "intuitive" doesn't mean that it is mystical, illogical, or unreasonable. To the contrary, insights such as first impressions are partially derived from the largest data base in the world—the content of the subconscious mind. Countless facts, prior observations, experiences, values, and skills are stored there, below the level of immediate awareness. When a new person is introduced, a built-in program kicks in and evaluates the perceptions about that person. With lightning speed, the answer comes forth as an "insight" or "feeling."

Intuitive perceptions aren't always clear. First impressions are sometimes uncertain, and feelings about an investment can be equally hazy. The objective is to provide your mind with enough important information, give it focus, and then let it do its work. The simple, deductive, problem-solving approach is too limited: there is just too much information. We have to move toward a different level of mental functioning, giving the mind rein to link together many different ideas synergistically and to draw conclusions that are greater than the sum of their parts.

Simply stated, our *intuitive capability,* needs to be tapped in order to conquer the problem of information overload. If you can use with confidence the judgments that are formed below your immediate level of awareness and if you can develop and learn to trust your intuitive capability, then the apparently complex problem of designing your financial future becomes much easier and more pleasurable. (For a more detailed discussion of how to develop your intuitive abilities, see Chapter 3.)

PROBLEM SOLVING IN REVERSE: FOCUSING ON THE SOLUTION

If you want your mind to create a synergy out of your abilities, knowledge, perceptions, and creative capabilities, you need to give it focus; you need to let your mind know what outcome you want it to help you achieve. In other words, one of the best ways to get intuition working for you is to plant the solution in your brain and then work backwards. If you can successfully focus on the solution or outcome that you are seeking, your mind will automatically provide support—you will become motivated and optimistic about achieving your goals. Rather than focusing on a *problem,* which has essentially negative connotations, your focus will be on a future *solution.*

By focusing on the solution, not the problem, you will be drawn toward positive achievement.

To focus on a solution, you can use the technique of visualization—picturing in your mind what you want, so that your intuitive ability can help create your vision. This technique is well known in sports, where teams collectively visualize how they will feel when they win the game. Many stars in tennis and golf talk about how they "see" themselves hitting the perfect serve or making a thirty-foot putt, first in their mind and then in their game.

I've used visualization throughout my life. I saw myself in a dream home on a hill and I made that dream happen. I saw my daughters having their choice of colleges and that dream came true. I saw my books being published and you are reading these words.

Now you are going to visualize your goal, making that important first step.

What is your goal? Providing an education for your child? Acquiring a vacation home? Taking a trip? Let's use the education goal as an example. Begin by seeing graduation day. Make your visualization of the event as vivid as possible. Picture your son or daughter in cap and gown, college diploma in hand, surrounded by family and friends in a photo session. Picture yourself looking fashionable in the kind of clothes you have always wanted. Close your eyes and feel the joy, the sense of achievement, that you are sharing with your family. You have successfully provided for your son's or daughter's education. Your goal has been reached and you are grateful.

Now that you have visualized the goal, you *know* how it feels to reach it. On a subconscious level, your mind is already looking for ways to accomplish your goal and place it alongside your other goals. The next step is to feed your mind information so it can begin to put everything together.

Some of the information you need will require contacting various schools and inquiring about costs. Your child may be Stanford University material, but are the costs realistic in light of your finances? Ask the question, but don't consciously answer it; there may be ways to make it work that you don't know about. Next, make a list of possible schools. Include in the list some schools that at present could only be attended on a full scholarship, some less expensive schools that you might be able to swing, and those schools that you know are affordable. Six or seven schools in each category should be enough to get a handle on costs. You'll be investing about two hours' worth of work.

After you establish a total current cost, consider the effects of inflation. The cost of education at private institutions has risen faster than inflation (as measured by the Consumer Price Index) over the past several years. Prices at publicly funded schools have also risen significantly. For most schools, you should plan on a 5 to 6 percent increase in costs *per year* for the next decade; many universities are using a 7 percent inflation factor to estimate costs. Some simple calculations will tell you approximately how much you will need to reach your goal. Now it's time to start considering a plan.

AN EASY AND SAFE FINANCIAL STRATEGY

Assume you find that a full college education costs $25,000 in today's dollars. In 15 years, at a 7 percent inflation rate, you will need $68,975.78. Don't panic! I realize this is a lot of money, but you *can* make it happen. Keep your eye on the cap-and-gown day.

The planned purchasing of zero-coupon bonds provides an affordable, easy, and safe strategy to reach future financial objectives.

Zero-coupon bonds are one way to meet these costs. Zero-coupon bonds won't pay you any cash or yearly interest income, but they can be bought at a deep discount—well below face value. When you buy one, you know exactly how much money you will receive on the date of maturity. For example, bonds that mature in 17 to 18 years and yield a little over 8 percent can be purchased, as of this writing, for approximately $275. (In other words, you can buy the bonds now for $275 and in 17 years cash them in for $1,000.) If you set a goal of purchasing some of these bonds each year, you can reach your target.

Assume your child is three years old and will enter college in 15 years. In this case, you could try a staggered purchase plan. Starting now, purchase by the end of a year six zero-coupon bonds that mature in 15 years; your cost will be approximately $1,650. Next year, purchase seven bonds that mature in 14 years. The third year, purchase eight bonds that mature in 13 years. The fourth year, purchase nine bonds that mature in 12 years.

As the maturity date on zero-coupon bonds comes nearer, their cash value increases, so your investment in them will cost more each year under this staggered plan. To keep your yearly cost down, cut back the purchase to eight bonds by the fifth year. After nine years, you will have purchased 66 bonds. You will have a total of 66 zero-coupon bonds worth $66,000 at maturity. This amount is very close to your goal.

As a way to plan for college, zero-coupon bonds are very safe, and the amount of money you will have in the future is assured. That's the good news. The not-quite-as-good news is that, because they are so safe, your return on investment is relatively small. During the nine years you will buy bonds, you will have spent approximately $26,000. Considering that you planned on a $25,000 college bill in today's dollars, you will have not quite kept up with inflation. But if your tolerance for risk is zero, purchasing zero-coupon bonds is a good plan.

One way to increase the return on your investment is to diversify your choice of investment vehicles: put your money in more than one investment. For example, you could keep some of your investment safe in zero-coupon bonds and, after several years of buying bonds, change course and invest in a balanced or growth mutual fund, which usually offers higher returns. If you combine your average 8 percent return on bonds with, let's say, a 12 percent return in a mutual fund, you will increase your yield and stay ahead of inflation—and you will need to save less money to reach your goal. But remember, with mutual funds, there is *no* guarantee that you will receive 12 percent return! Still, a high-quality, blue-chip mutual fund with a good track record should give you a better return than bonds. (Mutual funds are discussed in Chapter 10.)

If you decide on this combination of financial products, then it's time to take a closer look at the next nine years. Paying for your child's education isn't your only concern. What about your retirement? What about that dream vacation to Europe? Look at other investment vehicles and consider the possible ways you could reach *all* of your goals. After you've read about the various investment vehicles discussed in this book, you'll be able to decide on a plan that fits with your new knowledge and your tolerance for risk. Bonds, for example, don't earn as much as stocks, but as a bond owner rather than a stockholder you will sleep better when the stock market takes a nose dive.

Another approach is to purchase mutual funds when the stock market is in an area of strength. (You will find out more about stock market timing in Chapters 8 and 10.) Sell the funds when the cycle moves into an area of weakness, and convert your investment into cash. When the market moves lower, you can just watch. When the weakness phase is finished, begin purchasing mutual funds again. Using this strategy, you could purchase stock market mutual funds for the year 1992 and money market mutual funds in 1993. (I'll demonstrate the reasons for the timing in Chapter 10.)

For 1994 and perhaps 1995 you would purchase zero-coupon bonds. Using your knowledge of cycles, as well as your rational and intuitive guidance, you would then consider purchasing stock market mutual funds again in the years 1995 and 1996 and money market mutual funds in 1997. By purchasing mutual funds for two years and zero-coupon bonds for two years, you have a simple and profitable timing strategy. You would have a choice of selling the funds during the years of weakness or riding through the storm. (Don't forget, cycles indicate that the market will eventually recover.)

THE SIMPLEST PLAN: BUY FIVE BONDS A YEAR

The simplest of all plans would be to buy five zero-coupon bonds every year for the next ten years, while making sure all the bonds you buy mature in the same year—the year you expect your child to enter college. (If you are aiming at another financial goal, have the maturity date of your bonds coincide with the timing of your financial goal.) With this plan, when your bonds mature, you will have $50,000 in cash to apply toward college expenses. The additional expenses can be met while your child is actually attending college.

If you invest in zero-coupon bonds, make a commitment to hold the bonds until maturity. As interest rates rise and fall, zero-coupon bond prices fluctuate more than conventional bonds. You may take a loss if you don't hold them until they mature. Use this potential "penalty" as an added incentive to keep the bonds until you reach your goal.

There are many other ways to meet college expenses. Several states issue tax-exempt bonds geared toward parents who are trying to build a tuition fund. Washington, Missouri, Iowa, and Minnesota have passed legislation allowing such issues, and North Carolina has issued tax-exempt bonds that work much like zero-coupon bonds. Tax-exempt bonds are especially attractive for people in upper income brackets.

Prepayment plans are another option. Parents of a three-year-old could pay the University of Wyoming a lump sum today of, say, $6,500, and the school would guarantee to cover the entire cost of four years' attendance for the parents' child in later years.

This is a simple, worry-free method to cover the costs of tuition, room and board, and academic fees. For people with the required amount of cash at hand, this method might make good financial sense. A four-year program at the University of Wyoming today costs approximately $15,000, so the plan effectively starts at a discount. It is also relatively risk-free. If your son or daughter doesn't go to the prepaid university, you get back your initial deposit plus accumulated interest. Michigan also has such a plan.

The numbers presented here are simply to illustrate the concepts. As time passes, the figures will change, but the concept will remain sound. If such a plan suits your needs, call universities in which you are interested and ask whether they have this plan. If they do, be sure to ask these three important questions: (1) What happens if the student doesn't attend the school? (2) How much money is returned if your son or daughter enrolls but drops out at a later date? (3) Can the funds be applied to various schools within the state university system?

Although visualizing a positive outcome, obtaining information, and setting goals are all very important, none of them will do any good unless you take the next step—*action.* Whether your financial plan is for a college education for your child, early retirement, or a world cruise, make a commitment to do something *this week* to reach your goal. Decide on a series of actions. Determine what month or months you will buy the bonds and how. Will you use your Christmas bonus? Your tax refund? An automatic transfer from your paycheck into a credit union? Keep reading, but start making your action plans *today.*

ANOTHER ALTERNATIVE: REAL ESTATE

Making real estate investments—buying rental property—is another way to achieve financial goals. Many professional financial planners ignore this alternative, probably because they aren't licensed in real estate and therefore can't make commissions on property sales. In all fairness, they may shy away from it because owning real estate carries more risk than do vehicles like zero-coupon bonds.

Investing in rental property is often overlooked as a method to plan for financial security.

If you are interested in owning rental properties, be aware up front that you will be reducing your leisure time; being a landlord will take up, at a minimum, a few hours on weekends now and then. It may entail making occasional arrangements and payments for repairs and other expenses. If you like real estate, as I do, this will not seem like work. For years, even though I was making a lot of money, I considered real estate a hobby—it was fun. If you can afford the fees involved, these problems can be overcome by using the services of a good property management firm. If you don't mind the side effects, real estate may be for you.

I'll give you an example, but remember that real estate values vary tremendously across the country, so the numbers presented here are only intended to show you the method, not the actual return. For your own purposes, use numbers that match the economic environment of the area in which you intend to invest.

Assume you are interested in real estate. You have done a little homework and located a good buying area where vacant properties rent within a few weeks. You find a single-family dwelling available for $50,000 (still possible in parts of the country). (There will be more about local economic considerations of real estate in later chapters.) A 10 percent down payment will cost $5,000—equivalent to the cost of several years of buying bonds. Interest rates are 10 percent. You decide to buy.

Before you go to the bank, you do a little research and a few calculations, perhaps enlisting the help of a reputable realtor. You find that you can get a 15-year, 20-year, or 30-year mortgage, which would cost $483.57, $434.91, and $394.91 per month, respectively. You would also have to pay for taxes and insurance. Your research shows that rents of comparable homes in the area will cover the monthly payment of a 15-year mortgage, plus taxes. You decide to go with the 15-year mortgage.

Now you own a $50,000 property on which you have a 15-year, $45,000 mortgage. Your research indicates that rents are increasing; in a short time, your rental income will cover not only the monthly payments, taxes, and insurance, but also the *maintenance* on the property.

You have made a commitment to own this piece of rental property for the next 15 years. Fifteen years from now, your son or daughter will attend college or you will be thinking of retirement. You have purchased a nest egg that will grow. Let's assume that the price of the rental appreciates 4 percent a year for the next 15 years. (This is very conservative. Assuming you pick the right area, within the right cycle phase, rental values have been known to go up faster than the inflation rate, which can be expected to run in the 5 to 6 percent range.)

In 15 years, your rental will be valued at $90,000! Because you took a 15-year mortgage, the property should be paid for, which will give you $90,000 in equity. If you took a 30-year mortgage, you will owe the bank $36,747, but you will hold $53,253 in equity; at resale, after closing costs, you will net about $50,000. If you took out a 20-year mortgage, you will owe the bank $24,561.41 after closing costs, leaving you a net of about $60,000. That amount will go a long way toward paying for your child's college expenses or meeting another financial goal.

You have earned this money by being patient—by holding the property for 15 years—and by taking the trouble to manage your rental property. You have turned $5,000 plus expenses into an amount between $50,000 and $90,000 or more. This could represent more than 1,000 percent return on your money.

The tax benefits that accrue to owners of rental property could save you $500 or more in taxes each year you own the property—a minimum of $7,500 more over the 15-year period. Depending on the tax laws at the time, you may also pay less tax on the money your property earns.

I know this formula works, because I have done it. My daughters are now completing their college education with money made from my real estate investments. If you are planning to retire in 15 years, buying rental property with a 15-year mortgage is an outstanding financial planning strategy. In 15 years, the property is paid for. After that, the rent money will belong to you, not the mortgage company. You can use this money to supplement other sources of retirement income. In addition, you are protected against inflation; you simply raise the rent as the inflation rate increases.

None of the approaches I've outlined is intended to be an actual plan for you to employ. Each one may or may not be suitable for you, but the point is that there are a myriad of approaches, all of them less complex than they might seem at first. As you read on, you'll understand more and more about how to design your own financial plan and achieve your investment goals. If you let these examples sink in and give structure to your thinking, you'll find it easier to form a plan as unique as you are.

UNDERSTANDING INVESTMENT RISK

Every investment carries *some degree of risk,* but some carry more risk than others. Some people can tolerate risk, both mentally and financially; others have a very low tolerance. It is therefore very important to be aware of each investment's potential risk/reward ratio and of your own level of risk tolerance.

It is essential to understand the potential risk, as well as the reward, in every investment you consider.

As a starting point, consider the investment vehicle risk pyramid shown in Figure 2.1. On the bottom of the pyramid are the safest, most risk-free investments: insured checking and savings accounts, Treasury securities (bills, notes, and bonds sold by the federal government), life insurance cash values, EE and HH bonds (newer versions of the old savings bonds; EE bonds come

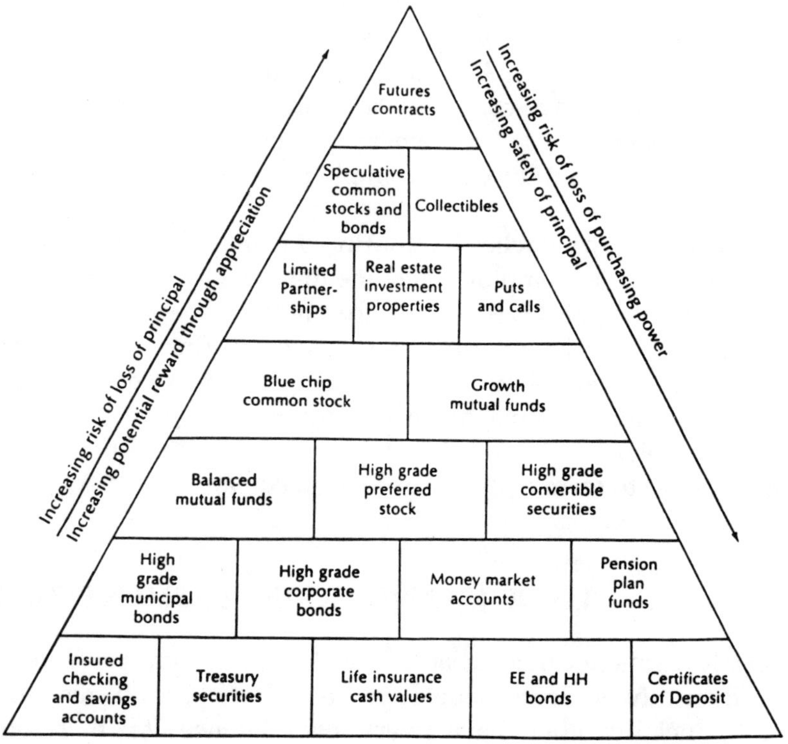

Figure 2.1 Investment Vehicle Risk Pyramid. Copyright by College for Financial Planning®. All rights reserved. Reprinted with permission.

in denominations as small as $50, and HH bonds start at $500), and certificates of deposit. In terms of safety of principal, there is no substitute for cash.

On the next level are investments with high liquidity—vehicles that can quickly be converted into cash. This group includes high-grade municipal bonds (bonds sold by cities to the public and given top rating by services such as Moody's and Standard & Poor's), high-grade corporate bonds (similar to municipal bonds, but sold by corporations), money market accounts, and pension plan funds. Although bonds are secure if held to maturity, they *do* vary in value from day to day. In that sense, bonds bought for liquidity can expose your investment dollars to a substantial degree of risk. In fact, many speculators make their living by buying and selling bonds on a day-to-day or week-to-week basis.

Medium-risk investments are found in the two middle layers of the risk pyramid. These include balanced mutual funds, high-grade preferred stock (stock issued by well-established corporations that carries privileges beyond those of common stock), high-grade convertible securities (corporate bonds that can be converted to stock at the discretion of the bondholder), blue chip common stock, and growth mutual funds.

At the top of the pyramid are six investments that present still higher degrees of risk. Real estate investment is one of them. If you are asking yourself why I have suggested real estate when it carries so much risk, the answer is that I would place residential real estate that is held for more than ten years in the same category as blue chip common stock. It is placed high in the pyramid because it is a nonliquid investment. If you want to convert your real estate to cash—sell it—it can take months to get the price you want. It is a relatively liquid holding at *some* price, but no matter what kind of bargain you offer, it takes time to close a sale in real estate. Common stock, on the other hand, can be converted into cash in a few days or less, simply by calling a broker and placing a sell order.

The other investment alternatives near the top of the pyramid are worth mentioning. Most of them should send up an intuitive red flag in your mind. Limited partnerships, for example, should most often be avoided. A limited partnership is an association of individual investors who pool their money to make an investment, such as buying an apartment building. On the surface this seems like a good idea. Many limited partnerships, however, only earn money for the people who run them (the general partners) and the brokers who sell them. In the fine print of many a limited partnership prospectus, you will see that the general partner and the management staff are earning enormous fees, even if the partnership itself isn't making any money or, worse yet, is losing money. For most investors, it's a "heads I win, tails you lose" situation. I'm not saying all limited partnerships are this way, but enough of them are that I stay clear, and I advise you to do the same.

In addition, limited partnerships have one of the highest commission structures in the investment industry. Commissions to selling agents are often in the 8 percent range.

This should tell you two things. First, those higher commissions exist as an incentive to selling agents or brokers. In other words, the brokers need an added incentive to "push" the product on the market. That alone should make you wary. Second, assuming that the commission is 8 percent, you automatically lose equity in your investment when you purchase it. It's as if you are buying a new car for $20,000, and the minute you drive it off the dealer's lot it is worth only $18,400 (which, by the way, is probably true!).

An even bigger drawback is that limited partnerships are not normally very liquid investments. Turning your shares into cash can be a nightmare. There is a very limited secondary market for selling limited partnerships, and prices vary on a daily basis. (A secondary market is one in which shares of the partnership are traded, bought, and sold, after the introductory selling of shares.) If you are forced to sell your shares in this arena, you will usually receive only a fraction of your initial investment. With single-family homes, at least you can improve a property to attract a buyer. There is almost nothing you can do with limited partnership shares. You are at the mercy of the general partner and the marketplace.

Collectibles are also found toward the peak of the investment vehicle risk pyramid. The world of collectibles is fascinating. It includes everything from 1950s automobiles to movie memorabilia, coins, dolls, baseball cards, and more. An original autograph by John F. Kennedy could bring $1,000. A glass marble of the rare, single-ribbon variety can bring $100. Prices for Elvis Presley collectibles are as high as his pants were tight. If your mom still has your 18-inch Elvis doll, dressed in plaid shirt, jeans, black belt, and blue suede shoes, you could cash it in for $2,000—if you still have the original pink-and-white box. Almost anything from the 1950s era should appreciate in value after the year 2000.

I wouldn't include collectibles in an investment plan for a critical purpose such as a secure retirement or college tuition. I don't actually consider collectibles a pure investment because a high degree of emotion is usually involved in their ownership. It's not easy to sell a collection that has been in your family for a hundred years, or that you've spent a lot of time and passion assembling. Collectibles can be considered an asset because they are valuable, but few of us can part with them painlessly.

Collectibles also aren't very liquid. They may be worth money to the right buyer, but finding that buyer can be a problem if you need money right away. If you have solid knowledge in a certain field of collectibles and can buy and SELL without emotional involvement, then they can be an enjoyable way to make money. Although collectibles should probably stay a hobby for most of us, there are a few experts who make a living dealing with what they know and love. If you are good at spotting future trends, you may already have a basement full of "valuable stuff."

A discussion of options (puts and calls), speculative common stocks and bonds, and commodity futures will be presented in later chapters.

Knowing the structure of the investment risk pyramid is just one dimension of the knowledge required to understand risk and put the odds in your favor. The cycle of your chosen investment vehicle is another, crucial dimension. In Part Two, I will present the most important cycles of key investment vehicles, to help you tailor your financial plan for optimum profits.

TAPPING YOUR RESOURCES

With this general overview of financial planning in mind, it is time to start filling in the blanks, providing the information you need to combine knowledge of cycle trends with your intuitive and problem-solving skills. The opinions and knowledge of others are very important, but ultimately *you* must design your future.

You already have tremendous power within you. You possess a wonderful form of creation, your imagination, and it can change your life. The key is to use it. When was the last time you consciously took some time to create the life you want?

Just as some people set aside time for their favorite television programs, I have planned times for my "visions." For me, the best time is just after I awaken. I schedule 15 minutes or more to create clear visions of my day and my future. Then I take at least one action step THAT DAY toward achieving those visions. The step can be as simple as writing a letter, making a phone call, or buying a book.

I also surround my visions and actions with a blast of positive energy. I know that my intuitive abilities will guide me toward the next steps. This positive expectation creates the environment necessary for me to unleash my own personal power.

In our abundant universe, there is prosperity for all. It has been said that there is enough fruit and vegetation rotting in the Amazon to feed the world. With resources literally lying around, left to rot, just think of all that is available to be used and enjoyed. Use your intuition as a guide to tap into your own abundant personal resources.

You create the quality and texture of your life with your thoughts. Neurospecialists estimate that each of us has some 40,000 to 50,000 thoughts per day. By choosing to concentrate even 1,000 to 2,000 of those thoughts on attaining your financial dreams, you will be creating a laser beam of energy that is focused on your goals. By concentrating the rays of your thinking through the magnifying glass of an action plan, you can ignite the light you've seen only in your dreams.

In your creative mind, your imagination, you already have enough information to start developing your financial future. Look not only at today and tomorrow, but at a time that is three, five, ten, or more years into the future. Visualize what you want, put your vision into action, and keep feeding those thoughts with optimism and positive expectation. Take one step each day to reach your goals. As you continue, your subconscious, your own creative energy, and your intuition will help you establish what you need to fulfill your dreams.

You have the tools to create your future. Begin today!

Chapter

3

Developing Your Intuition

The really valuable thing is intuition.
ALBERT EINSTEIN

Albert Einstein rewrote our basic understanding of the universe when he presented his general theory of relativity. An essential key to the theory is the relationship between matter and energy, in which energy equals mass times the velocity of light squared. Einstein found he could describe this relationship by a very simple looking equation, $E = MC^2$. Einstein said that he didn't *derive* the equation, but rather that it *came* to him. After countless hours of study, thought, and musing, one day he simply wrote the equation down, *knowing* it was right, and then backtracked to derive its mathematical proof. His discovery was based on *intuition.*

Everyone has intuition. Whenever you make a decision, you are, to some degree, using your intuitive abilities. If you reflect on some of the best decisions you have made in your life, you will likely find that, like Einstein, you didn't arrive at the decision by a conscious evaluation of all the facts. Instead, you relied on a "feeling" or a "hunch," but somehow you felt sure you were right.

Intuition is a way of communicating with the world, with yourself, and with others, without necessarily going through a rigorous process of deductive reasoning. If you are a parent, for example, you learn to "sense" your infant's needs without the benefit of words. You become aware that your toddler needs something more than a nap. When your teenager walks through the door after school, you definitely know when something is weighing on his or her mind.

Intuition is a way of communicating with the world, with yourself, and with others without following a rigorous path of deductive reasoning.

Pets offer us loving, nonverbal communication. You know when your cat is hungry, even if she is not pacing back and forth in front of an empty food dish. You know when your dog is anxious about another animal in the yard, even if he isn't barking at it.

Perhaps you have an intuitive feel for the weather, as I often do. You may find yourself "sensing" the coming of a storm when your subconscious becomes aware that the air is charged with static electricity and that the smell and density of the air are changing. You merge all of this information at a subconscious level and say "A storm is coming," without knowing how you reached that conclusion.

Sometimes, there seems to be no logical explanation for our intuition about the weather. I once invited a special business partner to spend some time with me in Kentucky. We planned to go to the horse races at Keeneland, one of the most beautiful tracks in the world. We had two choices: we could go on a Friday or on the following Tuesday. The newspaper had forecast cold, rainy weather for Friday and warm, sunny weather for the following week. Accordingly, we planned to go to the races on Tuesday.

When I awoke on Friday morning and looked at the sky, I *knew* it was going to be a beautiful day, and I had a very strong feeling that it would be cold and wet on Tuesday. We changed our plans and headed for the races. The day was perfect. I wasn't surprised when Tuesday turned out to be wet and one of the coldest days of the season. My intuition had proved to be a better weather forecaster than the National Weather Service.

You may be wondering what pets or the weather have to do with making successful financial decisions. There is definitely a connection. If you accept that you can *sense* the weather or can have an accurate "feeling" about your pet's needs, then it is only a small step to accepting that you can also sense or feel when financial decisions are positive or negative and can gain the confidence to *apply your intuitive ability* when making them.

If you are intuitive in one area, you can learn to transfer that skill to your financial investing and to all other aspects of your life. You can transfer your intuitive abilities as a parent, pet owner, or weather forecaster to enhance your financial judgment, as well as all the decisions you make in life.

INTUITION, GENIUS, AND YOU

Centuries ago, King Hiero II of Syracuse presented a problem to Archimedes, the Greek physicist. The king, suspecting that his crown might not be pure gold, charged Archimedes with the task of determining its purity. Archimedes was puzzled. How could he determine the gold content of the crown without destroying it in the process? He found the answer in a bathtub.

Archimedes knew that gold was denser than silver. As he watched the overflow from his tub, in a flash of insight he realized that an equal weight of silver and gold would displace different amounts of water—silver would displace more than gold. As the story goes, he was so excited by his discovery that he streaked out of his home without his clothes, shouting, "Eureka!" (Greek for "I have found it!"). He demonstrated to the king that his crown displaced more water than an equal weight of pure gold, thereby proving that it was made of an alloy, not pure gold.

Scientists are well acquainted with this "Eureka factor"—a sudden illumination, an instantaneous understanding that integrates all the pieces of a previously unsolvable puzzle. Although the scientific method of looking for a solution is strictly controlled and orderly, the solution itself usually comes in a "flash of insight." As Einstein put it, "There are no logical paths to these [natural] laws. Only intuition, resting on sympathetic understanding of experience, can reach them." He called the theory of relativity "the happiest thought of my life."

"There are no logical paths to these [natural] laws. Only intuition, resting on sympathetic understanding of experience, can reach them."

Intuition is a state of "knowingness," a feeling so strong that it makes most outside information seem almost irrelevant. For example, the scientific community spent two years preparing to test Einstein's theory of relativity during the solar eclipse of May 29, 1919. If the theory was correct, starlight would be "bent" by the sun's gravitational field, and this effect would be measurable while the sun was darkened.

According to biographer Jeremy Bernstein, Einstein was in Princeton when the results of the test were released. He had been speaking with a student and casually handed her the telegram from Sir Arthur Eddington, which confirmed the results. The student was astonished by his apparent indifference to the success of the experiment. "What if the theory had not been confirmed?" she asked. Einstein replied, "Then I would have been sorry for the dear Lord. The theory is correct." It was never determined whether he was referring to Lord Eddington or the Almighty; either way, he was sure of his theory.

Although most psychologists virtually ignore the subject of intuition, Carl Jung considered it one of four basic and equal psychological functions; thinking, feeling, and sensation were the other three. Jung regarded intuition as a mental element in all of us that allows us to sense possibilities and information not otherwise apparent—an ability to see that which is hidden.

Women trust and use their intuition much more than men use theirs. The commonly used phrase "Women's intuition" unfortunately gives rise to misguided scorn, ridicule, and humor. "Women's intuition" is nothing more than *human* intuition applied on an emotional level. The only reason that women are sometimes considered more intuitive than men is that our society teaches men to suppress their feelings, while women are encouraged to express theirs.

Research confirms that women tend to be particularly attentive to nonverbal communication such as body gestures and facial expressions, but there is no evidence that this is an inborn trait. It seems apparent that men *and* women who are in touch with their feelings tend to be more comfortable with the use of intuition.

An intuitive insight is more than just a belief. It is *knowingness.*

An intuitive insight is more than just a belief; it is *knowingness.* Even though the intuitively derived idea, discovery, or solution may not be immediately supported by data, there is no doubt that it will be. Philip Goldberg, author of *The Intuitive Edge,* feels that an element of surprise is associated with intuition, "as if the intuiter were a magician pulling knowledge out of his own hat, shocking himself." For me, intuition isn't a feeling of surprise as much as one of effervescence, a tingle of joy that fills me when I *know* I have become aware of something important. Sometimes, my new knowledge is immediately applicable to my life. At other times, I am only aware that the information is "in process" and that other elements of clarification will be forthcoming.

The Intuitive Experience

The actual intuitive experience may be difficult to define, but many have described their feelings of intuitive enlightenment. Philip Goldberg quotes Mozart, for whom the experience usually occurred in times of quiet solitude:

> When I am, as it were, completely myself, entirely alone, and of good cheer—say, travelling in a carriage, or walking after a good

> meal, or during the night when I cannot sleep; it is on such occasions that ideas flow best and most abundantly. Whence and how they come, I know not; nor can I force them.

Many athletes describe achieving an "extraordinary state of mind" while performing at their best. John Brodie, former quarterback of the San Francisco 49ers, calls it a state of "heightened focus and perception." Larry Bird, the Boston Celtics' star, says, "It's scary, when I'm at my best I can do just about anything I want and no one can stop me. I feel like I'm in total control of everything." When in this state, he often releases his shot toward the net and immediately turns and runs back to the other end, without ever looking back. "I already know it's all net," he says.

H. Ross Perot, founder and chairman of Electronic Data Systems, actively uses intuition in his business and in his decision-making process. In 1978, when two of his employees were taken prisoner in Iran, Perot personally directed a commando force to free them. He didn't have enough information to know exactly how the rescue would be accomplished, but he was *absolutely sure* it would occur. When asked to describe intuition, Perot replied, "It means *knowing your business*"; he gave special emphasis to the last three words, then added, "It means being able to bring to bear on a situation everything you've seen, felt, tasted, and experienced in an industry." In a world full of copies in triplicate, Perot doesn't even allow written memos in his company. He feels written reports stifle creativity. "They discourage the reader from responding intuitively," he says.

Ray Kroc followed his intuition and made a fortune. After serving in the Red Cross Ambulance Corps in World War I, he tried his hand as a piano player in Chicago bars, then became a salesman. In 1937, he bought the exclusive sales rights to the "multimixer," a machine that would make six malts or milkshakes at one time.

He lived a pretty normal life for the next 15 years. In 1952, two brothers, Richard and Maurice McDonald, ordered eight multimixers for *one* restaurant in San Bernadino, California. Wondering why any single establishment would need to make 48 malts at once, Kroc flew to California to deliver the mixers himself. "When I got there," he said, "I saw more people waiting in line than I had ever seen at any drive-in. I said to myself, "These guys have got something."

Ray Kroc trusted his intuition, and the result was the McDonald's empire.

Kroc persuaded the McDonald brothers to allow him to franchise their hamburger outlets nationwide. Within five years, there were 228 McDonald's franchises in operation. Although the businesses were doing extremely well, Kroc was getting less than 2 percent of the gross and had to give the two brothers about 25 percent of that. He offered to buy the McDonald brothers out, and asked them to quote him a price for everything, name included. They wanted $2.7 million and the right to keep the original San Bernadino restaurant.

Kroc's attorney strongly advised against paying such an "outrageous" price. Kroc recalled, "I'm not a gambler and I didn't have that kind of money, but my funnybone instinct kept urging me on. So I closed my office door, cussed up and down, and threw things out the window. Then I called my lawyer back and said, 'Take it!'" The result of listening to his "funnybone instinct" is the McDonald's fast-food empire.

I don't have a story to match Ray Kroc's, but my intuition has served me well in negotiations with businesspeople far better equipped than I am in terms of data and background resources. I have had "bad feeling" about a prospective business deal days before I had any knowledge that my potential partners had conflicts of interest. In negotiating one international trading contract, I *knew* something was wrong with an agent who was working with me. Two days later, I discovered he was also working with a competitor.

When it has felt right, I have purchased property outside of my own state, sight unseen, and have profited every time. I have also refused to complete a purchase when it felt wrong. When renting property, I can usually tell whether the person leaving a message on the tape machine will be my next tenant. I have successfully assessed investment proposals simply by listening to information presented over the phone and then examining how I felt as I listened.

I have also used my intuitive abilities to help others. I probably saved one friend at least $400,000. Judith had spent most of her 25-year marriage raising three children while her husband built a substantial medical practice. They had invested in a number of apartment buildings, limited partnerships, and land. When Judith and her husband decided to divorce, I was trying to help her negotiate a fair settlement that would be easy for her to handle as a single woman.

Three years and several different law firms later, the property settlement was about to be completed. Judith called from out-of-state, asking me to review the final offer. I told her I liked the feel of the two apartment buildings she was to receive, but I did not like the feel of an interest in some land she had been offered. I told her not to take the land, to trade it for a note or anything else. Just before the settlement was complete, it was revealed that the land was fully mortgaged under a blanket encumbrance by an out-of-state bank. By refusing the land, Judith received $400,000 in cash, including 10 percent earned interest, some four years later. I had absolutely no data to support my "feeling," but my intuition proved correct.

HOW TO BEGIN DEVELOPING YOUR INTUITION

A good first step toward developing your intuitive capability is to acknowledge your feelings. Because intuitive communication often comes in the form of a "feeling," the more you are aware of your own yearnings the better able you are to connect to your own source of intuitive power.

On a day-to-day basis, examine your dominant emotions and your state of mind during the mornings, afternoons, and evenings. You will probably discover a pattern. Your morning emotions might be feelings of eagerness, anticipation, happiness, excitement, or pleasantness. In the afternoons, you might feel busy, efficient, creative, or accomplished. In the evenings, you might feel tired, relieved, reflective, or content. There will undoubtedly be many different combinations, but strive to discover which ones dominate, at what times, and in response to what events. Practice this every day until it becomes a habit, until you become consistently aware of your feelings.

Your intuitive abilities are closely intertwined with your emotions, so becoming clear about your emotions is a very important first step.

I hope your life is filled with feelings of joy. But even if you must acknowledge everyday emotions such as frustration and stress, you are setting the stage for your intuitive development. Because your intuitive abilities are closely intertwined with your emotions, becoming clear about your emotions is a very important first step.

Some situations hold us back from intuitive development more than others. If you find your emotions pointing to a large amount of conflict in your life, developing your intuitive abilities may be more difficult. Conflict of any kind is an emotional drain. Mozart said that his ideas flowed best and most abundantly when he was "of good cheer." It takes a centered, focused life-style to create an environment in which intuitive insight can flourish.

The intuitive voice is a quiet voice. Its guidance rarely shows up on a megascreen complete with moving figures and a message that says *POW!* It is more a sense of presence, a feeling, a gentle nudge in the best direction for that moment in time. Listening to your inner voice is all but impossible when you have turmoil all around you and your emotions are screaming for peace. If there is conflict in your life, it will be necessary to resolve it or at least to distance yourself from it before you can find your own intuitive source of power.

HOW TO RECOGNIZE INTUITION

The kind of primal awareness found in some jungle tribes—a sense of danger when nothing is visible—is a highly developed form of intuition at the physical level. This awareness is different from instinct. Intuition is a fully conscious state: we sense and *know* what is taking place. Instinct remains at the unconscious level.

When I first began to listen to my own intuition, physical signals were my clues. If my intuition was alerting me to be cautious, I would tend to get a weighty feeling in my chest. At other times, I would feel a modest restriction of the energy flow in my body, as if a shield was being constructed for my own protection. When my intuition was alerting me to something positive, I would feel anticipation and a twinge of excitement mixed with joy, as though I had just won some small cosmic prize.

Intuition glides into our awareness in many forms. Often, with very little physical sensation, we merely have an instant knowing. Philip Goldberg describes this as "a faint body sense, some barely perceptible shift in how you feel, like a small child tugging at your sleeve."

Intuition is difficult to describe, and the idea of using intuition is not always accepted. Many people end up passing it off as "just a feeling." Unlike episodes of "Star Trek" in which feelings are an acknowledged part of decision making, our culture has been slow to speak openly of intuition. We accept those leaders and corporate presidents who have a "knack" for doing the right thing because we are drawn to success. If the explanation of that success involves an intuitive or nonrational process for decision making, we pass it off and concentrate on the quantified rational data taught in business schools. Many intuitive people, when pressed for more details of their decision-making process, end up saying, "It was just a thought." But Philip Goldberg points out, "Intuition is a thought, and thought is frequently a faint, ephemeral, smoky abstraction that can only be described as a feeling."

TEN WAYS TO CONTINUALLY DEVELOP YOUR INTUITION

Have Fun

When you view the world with a sense of playfulness, you automatically encourage creativity and intuitive development. Do you remember how you viewed the world as a child? Do you remember the games you invented, the countless, fascinated hours that you spent alongside a creek, with nothing more to play with than rocks, mud, twigs, and perhaps an empty can? Children dream of the impossible, they imagine the new, their every experience is fresh; they are constantly learning, growing, and progressing at a much faster pace than adults normally do.

For young children, using intuition comes naturally, but something happens when they enter the serious world of adulthood.

In third grade, you probably raised your hand eagerly when you had the right answer, and you often got the right answer without doing any homework. In high school, where kids who always had the right answers were branded "nerds," you began to keep silent. Adults started to take what you had to say more seriously, and questioned the sources of your information. You suddenly had to *prove* yourself. If you "just knew," it wasn't enough, so you may have stopped using your intuition. The wonderful source of guidance you so readily used as a child—your intuition—was stifled instead of being developed in conjunction with your other knowledge. You can reconnect to that playful, free-thinking child that has grown silent within you; when you do, your intuitive abilities will rebound.

A friend told me a true story that illustrates the point quite well. In the course of taking a high school trigonometry test, something seemed to click in his brain. When he looked at the blank test paper, it was as if the correct answers were already written down. To his own amazement, when he finished the test and walked up to the teacher's desk to hand it in, only 12 minutes had passed. The class saw him handing in the test and gasped in disbelief. Only two of the other 26 students finished the exam in the allotted time. The teacher accused him of cheating, but admitted to having no evidence. In spite of his innocence, instead of feeling elated over the event, he felt guilty. The experience never happened again, but, for a few minutes in high school, this otherwise normal student understood the meaning of genius. His intuitive powers were at work.

Reestablish Your "Sense of Humor"

Humor provides another link to intuition. When something strikes you as funny, it is usually because you see the ordinary from a different, even bizarre, perspective. The patterns you have to expect as normal are presented in a completely different light. A good comedian sets up what appears to be an ordinary setting, and then delivers a single statement—the punch line—that makes the ordinary become ludicrous. As you laugh, you gain a new perspective. The more often you allow yourself to see beyond the usual way of observing things and to think in unconventional ways, the greater the probability of quantum leaps of understanding.

Living out a personal fantasy several years ago, I began doing comedy at a local comedy club's "open mike" (amateur) night. Because most comedy clubs insist on original material, I had to be a writer as well as a storyteller in this environment.

What a challenge! It took a long time to think up enough material for an eight-minute routine. Like Archimedes, good material often came to me while I was in the bathtub. I also discovered great ideas while driving. (When you aren't listening to the radio or in a hurry or in bumper-to-bumper traffic, a car can be a great place for creativity and intuitive insight.)

Staying alert to humor makes every day more fun, and some of that creative perspective spills over into other aspects of life. One of the keys to harnessing intuitive power is to enable your mind to roam freely and to examine a problem from all possible angles. Humor is a great facilitator of this process.

Knock down the Walls of Formality

This is a great way to encourage intuition. Formality can discourage inventiveness and insight; by its very definition, formality means form and structure. Intuition partially involves a synthesis of information grasped at random, and too much form and structure will impede intuitive insight. No one truly knows all of the potential sources your mind can tap into, but if you limit your mind by always trying to constrain your mental functioning within the bounds of deductive reasoning alone, the natural processing breaks down and you lose mental power.

I'm not suggesting that deductive reasoning is bad or wrong—far from it. But it is only one element of thinking, and it should be fed and augmented by your intuition. Think of your mind as the most powerful supercomputer on earth. Your subconscious is the supercomputer's central processor; it takes your daily input—sensory data, what you read, what people say to you, and so forth—and provides output superrapidly and automatically. When you combine this process with your intuition, you are using all your resources.

One of the best ways to knock down your mental walls of formality is to knock down the physical walls of formality. Within many successful Silicon Valley companies, where new discoveries and innovations are almost a daily event, formality has been all but abandoned. Jeans and tee shirts have replaced three-piece business suits. Management decisions are often made by consensus, in an after-hours social setting, and are based on input from people at all levels in the company. These companies know that formality stifles the creativity and innovation that are at the very core of their businesses' success.

Giving up Control

A sense of security comes from feeling in control of the problem-solving process. Because intuitive insight is something that "comes to you," it is important not to mentally confine possible solutions within a narrow range. When faced with a problem, think of all of the pieces of the solution as being available to your mind. If you were to try and consciously locate all the right pieces from the billions of bits of information available, you would be faced with a hopelessly complex jigsaw puzzle. But if you envision the solution as within your grasp, then your intuitive and other mental powers will do everything possible *automatically* to put the pieces together. You'll move to a completely different plane of mental functioning.

When you envision the solution within your grasp, then your intuitive and mental powers will do everything possible *automatically.*

We live in an action-oriented society; we are proud of the way we "make things happen." Perhaps that is why our culture has given intuition so little attention. Giving up control, "allowing things to happen," may seem to go against everything you have ever known or tried to do. Yet, you must release the full range of your mind's abilities in order to achieve the kind of quantum leaps in understanding that underpin your intuition. If Einstein had not let his mind roam, if he had limited his mind with structure and formality, he would probably never have made his profound contributions to science.

When you need a solution, ask for it, and then release your mind. Avoid dwelling on the problem or on the solution for a while. Give it a day or so to incubate. When you come back to it, you will find a whole new energy surrounding the situation. When discussing intuition, virtually every great thinker has commented that a solution that was sought came only after the problem was released.

When giving up control, it is especially important to be aware of your emotional involvement in the situation. When your search for a certain outcome feels pressing, or you have strong emotions tied up in a specific decision, it is more difficult to experience your intuitive guidance.

Expand Your World

The larger your base of experience, the greater your opportunities to develop new insights. Dare to be different. Be a leader. Be someone who is loving, compassionate, and vulnerable, and you will discover your inner personal power. For one week, try to do things differently. Drive to work a different way, create a dish you haven't made before, read a book on a subject that has been "in the back of your mind." Break some habits, give a party, eat some tofu, go to an opera or a rock concert, visit the big city, or go camping in the wilds. Take a balloon ride, play in the park, visit a state or country you've never been to before. Ride a bike, rent some roller skates, dress up for Halloween, write some poetry, sing a song, take up dancing or horseback riding or rock climbing or absolutely anything you've ever thought you might like to try. The spirit of taking risks and experimenting with new experiences and personal frontiers creates an environment that encourages insight.

Once you've loosened the potentially rusty gears of your routines and can accept change with more comfort and enthusiasm, you have set the stage to harness the power of your intuition.

Expand your experiences with a sense of discovery and adventure. Flexibility will give you more freedom and a broader range of choices. Your life-style can be fertile ground for insight when it is enthusiastic, eager, aware, and adaptable.

Observe the Pictures in Your Mind

When you are relaxed and calm, close your eyes and look at the pictures in your mind. Whether awake or asleep, everyone has them. If you are trying to make a decision about travel plans, an evening out, or which class to take when several are offered, allow your mind to bring you images of the various choices. Often, these images will provide the clues and the insight you need to make the best choice.

Imagine That You Are in a Play

If you are considering a problem, set up an imaginary play in your mind. Bring in the cast of characters from your real-life setting. Don't consciously set up the plot; watch the play unfold in your mind. Create dialogues with the other players. When the play begins, ask for the solution to come at an appointed time. If the solution is not immediately available, direct the players to take a break. Leave your mental stage and go about another task. If your mind comes back to the play, just observe the action. The solution may come to you before you bring up the curtain for the second act.

Try Carrying on a Mental Conversation

Just for fun, do this with yourself or someone involved in a decision you are trying to make. Mentally ask a question and see whether an answer comes to you through your feelings. Try something simple like, "Are you relaxed or stressed? Did you have a good day?" See whether you sense an answer. You may feel silly at first, but no one needs to know what you are doing—unless you want to tell them. You may not get clear answers in the beginning, but who knows what the outcome of your mental conversations will be?

Treat Intuition like a Hobby

Read what you can find on intuition. Spend time thinking about it. Observe how much intuition is a part of your life. Talk to people about your intuitive experiences, and listen to them when they describe theirs.

Develop your own ways to increase your abilities. I find it helpful to have some quiet time every day (I call it "listening with a silent mind"), to get adequate rest, to drink almost no alcohol (it interferes with my focus), to adhere to good eating habits (I have chosen a meatless diet), and to exercise regularly (I do aerobics, running, dancing, tennis, and yoga, but not all in the same day). I also make it a habit to awaken at least 20 minutes before I need to be out of bed each day. I use that time to allow my thoughts to "float." On many mornings, during those 20 minutes, I find solutions and information I have been searching for. I also use this time to dream about and design my larger life-goals. I create wonderful futures in my mind.

The time before I go to bed is also important. What I put in mind at this time will be in process as I sleep. Before I go to bed, I *don't* watch television! Television can be great for information and entertainment, but I don't recommend its content or presentation as the best seed to plant in your mind before sleeping. I believe it can interfere with intuitive development.

Keep a Journal of Your Intuitive Experiences

Your own thoughts and experiences, written in your own words, will help you to accept the validity of intuition and will give you a record to examine when you look back at how you have made important decisions in your life.

APPLYING INTUITION TO YOUR FINANCIAL DECISIONS

In Chapter 2, I discussed the concept of intuitive financial planning. I outlined how to problem solve in reverse: focus on the outcome, feed your mind with information, and then muse over all the possible steps to take until you *know* which among them are the best.

Probably the single most important piece of advice I can offer with respect to making your financial decisions is to *listen* to your intuitive "voice."

Probably the single most important piece of advice I can offer with respect to making your financial decisions is to *listen* to your intuition "voice." Pay attention to the way you *feel* as you go through the decision-making process. For example, if you are listening to a broker's description of a bond or mutual fund investment over the phone, ask yourself how you feel about both the person speaking and the information being delivered. Do you feel trustful, or is there something about the person that makes you uncomfortable or perhaps even suspicious? Does he or she make you feel pressured to act right away? If so, say "Thank you for your time" and back away for a while.

If a particular investment feels good to you, there are probably some very important reasons why. If you have practiced using your intuition and it has served you well in the past, your intuitive judgment alone may be enough to support a final decision. In most cases, however, when you first get a good feeling about an investment, some mixed feelings are still tagging along.

Whenever you have substantial doubts, don't force yourself to act. Feed your mind with facts and figures about the investment. Do some deductive analysis, but don't make a decision. After you've done some research, envision the ultimate outcome you desire, ask for and expect a resolution (but not a *specific* one), and then move on to another task for a day or two. After the respite, at a preset time, evaluate your feelings again. Does the investment frighten you, or do you feel confident about it? Does it excite you? If you feel excitement, is it similar to the excitement of gambling, or is it more like the excitement you felt after hitting the best drive of your life on the golf course?

If all your feelings are positive, it's most likely time to take action. If your feelings are mixed, give yourself some more time. If your feelings are predominantly negative, then leave that particular investment alone. *Never, never* force yourself to make a decision. More often than not, if you back off and wait and/or do a little more research, some piece of information will come to you that makes everything fall into place, and the decision will seem almost self-evident.

I was told a story about a very effective commanding officer on an Air Force base; I'll call him Colonel Smith. One Monday, a captain went into Colonel Smith's office and told him about a problem in the supply group. Having related the problem, the captain stood expectantly, waiting for some kind of reply. After a brief pause, Colonel Smith said, "See me at 8 A.M. on Thursday." "Yes, sir," said the captain. He looked at the pile of papers on the colonel's desk, wondering how he could possibly handle the tremendous work load. "Begging your pardon, sir," he said, "just out of curiosity, why Thursday morning?" Colonel Smith replied simply, "I understand the problem. Wednesday at noon is my hour to contemplate supply problems. By Thursday morning, I'll probably have a good answer; otherwise, we'll speak more about it then."

Although at first glance this type of approach may sound very structured, Colonel Smith was tapping into his intuitive powers. He effectively handled what to many would have been an overwhelming work load by placing problems in his mind, allowing himself time for focused contemplation, and expecting a positive outcome. He didn't torture himself with details or draw charts and schedules; he simply let his mind function at its full intuitive power.

Like Colonel Smith, you should approach your investment decisions with confidence that your mind will serve you well. Pay attention to the way things develop and how you feel about them. If you decide to buy a piece of real estate but start running into all kinds of stumbling blocks, you may want to reconsider that specific purchase. If, for example, your credit is good but the loan officer at the bank wants an overabundance of personal and financial information or treats you as though you are the age of your firstborn child, it may be time to back out or to look for another banker, or possibly another property.

In my experience, when an investment feels right to me, associated events seem to fall into place in a natural, orderly way. On one such occasion, I went to see a loan officer about obtaining a mortgage on a property I really liked. The loan officer told me that he had spoken to his superior, his superior had a friend in the banking business who knew me, and consequently the loan was preapproved. Things don't always go that smoothly. Obtaining the investment that you want may take more effort than you anticipate, and you may feel frustrated at times. But if *everything* seems to be "going wrong," it is probably time to rethink the purchase.

INTUITION AND PERFECTION

Don't feel that you must always be right if you decide to develop and utilize your intuition. It is, after all, just one more source of information, although a very powerful one. You may have doubts about what you are sensing. Don't worry about your doubts! They will help you to refine your information until you achieve a point of certainty. Use your doubts to strengthen your resolve to reach your goals, to create a sense of challenge and adventure, to test how much you believe in yourself. When doubts give you strength, they have performed a very valuable service. Stay focused on your goal, and continue to see yourself with a successful outcome and to ask for information. Your doubts will soon disappear.

I have not always been in touch with my own intuition. There have been times in my life when I was so focused on what I *should* do that I lost sight of what I *wanted* to do. I shrouded my intuition with activity. I know now, without a doubt, that the quality of my life is enhanced when I am in touch with my intuition. Being in touch with that extra 90 percent of the brain, or whatever we are tapping into when we use our intuition, makes life easier.

I use intuition like I use cycles. I may not be able to explain why cycles work, but I do know how to use them to make better financial decisions. In the same way, I don't know how intuition works, but I know that the more I use it, the more the quality and character of my life improve. I use intuition in every aspect of my life, not only in my financial decisions. So can you. Accept your own personal power—the power to build wealth and, even more, the power to create the life you want. You already have everything you need.

Chapter 4

The Long Economic Wave and Where It Says We're Going

> **By the Law of Periodical Repetition, everything which has happened once, must happen again and again and again—and not capriciously, but in a regular period, and each thing in its own period, not another's, and each obeying its own law . . . The same Nature which delights in periodical repetition in the skies is the Nature which orders the affairs of the earth. Let us not underrate the value of that hint.**
>
> **MARK TWAIN**

I love classical music. I will never forget the beautiful melodies my mother played on the piano or the sounds of Chopin coming from her collection of 78-RPM records. Today, classical music plays an important part in my life, especially the best symphonies of Beethoven, Mahler, and Rachmaninoff. There is a motif to them—a basic musical theme threaded gently together that teases and haunts you as the movements unfold, carrying you through a full range of emotions, from the depths of melancholy to the heights of joy. In some passages, this motif is strong and quite pronounced; in others, it is almost unnoticeable but you can feel yourself under its influence.

All the varied experiences, patterns, challenges, and joys of your life also have an underlying theme or motif. That melody is the sound of your own personal dreams and aspirations.

It is easy to stop listening to this song. As the pace of our life-style quickens and we strive for more and more, faster and faster, we often lose sight of what we really want.

We need to think beyond this year, or next year, or the next five years, or the time when the kids go to school, or the mortgage is paid off, or any other short-term goal is reached, and start thinking of our entire life as a whole. Each stage of life has its goals, tests, satisfactions, and disappointments, but they all contribute to the making of one unique person—you! When you see yourself as a whole and complete person living a whole and complete life—not just moving through isolated, separate life experiences—you will find much greater peace and clarify in the present moment and will draw from it greater vitality. As George Burns says, "I don't want to be sixteen again, I want to be a hundred. I have been sixteen."

Viewing your whole life as a continuity, a cycle, helps with both major and minor decisions. My recent choice to return to graduate school was eased by this life cycle perspective. Plowing through the admissions packets and talking with economics department deans, I saw immediately that the prerequisites (six math courses and four economics courses) were going to take more than a few months. My degree wouldn't be completed for *years,* and I am no longer a kid. But I stopped those thoughts in their tracks. I'd already made the decision to live a long time (till a hundred!), which meant I still had over half my life ahead of me. Entering graduate school was no different from entering the university in my youth; I was just a slightly older youth. After all the responsibility and busyness of motherhood and childrearing, I was preparing now for the rest of my life, the years when I could create the dreams that had been dormant since my youth.

Taking a whole and complete view doesn't mean trying to plan out every moment of your life. You can't know the exact form your life will take. But with the larger view, you can come to a clearer understanding of who you are and how you fit into the greater cycle of humanity. You'll be more centered and focused, which will help you to create a more centered and focused life-style.

Success with your financial investments is an integral part of the life-style you want. Just as you can find peace and perspective from listening to the symphony of your own life cycle, so you can make sounder and more satisfying financial decisions by understanding the long economic cycle or wave.

Think of the long economic cycle or wave as the motif around which other economic cycles interplay. Stock prices, interest rates, real estate, commodities, and the 7- to 11-year cycle in the general economy—all are influenced by the long economic wave. If you understand its influence, you will be able to use other, more specialized cycles to achieve optimal financial performance, and you will find integration in your financial decisions.

When you understand the influence of the long economic wave, you will be able to achieve optimal financial performance.

Although the first references to the long economic wave date back to 1901, it was the work of Nikolai Kondratieff, a Russian agricultural economist, that captured the attention of Western economists. Kondratieff's theory sparked my interest in cycles in the 1970s.

A DISCOVERY IN HARDSHIP

Nikolai Dmitriyevich Kondratyev, or Kondratieff, was born in 1892 in the village of Goluevskaja, located about 185 miles northeast of Moscow. Because he was the oldest of eight children and had a superior intellect, he was given the responsibility of educating his brothers and sisters while he carried out his own studies. At age 17, he entered St. Petersburg University to study economics. Upon graduation, he joined the faculty in the department of political economics and statistics.

In 1917, following the Bolshevik Revolution, he was appointed Deputy Minister for Food in the government of Alexander Kerensky. When the communists threw Kerensky out of power a few months later, Kondratieff lost his position and spent several months in prison. Kondratieff was not a member of the communist party.

In 1920, in spite of his lack of party membership, Kondratieff became head of the Institute for Business Cycles, in Moscow, where he spent the majority of his time researching and writing about agricultural topics. As one of the authors of the first five-year plan for agronomy, he staunchly opposed the nationalization of agriculture in the Soviet Union.

Kondratieff's first reference to the possible existence of a long economic cycle appeared in 1922 in a study entitled "The World Economy and Its Conditions During and After the War." Working with very limited statistical data, his conclusion was tentative: "We consider the long cycles in the capitalist economy only as probable." Both he and his colleagues agreed on the need to acquire more data to investigate the possible existence of the long economic wave.

By 1924, Kondratieff was a respected economist in the international community and belonged to organizations such as the American Economic Association, the American Association of Agricultural Economics, and Britain's Royal Economics Society. In 1924, his interest in cycles was apparent when he wrote: "The idea that the dynamics of economic life in the capitalistic social order is not of a simple and linear but rather of a complex and cyclical character is nowadays generally recognized. Science, however, has fallen far short of clarifying the nature and the types of these cyclical, wave-like movements." A year later, he published his most famous article, "Long Economic Cycles," an exposition of his theory of the long economic wave, now dubbed "the Kondratieff wave."

Unfortunately, a great deal was lost in the initial translation of the work. As J. J. van Duijn, author of *The Long Wave in Economic Life,* puts it, "What we got was a mutilated version of Kondratieff's theory and his interpretation of historical data." Not until 1984, when Guy Daniels wrote a new translation directly from the original Russian version, was justice done to Kondratieff's work.

In 1928, Kondratieff's theories brought him political trouble; he was dismissed from his post as director of the Institute for Business Cycles. In 1929, the Soviet government's official encyclopedia stated, "This [Kondratieff's] theory is wrong and reactionary." He was arrested on June 30, 1930, and charged with being a member of the illegal Working Peasants Party.

He was not alone. As Alexander Solzhenitsen described in his novel *Gulag Archipelago,* Kondratieff was one of as many as

200,000 other "detainees" who were imprisoned at the whim of government officials. One account indicates that Kondratieff fell into political disfavor because he said that a depression in capitalistic economies was cyclical and therefore self-correcting, a direct contradiction of the communist dogma. His only "crime" was his willingness to speak out. Without a trial, he and thousands like him were sentenced to serve prison terms under the harshest conditions.

Kondratieff spent two years in a Moscow prison before being transferred to Suzcal, a small town about 80 miles from Moscow, to serve the rest of his seven-year term. At first, conditions there were tolerable. Many other intellectuals were imprisoned with him; his roommate was an economist, Ya. M. Yurovsky. During his prison term, Kondratieff was able to read and work, and he produced a long manuscript on economic dynamics, which exists today but has never been published.

At the end of his seven-year term, Kondratieff was sentenced to a second prison term. As the intellectual and physical conditions at the prison continued to deteriorate, Kondratieff was denied access to the prized scientific journals that had formerly been allowed. He fell ill and was transported back to Moscow in 1938, when Stalin's reign of terror was fully underway. Nikolai Kondratieff was shot on September 17, 1938, at the age of 46.

"Posthumous Justice" was the headline of an August 16, 1987, edition of the *Moscow News*, a Russian weekly printed in Russian, German, French, and English. The article reported that, on July 16, 1987, the Supreme Court of the USSR had repealed the conviction of 15 citizens who had been tried during the years 1931, 1932, and 1935. "Let us remember the names of these fifteen well, for they are the pride of Soviet science," the article went on to say. "Their works will again be published, articles and books will be written about them. Their names will once more appear in textbooks."

The report went on to explain that the Working Peasants Party, of which Kondratieff was supposed to be a member, never even existed. The hundreds of thousands of people who were arrested in 1930 through 1932 were the victims of a political sham. It is little comfort to the few who are still alive that the Soviet government eventually wiped their records clean. A destructive and horrible waste cannot be reversed. Who knows what further advances and discoveries Kondratieff might have contributed to the body of economic knowledge? How much other knowledge was lost forever in the death camps of the Soviet Union? We can be grateful for the amount of Kondratieff's work that was preserved.

KONDRATIEFF AND CYCLES

Unlike the Kitchin and Juglar economic cycles that fascinated Schumpeter (see Chapter 1), Kondratieff's work focused on the granddaddy of them all—the 50-year (now thought to be 54-year) economic cycle found in countries with essentially capitalistic economies. Kondratieff found that there was a close relationship, dating back to the 18th century, among the turning points of the long economic cycle in the United States and European countries. The charts he developed compared the economic turning points of France, England, the United States, Germany, and, as he put it, "the whole world." He found evidence to support the existence of three successive 50-year cycles or waves.

Because the first cycle began almost 200 years ago, the data or records supporting it are obviously incomplete. The statistics for the second and third cycles, however, are more convincing.

In his 1925 work, "Long Economic Cycles," translated into English and published in the *Review of Economic Statistics* in 1935, Kondratieff summarized his findings:

> Although for the time being we consider it to be impossible to fix exactly upon the years that marked the turning points of the long cycles, and although the method according to which the statistical data have been analyzed permits an error of 5 to 7 years in the determination of the years of such turnings, the following limits of these cycles can nevertheless be presented as being those most probable:

First Long Wave:

1. The rise lasted from the end of the 1780s or beginning of the 1790s until 1817–1819.
2. The decline lasted from 1810 to 1817 until 1844–1875.

Second Long Wave:

1. The rise lasted from 1844–1851 until 1870–1875.
2. The decline lasted from 1870 to 1875 until 1890–1896.

Third Long Wave:

1. The rise lasted from 1890–1896 until 1914–1920.
2. The decline probably begins in the years 1914–1920.

More recent research indicates that the cycle is not a 50-year wave, as Kondratieff thought, but a 54-year wave that can vary as much as plus or minus six to eight years in actual duration, as shown in Figure 4.1. Based on these newer findings, we are nearing the end of a Kondratieff area of weakness and are on the verge of a 25- to 30-year period of economic prosperity.

We are nearing the end of a Kondratieff area of weakness and are on the verge of a 25- to 30-year period of unparalleled economic prosperity.

"Where," you might ask, "has the down period been for the past two decades? After all, haven't we seen, overall, a dramatic

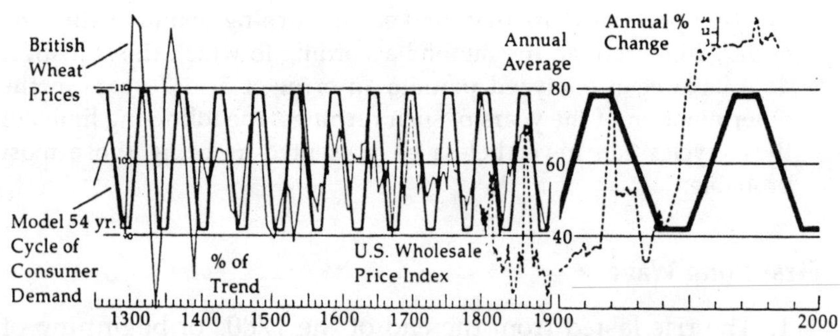

Figure 4.1 The Idealized Kondratieff Long Wave. Adapted from Recept 2000: The Timing Tool, © BV Institute Inc., Boulder, CO.

period of economic growth?" My preliminary answer is that we have had overall strength in the past two decades, but it has been a *relative* period of incubation, in preparation for the incredible decades to come. Before I discuss the coming decades in more detail, let me review where some economists have taken Kondratieff's thinking.

RENEWED INTEREST IN THE KONDRATIEFF LONG WAVE

During the past decade, interest in the Kondratieff long economic cycle has been renewed. In October 1983, a conference sponsored by the International Institute for Applied Systems Analysis was held in collaboration with the Institute for Regional Economic Development. There was a follow-up conference in June 1985.

In the United States, a great deal has been written about Kondratieff and his theories. Most of the discussion focuses on the causes of the cycle, not its validity, which implies a broad acceptance of the cycle theory's merits. The idea that draws the most attention is what economists call the "bunching" of investment—the grouping of technical innovation and production during certain years or decades.

Professor Jay W. Forrester and his colleagues at MIT have developed detailed computer simulation models that help explain the long-term cycle movement based on the bunching effect. Forrester's work was summarized by Scott Erickson in *Futurist* magazine as follows:

> According to Forrester, during times of prosperity profitable industrial sectors are overbuilt and grow beyond the size needed for long-term equilibrium. Productive capacity is expanded beyond market opportunity creating large debt. This overexpansion is ended by recession and depression, during which excess productive capacity is physically worn out and financially depreciated until the state has been cleared for a new era of rebuilding. Decreased profits during this period make it difficult to repay debt, forcing some individuals, businesses, and nations to default.

On March 17, 1992, commemorating the birthday of Kondratieff, a conference was held in Moscow and St. Petersburg.

Sponsored by the Institute of Economics of the Russian Academy of Sciences and the Russian Academy of National Economy, the conference was attended by over 600 people. During the conference, more than 50 papers were delivered on all aspects of the life and work of Kondratieff. Richard Mogey, Executive Director of the Foundation for the Study of Cycles, who presented a paper, states, "Russian scholars who were not allowed access to Kondratieff's work have actively been researching his writing and its implications. For Russians the ability to celebrate this centenary was not only a chance to right an old wrong but a chance to freely consider one of the most influential ideas in economics."

THE LONG ECONOMIC WAVE AND THE CYCLE OF HUMAN ENERGY

In more humanistic terms, I believe it is possible that the long wave Kondratieff referred to in the capitalistic process is not confined to capitalism. Unlike the smaller economic cycles, these long waves seem to push and pull at the forward movement of civilization itself. They may be long waves in the energy cycle of human activity that are simply more visible and easier to measure in the realm of economics.

The Kondratieff wave may actually be a manifestation of a long wave in the cycle of human energy.

"The wave" that stadium fans perform during football and baseball games represents how human energy moves in cycles. At the low ebb, a small group of people may start, encouraging those next to them to join in. The energy of the wave starts to transfer, growing as it reaches each successive section of the stands. The psychological momentum builds and intensifies until the whole stadium is drawn into the activity, and the wave peaks in a roar of excitement. Some people will remain seated on the next circuit; a touchdown or home run by the visiting team may stop all enthusiasm for a while. But there is always another wave coming. The energy begins, builds momentum, peaks, loses momentum, and ebbs, in a repeating cycle.

Throughout the past two centuries, this type of pattern has been repeated in human history. Some major event, discovery, or set of discoveries has set off a cascade of events resulting in approximately 30 years of growth and relative prosperity, followed by roughly 25 years of slower growth and relative economic weakness. In the early stages of the strength phase of the cycle, technological advancement based on the discoveries in the previous period of weakness begins to take hold. As the advances gain wider use, people begin to accumulate more wealth and the momentum of their confidence and enthusiasm starts to build. Typically, the momentum continues to grow until the confidence and momentum are nearly universal.

In the latter stage of the strength period, widespread speculation and massive borrowing to finance economic expansion usually occur. The result is the bunching effect described above. Because of the inherent inefficiencies created by overexpansion, some significant event causes the house of cards to tumble, often in a flurry of panicked activity. Public disillusionment takes hold, and the cycle phase of weakness begins.

The down phase of the Kondratieff wave is an incubation period for human energy. Facing political, social, and economic problems stemming from the previous period of strength, the bulk of humanity becomes entrenched in the pursuit of day-to-day survival. People tend to be more sedate and contemplative, but the search for solutions to the problems of humanity continues. New ideas, concepts, and innovations are being spawned that will feed the next phase of strength and growth.

INCUBATION PERIODS AND NEW PROSPERITY

The period from about 1760 through the mid-1780s marked the incubation years of the Kondratieff revival that began about 1785, when the United States had just gained independence.

The revival was led by England, with major advances in cotton processing technology for the textile industry. The invention of the spinning jenny, a machine that could spin more than one thread at a time, was followed by Cartwright's invention of a power loom run by steam. These advances were developed during the incubation period, but led the way to the Kondratieff revival that lasted from the 1780s until the early to mid-teens of the 1800s.

The next incubation began about 1815 (after the War of 1812) and lasted until the late 1830s or early 1840s. During this time, the demand for railroad transportation was developing in the United States, but the steam locomotive, tracks, and roadbeds did not become serviceable until roughly 1835. By 1837, approximately 1,500 miles of roadbed were laid across the American continent, and that number ballooned to 4,000 miles by 1842. This new mode of transportation, which opened new markets and new opportunities to farmers and manufacturers throughout the United States, led to a period of economic prosperity that lasted until approximately 1870.

Many people don't realize it, but the massive expansion of the railroads was largely financed and encouraged by the federal government. Not surprisingly, graft was rampant and railroad lines were laid where economies wouldn't support them. Consequently, the inefficiencies created during the boom time required a period of correction. In and around the panic of 1873, the United States experienced one of the worst recessions (then called a depression) in its history. The period from approximately 1870 to 1895 was another incubation period characterized by a Kondratieff cycle phase of weakness.

The major innovation that was to fuel the next period of strength was the development of a commercially feasible electric light bulb, which led to widespread use of electrical power. Although Moses Farner was lighting his house in Salem, Massachusetts, with electric lamps one year before the Civil War, not until 1879, when Thomas Edison developed an electric lamp that could be manufactured efficiently, was electrical power generally available. The first carbon filaments were soon replaced by tungsten, which produced almost three times as much light from the same electrical supply. Electricity carried the third Kondratieff wave. The revival of economic strength and prosperity lasted until the early 1920s.

The last complete incubation period that we can examine lasted until the mid-1940s. In 1923, Vladimir Zworykin filed a patent application on the iconoscope. As a receiver, Zworykin developed a kinescope. Although these two names may seem strange today, they were the basis for one of our most important modern technical advancements—television.

Even though the nation experienced the Great Depression during this incubation period, development of television continued. The first regular commercial telecasts were begun in New York City on April 30, 1939. Along with other developments in communication media, television spawned the communications age and carried us through a cycle phase of strength that lasted from the mid-1940s (after World War II) until the early to mid-1970s.

Throughout the era of "the fabulous fifties," Americans acquired homes, cars, telephones, television sets, and amenities that once were considered luxuries of the rich. People were full of optimism, enthusiasm, and hope. By the mid- to late 1960s, the signs of trouble had started to emerge. As America reached new heights of economic power, social unrest and rebellion among the young caused Americans to challenge the basic premises of their way of life. Blacks and other minority groups that had been held under the yoke of discrimination demanded change. Women, who had been briefly freed from their traditional and taken-for-granted role of homemaker during World War II, began demanding equality with men. Teenagers and young adults who had never experienced poverty challenged "the pursuit of the almighty dollar."

By the early to mid-1970s, the Kondratieff cycle phase of strength had peaked. Throughout the past two decades and into the present, we have been seeing social challenge and change in every area of the globe, including the United States. The relationship between men and women is changing and evolving toward parity; the structure and style of business management are becoming more decentralized, thus releasing the creative potential of employees; political change has restructured even the harshest national regimes. Slowly but surely, problems are being solved, and as those solutions gel, we will begin to see a revival of human energy and a period of accelerated prosperity.

On the scientific front, there have been few technological innovations; rather, existing technologies have been refined and perfected. The basic research that will lead to the next generation of technological advancement is being performed somewhere. What those innovations will be is anyone's guess, but they *will* come about.

In the early 1990s, according to an article in the October 8, 1990, issue of *Fortune* magazine, resources spent for research and development were at an all-time high. The article featured 12 young scientists (all under 40) who are making major inroads into such research areas as the structure of the cosmos, artificial intelligence, noninvasive treatments of heart disease, environmentally safe methods of crop fertilization, energy research, robotics, rearranging matter for productive purposes, and other subjects.

As these and other new discoveries are transformed into workable technologies, we will see a new era of prosperity that may make the prosperity of the 1950s look almost primitive.

As new discoveries are transformed into workable technologies, we will see a new era of prosperity that may make the prosperity of the fifties look almost primitive.

WEAKNESS IN THE 1980s

Some readers might say, "Weakness in the 1980s? What weakness? The 1980s were very prosperous." It is true that the United States consumed more VCRs, movies, and Big Macs than ever before, but the prosperity we enjoyed was purchased on a credit card. If the United States had not gone from the world's largest creditor nation to the largest debtor nation in just six years, would we have had such prosperity?

Our government, by allowing continued inflation, by guaranteeing billions of dollars in bad loans, and by operating at huge deficits, propped up an ailing economy and numerous deteriorating industries that otherwise would have suffered a deeper decline. It was a trade—debt for relative prosperity. The trade involved, however, was the exact type of "bunching" described earlier. Many industries—savings and loan institutions, banks, major airlines, insurance companies, brokerage houses—are paying for it now and others have faced bankruptcy and default.

Economic realities will continue to force the retrenchment of resources and assets, but, rather than occurring all at once, the retrenchment will be what the Comstock Partners, a research and money management firm on Wall Street, have termed "a rolling recession"—the recession moves from sector to sector and region to region throughout the country.

The period of retrenchment will come to a close toward the middle of the decade, when the long Kondratieff cycle will enter a new period of strength. The shorter cycles of the stock market, interest rates, and real estate will combine with the Kondratieff phase of strength (stock prices up, interest rates down, real estate activity up) to take us into a period of strength in the last half of the 1990s. After the start of the 21st century, the shorter-term cycles will move up and down in their characteristic patterns, but there will be underlying, broad-based support provided by the long economic wave until the early part of the century's third decade.

THE CYCLE IN PSYCHOLOGICAL EXPECTATIONS

In addition to a human energy cycle, the Kondratieff wave may represent a long wave in the psychological expectations of humanity. As evidenced by reports on consumer sentiment, there is little doubt that human confidence is susceptible to alternating periods of sureness and uncertainty. Both government and business constantly monitor the attitudes and actions of consumers in an attempt to characterize their confidence level. Evidently, what people expect is going to happen largely determines what *will* happen.

Perhaps the longer cycle of consumer confidence manifests itself in the Kondratieff wave. Because humans talk, trade, share, and compare in a social setting, the predominant attitudes shift in repeated patterns that can have a cumulative effect on behavior. Clarence Long tells us, in his book *Building Cycles and the Theory of Investment:* "The fact is, however, that the investment market is not an aggregation of isolated individuals but a social group composed of members wanting somewhat the same thing." This interaction may be the cause of the wide swings of negative and positive feelings that dominate society.

During the early years of an upward spiral, after suffering the relative hardships of the weakness phase of the cycle, people are grateful for whatever level of prosperity they may have; compared to the past, their future prospects seem much better. When their economic condition begins to improve, their attitudes continue to become more positive. Success and prosperity become widely expected. Public confidence picks up momentum; energy and enthusiasm permeate virtually all areas of economic and social life.

Business expands, and people accumulate more wealth. People who once were satisfied with modest incomes begin to spend and live more extravagantly. As expectations increase, people strive for more and more wealth at a faster and faster pace. Tensions build. The economy cannot fulfill everyone's expectations or demands, and a general state of frustration begins to develop. Capital, in the form of savings, is spread thin. The inherent weakness soon leads to a collapse, in terms of both economic prosperity and psychological expectations.

TODAY'S ECONOMY AND THE KONDRATIEFF LONG WAVE

According to the Kondratieff cycle, we should currently be in the last stages of an incubation period. By this reasoning, an analysis of the past 20 years should demonstrate relative economic weakness: falling incomes, lower profits, and a relative drop in the standard of living. Although these effects were long masked by inflation and deficit spending, there are strong indications that the Kondratieff pattern has been accurate.

Many incomes have not kept pace with inflation, which means that real purchasing power and real income for many individuals have fallen. Many households depend on two incomes to maintain or improve their standard of living. Taxes are currently on the rise, further reducing actual incomes. Many baby boomers believe it will be more difficult for them to achieve the level of lifetime prosperity that their parents enjoyed.

Debt at all levels has increased. Mortgage debt as a percentage of the asset value of owner-occupied real estate is approximately 18 percent higher than it was in 1970. Consumer debt as a percentage of personal income has increased 4 percent since 1970. Nonfinancial corporate credit debt (money borrowed by corporations other than financial institutions) is approximately 5 percent higher. Only 19 of the 50 states balanced their budgets in 1991, and federal debt is over $3 trillion.

Other signs indicate the economic weakness that the Kondratieff cycle predicted. In 1988, federal regulators closed or rescued 217 insolvent institutions, the highest single-year number since 277 savings and loans went under in 1938, during the Great Depression. Savings and Loans continue to be "rescued" and the S&L bailout will eventually cost American taxpayers more than $500 billion.

The stock market crash of October 1987 got everyone's attention. Although it didn't usher in another Great Depression, it did affect everyone in the country to some degree. Robert Samuelson of *Newsweek* commented:

> What's unsettling is not the certainty of doom. Rather, it's the sense that we're losing control. We think we understand the economy well enough to avoid disaster. Wall Street's panic has shaken that faith. No one expects an economic collapse, but then again no one thought stocks could lose a fifth of their value in a single day.

We have seen some areas of growth during this incubation period, which means that the Kondratieff cycle does not predict consistent boom times or depression during each cycle phase. When the Kondratieff cycle is in an upward trend, business expansions will be longer and stronger, and business contractions will tend to be shorter and milder. In a period of weakness, the converse will be true.

During the upward trend of the Kondratieff wave, business can do almost nothing wrong. Because the economy is in a period of growth, practically everything that is manufactured can be sold. The consumer's appetite is insatiable. Small businesses can form and flourish because venture capital is abundant and interest rates are low. The recessions during such times tend to be mild and short-lived, and inflation is usually moderate. The booms are long and strong. During the weakness phase, booms will appear in segments of the economy rather than in the economy as a whole. These events are exactly what has happened in the past two decades.

PROSPERITY: ON THE HORIZON

We are in a time of change. In an article called "The Transition Time Between Eras, The Long-Wave Cycle" (*Futurist,* August 1985), Scott Erickson says,

> We find ourselves in a time of transition between eras. Like other transitions between previous long waves, this calls for a time of "high thought." The 1980s and 1990s will witness the demise of the fourth long wave and the birth of the fifth long wave. We are now experiencing a surge of innovation in the business and economic sectors. Today's successful innovations will define the character of the next long wave. Our decisions about these innovations will help to shape the next long wave in years to come.

This pattern also applies to you. Your current investment decisions will shape your future financial independence. During the 1990s, our economy will move into the recovery phase of the long economic wave. You can use this forthcoming surge in human energy and financial abundance to make your own transition to a more prosperous life.

We are in a time of renewal. Use the energy of growth to create a beautiful financial environment for yourself.

Use the energy of growth to create a beautiful financial environment for yourself. Freedom is a basic human need, and financial freedom is both a means to fulfill that need and an extension of it. Consider all the good you can do for yourself, your family, and your community when you have achieved financial independence. These worthy goals, combined with the energy that is embodied in the Kondratieff growth period, will offer unparalleled opportunity for you to build your own prosperous environment.

Be creative and free with your interpretations as you create the symphony of your financial life. Remember that, just as musical harmony can result when three or more notes are played at the same time, so financial harmony can be found by integrating your knowledge of cycles, your informed data base of specific markets, and your intuitive abilities.

You determine the tempo at which the music of your financial future will be played. Don't rush your decisions or fail to act when the timing is right. Financial planning offers a tremendous outlet for practical and profitable creativity. It can be as enjoyable and exciting as anything you have ever experienced.

Your choices will be a unique expression of what you consider to be the most essential and harmonious aspects of your life. The financial plans of those around you may be different from yours. Stay with financial choices that match *your* temperament, *your* goals, and *your* time frame. Look ahead—not only to next month and next year, but to future decades. See excitement and prosperity for the rest of your life. Look forward to joy, peace, fulfillment, and a secure financial foundation. Begin to listen to your own song, your own melody of life. Everything you have ever wanted will follow.

You are absolutely worthy of everything you want. See your own prosperity, set your goals, listen to your intuition, and succeed.

Chapter

5

Why You Can Stop Worrying About Another Depression

Courage is grace under pressure.
ERNEST HEMINGWAY

Courage has many faces: the quiet determination of a parent or teacher trying to make a difference in a child's life; the bold endurance of a dedicated athlete practicing for countless hours in a quest for a gold medal; the simple tenacity that keeps us putting one foot in front of the other when unanticipated events in life seem almost too much to bear. The fountainhead of courage is the knowledge that the challenges and struggles we face in life are not insurmountable burdens, but opportunities in disguise.

The fountainhead of courage is the knowledge that the challenges and struggles we face in life are not insurmountable burdens, but opportunities in disguise.

The opposite of courage is fear, and fear can keep us from what we really want. It can cause hesitation, doubt, and procrastination. Because of money's importance for most of us, it's easy to understand how fear can undermine our confidence in our financial decisions and make us afraid to move forward.

Fear of another Great Depression is very real for many of us. Even if we didn't experience it ourselves, we have "lived" it through our parents' and friends' memories of hardship. This underlying fear of bread lines and soup kitchens and bank failures can paralyze us in our quest for financial independence.

Before 1929, "depression" was the word used to describe periods of economic weakness in the business cycle. Economists now describe downturns with the word "recession," as if to reassure us that the Great Depression of the 1930s was a one-of-a-kind event. But was it? Do cycles point the way to another major depression? Do we have anything to fear?

Franklin Roosevelt said, "The only thing we have to fear is fear itself." I once knew a professional football player who was 6 feet 6 inches tall and weighed about 260 pounds. He told me that the first time he had to run onto the field through a paper banner, he was afraid the banner wouldn't break! After he did it the first time, he was never frightened by the paper barrier again. In the same way, I think that fear of the unknown is the predominant factor at work in predictions of another Great Depression. If we break through that fear by acquiring knowledge of what the Great Depression was like and what caused it, then we need never fear it again.

There was a time when I was afraid. Now, I am confident we will never see the likes of the Great Depression again.

There was a time when I was afraid. In fact, I started my study of cycles after reading a prediction of a forthcoming major depression. Now, I am confident we will never see the likes of the Great Depression again. We will see periods of economic weakness and there will be similarities. But we *won't* experience *ever* again the depths and duration of hardship and poverty that occurred in the 1930s. This chapter considers the information that gives me such confidence.

APPLE PEDDLERS AND BOXCARS IN THE SAND

Some of the most vivid images of the Great Depression years originated in major American cities. Fifteen thousand able-bodied but homeless men searched for work in New York City in 1931. Those who could afford the fifteen-cent charge could stay overnight in a flophouse. The less fortunate slept on park benches, in partially hidden doorways, in small corners of subway stations, and in shelterless vacant lots. These weren't drunks, drug addicts, or beggars; they were strong, healthy people who had fallen through the few social supports available, and, because of the economic fate of their nation, simply could not find work.

For many who lived through those times, the Washington apple was to remain a lasting symbol of the hungry decade. During the fall of 1930, the International Apple Shippers Association discussed ways of selling their surplus apples. The association originated the idea of using unemployed men to peddle their apples on street corners in the Northeast. A press agent for the growers' association developed a catchy slogan to increase sales: "Buy an apple a day and eat the Depression away."

Early each morning, men without jobs—and without jackets—would line up to receive their daily quota of apples to sell. The apples were issued on credit, and the men would sell them for 5 cents apiece. After a full day's work, a man might end up with less than a dollar in his pocket. Today, "another day, another dollar" seems incomprehensible. During the 1930s, it was a common definition of a good day.

At first, more fortunate Americans rose to the occasion. In major cities throughout the United States, people bought apples in an effort to help hungry men. Gene Fowler, a noted Manhattan reporter, wrote: "Apple sellers crouched at the street corners like half-remembered sins sitting up on the conscience of the town." People were sympathetic.

Unfortunately, the sympathy didn't last very long. The public grew tired of apples and apple peddlers and stopped buying. Harassment by city officials combined with public disfavor and soon caused the apple peddlers to disappear.

Lines of hungry people at "soup kitchens" were a familiar sight. The bill of fare in these emergency kitchens was meager: bread, soup, and coffee. There was never enough to eat. Some men spent the entire day moving from one bread line to another, with wind, cold, and hunger their only companions.

Conditions throughout the country were much the same. "Hooverville" settlements —shanty towns named derisively for President Herbert Hoover—are among the realities described by Edward Robb Ellis in his book *A Nation in Torment:*

> In St. Louis the residents of a Hooverville built and dedicated a church made of orange crates. Near New Orleans jobless men lived in old houseboats. In Connellsville, Pennsylvania, unemployed steel workers kept warm inside the huge ovens they had once stoked. In Jersey City the police evicted 300 homeless men from a Hooverville and then burned their shacks. In Oakland, California, some desperate men lived in sewer pipes the manufacturer was unable to sell. In Los Angeles a local street railway company donated fifty ancient trolley cars to workless men to use as homes.

In a book entitled *Boxcar in the Sand,* Laurence Hewes describes the inhabitants and their dwellings in a Hooverville near Sacramento, California.

> Each had built for his family a rickety shelter of salvage lumber, boxes, cardboard, and tin cans. Each small holding was pitifully cultivated in a hopeless diversity of crops. Some had strawberry beds, others spindly orchards; here and there tobacco and cotton stalks evidenced either imagination or a cotton-belt origin. The entire settlement was a dreary, sodden mass; stagnant rain water stood three to six inches deep; outdoor privies had overflowed shallow wells; sickness was rampant. I stared at the dismal scene in a steady autumnal downpour. Lank men in patched denim pants puttered lethargically; a few in groups whittled and spat; half-clad urchins peered through windows or skittered through slop. There wasn't a dollar in the whole settlement; summer cannery and fruit pickings wages were long since spent and there would be no new cash until next season began.

An invisible scar marks all those who lived during the Great Depression.

An invisible scar marks all those who remember or were born during the Great Depression. Children of the depression years remember clothes that were never new and shoes that became way too tight. Adults who lived through it, like my parents, learned to save. No matter how big or small the item, it was to be kept. People saved worn but usable tires just in case new tires would be unavailable or too expensive when needed. They saved scraps of cloth, string, tape, wire, paper, thread, and, above all, food. No food item was wasted. Every last string bean, peach, or tomato from gardens was eaten or canned. These were indeed hungry years.

But even during the darkest days of the Great Depression, Americans were able to laugh at themselves. In fact, black humor become fashionable in the folklore surrounding the stock market crash. In the first days after "Black Friday," clerks in downtown hotels supposedly asked prospective guests whether they wished to rent the room for sleeping or for jumping. In Milwaukee, a man who committed suicide reportedly left a note willing his body to science, his soul to Treasury Secretary Andrew Mellon, and his sympathy to his creditors. Another popular joke concerned two men who were said to have jumped, hand-in-hand, from one of the upper tiers of the Ritz Hotel. They had a joint account.

WHY DID IT HAPPEN?

The questions of how and why a nation as strong as the United States was brought to its economic knees have nagged every generation since 1929. To this day, writers and economists debate the possible causes. There was no one, single cause. The Great Depression was a combination of many economic and psychological factors.

One significant contributing factor was the disparity of wealth that existed in the 1920s. Although there were gains in productivity during this decade, wages in mining, transportation, and manufacturing were actually falling. Nobel prize winner Friedrich Von Hayek termed the results a "shift to profits." The income generated from the prosperous business environment that existed in the 1920s went largely to established high-income groups. From 1919 to 1929, the share of disposable income received by persons in the top 1 percent income bracket rose from 12.2 percent to 18.9 percent. While the income of the wealthy was on the rise, almost 60 percent of America's 30 million families earned less than the estimated $2,000 a year needed in 1929 to buy the basic necessities. As a result, when the hard times came, very few had the financial resources to carry on.

Governor Huey Long of Louisiana (as quoted in Edward Robb Ellis's *A Nation in Torment*) described the situation very well:

> The wealth of the land was being tied up in the hands of a very few men. The people were not buying because they had nothing with which to buy. The big business interests were not selling, because there was nobody they could sell to. One percent of the people could not eat any more than any other one percent; they could not wear much more than any other one percent; they could not live in any more houses than any other one percent. So in 1929, when the fortune-holders of America grew powerful enough that one percent of the people owned nearly everything, ninety-nine percent of the people owned practically nothing, not even enough to pay their debts, a collapse was at hand.

Unlike today, in 1929 there were no solid, middle-class foundations for American wealth. Most of those who had money were heavily invested in the stock market. When the crash occurred in October 1929, their fortunes were gone overnight, and there was no one left to hold up the economy. The economic foundation of the country was wiped out.

Another major contributing factor was rampant stock speculation. As the famous English economist Walter Bagehot put it: ". . . at particular times a great many stupid people have a great deal of stupid money." Economist John Kenneth Galbraith called it a "mass escape into make-believe, so much a part of the true speculative orgy."

Business leaders, bankers, and intellectuals alike told the public it was safe to invest. In a *Ladies' Home Journal* article entitled "Everyone Ought to Be Rich," John Jacob Raskob, a top executive and director of General Motors and an associate of the du Ponts, wrote in 1928: "If a man saves $15 a week and invests in common stocks, at the end of 20 years he will have at least $80,000 and income from investments of around $400 a month. He will be rich."

People were making paper "fortunes," sometimes virtually overnight. In *A Nation in Torment,* Edward Robb Ellis described the speculative atmosphere:

> By word of mouth, by means of newspapers and radio, tip sheets and magazines, people heard of ordinary folks like themselves who cleaned up in the market. A nurse made $30,000 by betting on tips she got from grateful patients. A valet played the market and raked in a quarter-million dollars.

John Kenneth Galbraith commented, "Of all the mysteries of the stock exchange there is none so impenetrable as why there should be a buyer for everyone who seeks to sell." *Everyone* wanted to own stocks.

ECONOMISTS AND THE AMERICAN INVESTOR

In the fall of 1929, when uneasiness began to cloud the stock market euphoria, very few economic "experts" read the signs correctly. Early in October 1929, less than a month before the crash, Charles E. Mitchell, chairman of National City Bank and a director of the New York Federal Reserve Bank, said that the "industrial condition of the U.S. is absolutely sound . . . . Nothing can arrest the upward movement." On October 12, about two weeks before the bedlam began, he predicted, "I expect to see the stock market a good deal higher than it is today."

In the fall of 1929, when uneasiness began to cloud the stock market euphoria, very few economic "experts" read the signs correctly.

Some of the most respected minds in the country were caught napping. The Harvard Economic Society was an esteemed group of economists who formed an extracurricular enterprise that sold economic forecasts to businesses and investors. In the spring of 1929, the Society was mildly bearish and predicted a recession in the near future. By the summer, when the recession was not the least bit visible, the Society retrenched and confessed error, thinking that business must have been good after all. Following the crash, the Society again had trouble adjusting. In November, 1929, it said firmly that "a severe depression like that of 1920–1921 is outside the range of probability. We are not facing protracted liquidation." The Society stood by its prediction until it disbanded in 1932.

Not everyone was bullish in 1929. One of the most accurate forecasts came from the outspoken Rodger W. Babson, a 54-year-old economist and statistician. Since 1919, Babson had been training young men at the Babson Institute for careers in business and finance. By 1927, he had endowed the Institute with $1.2 million made in the stock market. Periodically, he issued reports to investors and predicted the behavior of the stock market. On September 5, 1929, supported by numerous graphs and charts, Babson predicted, "Sooner or later a crash is coming, and it may be terrific. . . . Factories will shut down . . . men will be thrown out of work . . . and the result will be a serious business depression." Wall Street labeled Babson "notoriously inaccurate," and *Business Week* ran an editorial on September 14 that joked about "an attack of Babsonmindedness" that depressed the stock market.

Few people wanted to listen to portentous statements or forecasts of gloom and doom. After the devastating reality of the crash, everyone was searching for a note of optimism. For example, there is little doubt that Wall Street urged John D. Rockefeller to make an optimistic forecast about the stock market. His statement ran, "Believing that fundamental conditions of the country are sound . . . my son and I have for some days been purchasing sound common stocks." The statement was widely applauded, although comedian Eddie Cantor was quick to note, "Sure, who else had any money left?"

People clung to the "words of wisdom" of the prophets of euphoria. These were Calvin Coolidge's, in his final message to Congress:

> No Congress of the United States ever assembled, on surveying the state of the Union, has met with a more pleasing prospect than that which appears at the present time. In the domestic field there is tranquility and contentment, harmonious relations between management and wage earner, freedom from industrial strife, and the highest record of years of prosperity. In the foreign field there is peace, the goodwill which comes from mutual understanding, and the knowledge that the problems which a short time ago appeared so ominous are yielding to the touch of manifest friendship. The great wealth created by our economy has had the widest distribution among our own people, and has gone out in a steady stream to serve the charity and the business of the world. The requirements of existence have passed beyond the standard of necessity into the region of luxury. Enlarging production is consumed by an increasing demand at home, and an expanding commerce abroad. The country can regard the present with satisfaction and anticipate the future with optimism.

THE WRITING ON THE WALL

The euphoria of the late 1920s masked several areas of economic weakness that pointed to an economic downturn. One of these was home building. In 1926, as the real estate activity and building construction cycles peaked, residential construction began a decline that would last through the remainder of the decade and beyond. The implications of weakness from this prime economic indicator went almost totally unnoticed.

Agriculture was another area that was essentially overlooked. Competition from foreign grain exporters, such as Argentina and Australia, and the loss of European markets after World War I were depressing prices and profits for farmers. Technical improvements were helping to produce higher crop yields, further glutting the market and driving prices down. All the while, prices for other goods moved sharply higher. Farmers were in a pinch, and many were destined for bankruptcy.

Ironically, the weakness of the banking system stemmed from the fact that banks were nearly bulging at the seams with money. From 1919 to 1929, industrial production rose 30 percent while wages and other producers' prices remained relatively flat or went down. For corporations, unit costs were low and prices were stable. Profits soared. In the early 1920s, profits were rolled into capital investment, which rose by more than 6 percent a year through the 1920s. Toward the end of the decade, there was almost no place to put money but in the banks.

With their abundance of cash, banks lent money to everyone and backed many highly speculative ventures. When they ran out of borrowers in this country, bankers went abroad, lending money to unsound German municipalities and unstable Latin American governments. In their fervor to lend, some banks actually *paid* money for the privilege of making a loan. One bank affiliate paid the son of the president of Peru $450,000 for his help in placing a loan to that nation. Later, the bank took a $90-million bath when Peru defaulted on the debt.

The banks also contributed to the speculative frenzy in stocks. Using the stock portfolio of depositors as collateral, bankers would loan money for the purchase of more stock. In doing so, they created paper money that fed the speculative flames. By 1929, the banking system was poised for disaster. Edward Robb Ellis aptly concluded,

> The economy was unsound. The corporate structure was sick. The banking system was weak. Foreign trade was out of balance. Business data were inadequate and often faulty. This constellation of conditions left the economy a flawed and loaded gun, and when the stock market crashed, the gun did not merely fire—it exploded in everyone's face.

ECONOMIC WEAKNESS VERSUS DEPRESSION

The scenario presented above seems frightening. With the people of the country full of optimism and with business apparently prospering, everything suddenly came crashing down. There are *many* reasons why we will not see this situation repeat itself.

First, the structure of American wealth—the standard of living—is now entirely different. A high percentage of American wealth today is distributed in a broad and relatively affluent middle class. During the 1920s and 1930s, the average American didn't own a car. Few, if any, electrical appliances were found in most kitchens. Most homes were equipped with one radio, not three televisions sets and a stereo VCR. People owned work clothes and, possibly, Sunday clothes. There was almost no leisure wear and little, if any, leisure time.

A steady job was considered a blessed asset. Only the very rich played tennis and golf. Vacations consisted of two or three days off from work, most often without pay. Higher education was for the fortunate few. Everyone was busy just trying to make a living.

Lessons Learned

Largely because of the experience of the Great Depression, specific checks and balances are built into our present-day economy to discourage financial panic. For example, although our system of unemployment insurance doesn't replace full pay and has a limited term, it does provide a stabilizing influence in a depressed economy. When people lose their jobs because of economic downturns, this money helps keep families afloat long enough for some type of recovery to begin.

Largely because of the experience of the Great Depression, specific checks and balances are built into our present-day economy to discourage financial panic.

Our system of home mortgage repayment also provides stability. In the 1930s, most mortgages on homes and commercial buildings had to be renewed each year and became due and payable at year's end. When money and credit availability lagged, banks couldn't or wouldn't refinance, so people lost everything. Today, most mortgages on homes and commercial buildings are repaid in small monthly installments over a period of 30 years. Only consistently nonperforming loans are subject to foreclosure.

A recent factor that protects against the possibility of a severe depression is that many American families are now supported by two incomes. More than half of all married women work full-time. If one wage earner loses a job, the other's income will support the family's basic needs, at least for a while. Women's salaries haven't achieved parity with men's, but they are getting there. Today's family has a 50 percent better chance to survive financially than the one-wage-earner family of the 1930s.

Another stabilizing factor lies in our experience with fiscal policy. Prior to the Great Depression, economists thought that the government should raise or lower taxes according to the level of spending, in order to balance the budget at all times. We have learned, however, that raising taxes can sometimes actually lower tax revenues. In 1932, President Hoover and the Congress passed a bill to raise tax rates; they expected to generate roughly one-third more revenue than in 1931. These policy makers failed to realize that higher tax rates would reduce consumer spending and further depress businesses, thus reducing total gross national product (GNP) and lowering net tax revenues. Needless to say, their tax policy made the Great Depression more severe.

That kind of mistaken policy won't reappear. Immediately after the crash of October 1987, the federal government flooded the economy with money so the crash alone would not cause a recession—or worse. I don't always agree with the fiscal policies of our government and the Federal Reserve Board, but I am confident that they know what actions to take to prevent another Great Depression.

The depth and diversity of our economy are other major stabilizing influences; they were at work to some degree even during the Great Depression years. Not all companies went broke, and some actually managed to make a great deal of money. Entertainment, advertising, and tobacco companies posted banner sales. As the nation felt the need for distraction, entertainment grew in variety and abundance. People bought newspapers for information as well as to read ads to help overcome their blues (at least they could read about new cars and merchandise even if they couldn't buy them). Today, we have so much diversity in business, so many opportunities, that a general decline among them all is highly unlikely.

The structure of the American work force is entirely different from that of 50 to 100 years ago. Your employment offers far more stability than that of your parents and grandparents.

Look back further, to the year 1869. About 45 percent of the work force owned a business, worked in a profession, or were self-employed farmers. Another 23 percent worked for someone else in agriculture, merchandising, financial enterprises, personal service trades, and government. The remainder of the work force, about 32 percent, was engaged in mining, construction, and freight transportation.

Members of this last group have always had the most difficulty finding stable employment, because the underlying industries respond so violently to movements in the business cycle. This group is the first to be hired when the economy looks good, and the first to be fired when the economy looks bad.

Fifty years later, in 1919, the composition of the work force had changed significantly. There were fewer folks "down on the farm." People moved out of the self-employed farming business and into the more unstable positions of construction and manufacturing. This first-to-be-hired and first-to-be-fired group made up 36 percent of working Americans in 1919. With over a third of the American work force dependent on employment in the cyclical trades, the financial collapse ten years later had a devastating effect on the laborers of America.

Today, technology has brought new changes in the character of the work force. The growth of white-collar occupations—managers, engineers, accountants, lawyers, secretaries, and salespersons—has brought new stability to the work environment. This group, which constituted only 28 percent of the labor force in 1900, had risen to 44 percent by 1957 and makes up the majority of the work force today. White-collar workers hold *positions* rather than jobs, they earn *salaries* rather than hourly wages, and they are more likely to find new positions if they are laid off than people involved in the trades.

When you combine the increase in service industries with the increase in white-collar jobs, you will find today's labor force is less volatile, even during cyclical ups and downs. Recessions come and go, but more people than ever before are employed.

Finally, Americans today are more psychologically prepared for economic weakness than they were in 1929. Even after Black Friday in 1929, the nation failed to recognize the full extent and scope of the problems before them. Consumers were still caught up in the heady atmosphere of the 1929 boom year. When they awakened to the economic realities, as Joseph Schumpeter wrote in *Business Cycles,* "People felt the ground give way beneath their feet." Public confidence, an essential element for any economic recovery, was deeply shaken.

Today, we are better educated. We know more about the business cycle. Individuals and businesses alike are more prepared to ride through periods of weakness and take advantage of intervening periods of strength. Americans are more sophisticated with regard to financial and economic information. We have seen recessions come and go. We have seen wars come and go. We know we will survive. We know that, ultimately, we will do well.

A CASE FOR OPTIMISM

At the beginning of this chapter I posed a question: Do cycles point the way to another major depression? The answer is a resounding *No!* Cycles do point to periods of weakness in the future, but these are periods of *relative* weakness. There is absolutely no evidence from cycle theory that we will see a worldwide economic collapse in our lifetime. The fact that we will experience economic weakness does not imply that our climb up the ladder of economic prosperity will be stopped.

Do cycles point the way to another major depression? The answer is a resounding *NO!*

When you look at a cycle chart of business activity, you see a horizontal wave that moves up and down. This depiction may be misleading. More precisely pictured, this cycle would be placed not on a horizontal plane, but rather on an upward-sloping axis. In other words, the cycle of business activity is not simply one of strength and weakness, but of strength and weakness *within the context of continuous long-term growth.* The means that, in the long term, you can expect to see a continual rise in our standard of living.

And even that concept is changing. There are those today who are choosing to work fewer hours so that they may enjoy more "quality of life." This is another form of prosperity and perhaps a new way to measure our "standard of living." The rate of consumption may decline in the future and yet we may all "feel" we are living better than any generation before us. As we become more gentle with nature, flow more freely with the natural rhythms of the universe, and listen to our intuitive voice, we can't help but feel prosperous.

You can use this information, this change in energy, to remain optimistic and courageous about your financial future. You can combine your knowledge of cycles with expectations of a positive outcome to produce the results you want in life. You can choose to remain optimistic and refuse to let negative images of the future bring you to the edges of despair.

By anticipating a positive outcome from your financial decisions and by combining your knowledge of cycles and intuition, you will draw positive influences and surround yourself with opportunity. *You* are your own best case for optimism.

Chapter 6

Cycles of Success

I found that money was like a sixth sense without which you could not make the most of the other five.

Somerset Maugham

I considered many lofty financial and philosophical discussions as themes for this chapter; instead, I found myself drawn to images and episodes from the *Star Wars* trilogy.

Like most *Star Wars* fans, I am enthralled with the action, the music, the special effects, the humor, and the ideas underlying "the Force." I am charmed by Luke, Princess Leia, Han Solo, C-3PO, R2-D2, and the Wookie. The bar scene on some distant planet, where Han buys a used spacecraft, is a classic.

The second movie in the series, *The Empire Strikes Back,* is for me the most interesting of the three. Luke is separated from Han, Leia, and the Wookie when an ice station they are visiting gets invaded by Darth Vader's imperial guard. Luke sets out on a mission to find the great Jedi master Yoda, who will teach him to become a Jedi knight so he can rescue the universe from the dark forces of the Emperor. Yoda turns out to be a wise, wonderful, and unassuming creature with patient wisdom about the sources of human power and how to find balance in life.

Luke's inner growth under the loving direction of Yoda is my favorite part of the movie. Luke eventually joins Yoda in his tiny home, after crashing his starfighter in a swamp as green and slimy as you can envision. Luke is certain that he is stranded and that his ship will never fly again. Yoda, in his wisdom, knows the essence of what is to come. He instructs Luke, primarily through example, about the simplicity of true wisdom and personal power. What struck me about his teachings was how they encased the very essence of cycles.

When you synthesize your personal power, when you integrate knowledge and intuition with the natural cycle rhythms found in all parts of the universe, your life takes on an entirely new perspective. In effect, you draw on "the force" of nature, creating a synergy of thought and action.

When you integrate knowledge and intuition with the natural cycle rhythms found in the universe, you draw on "the force" of nature, creating a synergy of thought and action.

CYCLES AND TEACHINGS OF A JEDI MASTER

This is the essence of what Yoda tries to teach Luke: by living *with* the forces of nature rather than opposing them, you create and live a positive "destiny," defeating the power of "the dark side"—that element within us that makes us prone to fear and anxiety. Often, however, our zeal for immediate results gets in the way.

In the movie, Luke is willing to work as hard as possible, as long as it doesn't take too long. His friends are in danger, and his measure of success is the speed with which he can prepare himself to save them. Constantly judging himself and his rate of growth, he pushes the learning curve by tackling challenges before he is ready—pushing, pushing, pushing, driven to succeed. Yoda watches in dismay and tells Obi-Wan Kanobie, "The boy has no patience."

And so it is with our financial and personal lives. If we can learn patience, if we can learn to tap the power of cycles and intuition, then personal and financial growth will follow with a minimum of fear and frustration. We can learn patience by realizing there is never just one "chance of a lifetime"—there are always other opportunities. We can avoid fear by "seeing" our future success within the context of the financial trends predicted by cycles. If, like Luke, we try to push the limits of growth, we will experience the process as a struggle rather than as a natural, harmonious progression of life.

If we impatiently try to push the limits of growth, we will experience the process as a struggle rather than as a natural, harmonious progression of life.

Before accepting Luke as a student, Yoda asks Ben, "Will he finish what he starts?" Finishing what you start means more than just working hard; it means staying the course, integrating goals and subconscious motivations for a common purpose, not just in work but in an approach to life. In our activity-saturated culture, we fill ourselves with good intentions, but when the process of goal achievement gets too long, too lonely, or both, we often retreat into "seeing what's on" television, into work, or into alleged "obligations."

Finishing what you start is important for several reasons. The first has to do with energy. I believe a certain hidden "energy" surrounds a task when your subconscious is aware that you are a person who finishes what you start. If you train your subconscious to be a finisher, to stay focused on solutions until they are reached, then you get an extra boost, an internal motivation that will carry you toward achievement.

If you train your subconscious to be a finisher, to stay focused on solutions until they are reached, then you get an extra boost, an internal motivation that will carry you toward achievement.

By contrast, if you repeatedly show your subconscious that you are a quitter, it won't take your good intentions and goals seriously.

In addition to providing you with energy, completing what you start will help you maintain mental clarity and focus. If your life is filled with scores of partially completed tasks, then you will live in a world of mental clutter. Imagine having all the uncompleted tasks in your life tossed into a gunny sack, like pieces of junk and unassembled parts. Imagine that sack tied to your waist, going everywhere you go, pulling on you with a useless weight. That "weight" will affect everything you do and every goal you set.

This residue of unfinished business clings to every new beginning like the slime that surrounds Luke's ship while he is in training. It's not a pretty sight, and it is holding you back from reaching your full potential. Whether the goal is to be a Jedi knight or to achieve financial independence, it is important to finish unfinished business. Decide what you want and what you don't want in your life. Pursue your goals to completion, and experience the accompanying joy when you realize them.

While training under Yoda, Luke spends a good deal of time asking questions, but he gets no direct answers. As a great master, Yoda is purposely evasive. He wants Luke to discover his own truths. In rarely spoken words, Yoda instructs Luke to be less concerned with answers and more concerned with his *knowing,* with *his intuitive knowledge.* He tells Luke that the answers to his questions will come to him when his mind is calm and peaceful, uncluttered by frustration, doubt, and fear.

Your initial response to this bit of guidance is probably anything but calm and peaceful: "In my busy life? You've got to be kidding!" I know this feeling all too well. With the amount of change we are all experiencing, it is not easy to enjoy life in a state of tranquillity. Yet, I know it is both possible and powerful.

Insight is born when your mind is in a state of clarity and focus, not when you are consciously striving for immediate answers.

What Yoda is really referring to is reaching a mental state of true clarity and focus. We all know the feeling that comes with sudden understanding and knowingness. Like the lightbulb shown in cartoons, the knowledge comes all at once, usually in a flash of wisdom following a period of contemplation when time seems nonexistent. If you recall and analyze such an event in your life, I think you will find that the insight didn't come when you were demanding answers, but rather when your mind was peaceful and at rest. If it helps, think of your subconscious mind as a computer that needs time to process all the information it takes in. Each time you demand an immediate solution, you are pressing a key that interrupts the processing. You lose focus and your mind gets off track; sometimes, it has to start all over again.

I feel fortunate to have realized how much more energy I can tap when my mind is in a state of clarity and focus. By learning to quiet my mind, by filling it with positive visualizations, by finding humor in events that seem negative, by exercising, and by feeding my body with nutritious foods, I feel that I have expanded what each day can hold. Some decisions that used to take weeks, I can now make instantly. Projects that formerly took months, I can now complete in weeks. My energy use seems wonderfully efficient to me, and a tremendous return on investment.

The whole approach comes back to accepting intuition, that state of knowingness that each of us can attain. Dr. Jonas Salk, whose contributions to medicine have saved millions of lives from the crippling effects of polio, discusses knowingness or intuition in his book *The Anatomy of Reality.* Dr. Salk believes that true evolution is evolution of the mind, and that developing intuition is the force behind this process. Dr. Salk expresses his personal access to insight this way:

> I am drawn and guided by feelings to move, to ask, to observe, and to reflect on what all of this means. I sense something strong and powerful that is acting with interior as well as exterior force. I feel it as I feel the wind although I cannot see it. My sail is full but I do not see what fills it. I am drawn toward certain people and in certain directions. Forces of attraction act upon me; they guide me as if I did not need a compass with which to verify my course. It is enough that I should yield and allow myself to follow what I feel.

Perhaps this is the perspective that Yoda tries to help Luke grasp—and the idea that draws so many viewers to the movie.

In his frustration with the process of becoming a Jedi knight, Luke accuses Yoda of "wanting the impossible." In his anger, he throws, for lack of a better term, a "psychic tantrum" and, to his surprise, watches as his negative thoughts cause his ship to sink into the muck. He predicts, "We'll never get it out." Yoda responds, "So certain are you? Always with you it can not be done." Luke says that moving rocks is one thing but moving the ship is completely different. "Only different in your mind," says Yoda. "You must unlearn what you have learned."

Unlearn the limiting beliefs you have adopted. *Do*, don't just try.

I'm not saying you can move rocks with your mind, but unlearning is one of the most stimulating things you can do. To reach higher levels of success, old ideas that limit your connection to your own source of power must be unlearned. You may hold many restricting beliefs about yourself. When you concentrate on what you can't do, rather than what you will do, your mind creates situations that verify your foregone conclusions. The financial world is filled with what seem to be intimidating decisions. You can turn this around by "unlearning" negative beliefs about yourself and about making money.

The knowledge and use of cycles can help with your unlearning process. With the road map of probabilities that cycles present, you can concentrate on your future success. You can let go of old beliefs and behaviors that have kept you from prosperity. You have already opened yourself to new ideas by reading this book. Start now to unlearn and to let go of beliefs like "I can't make successful investments." You *can.*

When I first encountered the concept of cycles, I had a bachelor's degree in education—no other specialized training. I now have a master's degree in economics: I wanted to find out whether economists knew more about money making than I did. They don't. You shouldn't let the financial world intimidate you. You have absolutely everything you need to be financially successful.

After his ship sinks in the muck and just before he walks away in despair, Luke is challenged by Yoda to bring it out of the slime using "the Force." Luke responds, "All right, I'll give it a try." Yoda then says, "Try not. Do, or do not. There is no try." This is first-rate wisdom for success. If you spend all your time trying, then you will end up trying. If you spend all of your time doing, then you will accomplish your goals. Self-made billionaire and philanthropist W. Clement Stone hands out cards that say "Do it Now!" Think how weak it would be if the cards stated "Try it now."

Perhaps the best two lines in *The Empire Strikes Back* are spoken just after Yoda successfully raises Luke's ship out of the swamp. Luke watches the process in amazement, walks around his ship, which is now on dry land, and says, "I don't believe it!" Yoda smiles his knowing smile and responds, "That is why you fail."

Believing in your own ability, believing that you are worthy of a prosperous life, is the single most important criterion of success. Without this belief, no matter what you do, something will come along to sabotage your plans. In *The Inner Game of Tennis,* a terrific book that is as much about life as about sport, Timothy Gallwey talks about playing the game as if you were already a professional. He describes taking a beginning tennis player and setting up a scene where the player is told he is needed as an actor in a video. The beginner is told the camera will stay on his side of the net, so he doesn't have to play like a pro, he just has to look like a pro. "No one will ever see where the balls land," Gallwey tells him. "You just have to play the part."

Guess what happens? The beginner plays five levels *above* his own ability. Just by trying to look like a pro player, he starts hitting professional-type shots. His subconscious mind lets go of the fact that he is a beginner and "allows" his body to emulate the movements and strokes of professionals he has seen play. For that brief moment in time, he "unlearns all he has learned" about being a beginner. He doesn't try, he *does.*

Cycles can give you the edge to believe in yourself; they can tap the buried knowledge and power of your subconscious mind. Because you can see the probabilities of future strengths in various financial areas, you can also see your own financial success during these times. Use the power of visualization to create what you want. Your mind, your imagination, is the fountainhead of what you will create in life.

Being patient, finishing what you start, accepting your own knowingness, acting confidently, and believing in yourself will help you obtain what you desire. When you combine these attributes with your own positive attitude, you will have found the keys to creation. Use them to succeed, to find peace of mind, to create the life you want. You are your own best Force for making money.

Part 2

How to Have Your Money in the Right Place at the Right Time: Applying Cycles to Your Financial Life for Optimum Profits

Chapter 7

How to Get the Money to Start Investing

The lack of money is the root of all evil.
GEORGE BERNARD SHAW

You *can* accumulate money for investing. The easiest way to do this is to keep more of the money you earn by paying less tax. Rather than think of only your "take home" earnings, think about the total amount of money you deserve for your efforts. By reducing your tax bill, you can build capital to invest for your future.

I would like to pay a million dollars in taxes someday. It would mean I had earned enough for a million-dollar tax payment to be warranted. If I ever do earn that much in one year, you can be sure I will pay the absolute minimum amount of tax legally required.

The less money you pay to the IRS, the more you will have for yourself, for your children, for charity, and for *investments.* You have the right to pay as little tax as possible. An opinion written on the subject in a United States Circuit Court of Appeals stated: "Anyone may so arrange his affairs that his taxes shall be as low as possible. He is not bound to choose a pattern that will best pay the Treasury. No one owes any public duty to pay more than the law demands." I changed "he" to "she" and took this judge's opinion to heart.

Saving on taxes can provide the capital you want for investing.

Saving on taxes can provide the capital you want for investing. If you are in the 28 percent tax bracket (see Table 7.1), 28 cents of every dollar you earn goes to the government, not to mention the additional burdens of social security, state tax, and the many other taxes you pay each day (sales taxes and federal excise taxes, for example). For each additional dollar you can take as a deduction, you in effect give yourself a 28 percent raise on that part of your income.

Find your tax bracket in Table 7.1 Use this number to picture exactly how much more money you are going to have next year

Table 7.1
1991 Tax Rate Schedules

Taxable Income	Marginal Bracket
Single	
Up to $20,350	15%
$20,350 to $49,300	28
Over $49,300	31
Head of Household	
Up to $27,300	15%
$27,300 to $70,450	28
Over $70,450	31
Married Filing Jointly	
Up to $34,000	15%
$34,000 to $82,150	28
Over $82,150	31
Married Filing Separately	
Up to $17,000	15%
$17,000 to $41,075	28
Over $41,075	31

than you have this year. Check your last year's tax return. Scrutinize how much money you paid in taxes. Picture having more of that money returned to you. With that image in mind, let's consider the different ways you can make the vision come true.

STARTING YOUR OWN BUSINESS

Perhaps the best way to reduce your tax liability is to increase your legitimate deductions, and one of the best ways to do this is to start your own business. *Don't panic!* You don't have to commit every waking hour of your day or invest huge sums of money to start a business of your own. The level of your hourly and financial commitment is completely up to you. The work you choose can be the most personally fulfilling of your life, and there is no limit on the scope of your vision. Best of all, when you operate your own business, *you* are in charge. If you have the time and energy to devote to it and aren't already in a career that provides you with personal satisfaction and your desired level of income, I strongly suggest that you consider starting your own business.

Starting you own business is probably the single best way to reduce your tax liability. It will also foster creativity and the development of your limitless productive potential.

Begin by thinking of things you like to do. What are your interests? Because you are going to be running this business in addition to your current work or obligations, it is imperative that you choose an endeavor you enjoy. If you enjoy your new enterprise, it won't seem like work!

The possibilities for businesses are absolutely endless. Napoleon Hill and W. Clement Stone have said, in their book, *Success Through a Positive Mental Attitude,* "What the mind can conceive and believe, it can achieve." Here is a list of a few of the many possibilities that exist for your own business:

Buying and Selling

- Antiques
- Art
- Boats
- Books
- Cars
- Clothing
- Collectibles
- Jewelry
- Musical Instruments
- Pets
- Records
- Sporting Equipment

Consulting/Services/Producing

- Cake Decorating and Baking
- Catering
- Cleaning
- Color Consulting
- Computer Expertise
- Day Care for Children
- Day Care for Elderly
- Delivery Service
- Fishing
- Foreign Language Teaching
- Interior Decorating
- Lawn Service
- Painting/Wall Papering
- Pet Boarding
- Photography
- Publishing/Desk-Top Publishing
- Sewing/Dress Designing/Alterations
- Speaking
- Teaching:
  - aerobics
  - acting
  - cooking
  - dancing
  - fishing
  - golf
  - meditation
  - music
  - nutrition
  - sewing
  - swimming
  - tennis
  - yoga
- Typing/Word Processing
- Writing

The list is limited only by your imagination. If you are interested in the prospect of starting your own business, a number of excellent books are available to help you foresee and make the decisions you will face. Gregory and Patricia Kishel, for example, have written several very helpful books, including *Dollars on Your Door Step: The Complete Guide to Home Based Businesses,* and *Cashing in on the Consulting Boom.* If you like the idea of running a business from your home (you wouldn't be alone: 28 million Americans now work at home—nearly 10 million more than five years ago), but no specific interests come to mind, you'll find over 100 ideas in Lynie Arden's *Franchises You Can Run from Home.*

If you pay *any* taxes at all, forming a small business can give you the opportunity to reduce or eliminate them. I recently gave a seminar, "Women and Wealth," to several groups of women at a major Fortune 500 corporation. A key feature of the seminar was a discussion of increasing personal income by paying less tax. One woman, Beth, was especially excited about the possibilities I presented. She and her husband had been married for three years and, although they both worked full-time, they had been unable to accumulate enough money to make a down payment on a home.

Beth was an attractive, well-groomed woman; on the day of the seminar, she was wearing a beautiful, kelly green dress. I commented on the color, which is one of my favorites. She told me she had been studying color consulting—the art of coordinating colors of clothing and makeup to suit an individual's natural skin tone and hair color. She had already "done" colors for a few people and all of them were pleased with the results. She asked me whether I thought color consulting would be a good business to start. Looking at how well she presented herself and hearing the enthusiasm in her voice as she spoke, I *knew* she would be successful. I explained the many ways she could use this business to earn profits and create tax deductions against her ordinary income.

Using Beth's case as an example, let's look at a few of the legitimate deductions she was allowed by starting her own business. Shown in Figure 7.1 is Part II of Schedule C: Profit or Loss from Business (Sole Proprietorship), a schedule that people who own their own businesses must attach to their Form 1040. The "Expenses" amounts they fill in are deductions that individual businesspersons can take. Their business profits or losses are included with their other income if they have a salaried job or a gain on their investments. If they show a business loss because of deductible expenses, they can reduce ordinary income, and *pay less tax.*

Part II Expenses

8	Advertising	8	
9	Bad debts from sales or services (see Instructions)	9	
10	Car and truck expenses (attach Form 4562)	10	
11	Commissions and fees	11	
12	Depletion	12	
13	Depreciation and section 179 expense deduction (not included in Part III) (see Instructions)	13	
14	Employee benefit programs (other than on line 19)	14	
15	Insurance (other than health)	15	
16	Interest:		
a	Mortgage (paid to banks, etc.)	16a	
b	Other	16b	
17	Legal and professional services	17	
18	Office expense	18	
19	Pension and profit-sharing plans	19	
20	Rent or lease (see Instructions):		
a	Vehicles, machinery, and equip.	20a	
b	Other business property	20b	

21	Repairs and maintenance	21	
22	Supplies (not included in Part III)	22	
23	Taxes and licenses	23	
24	Travel, meals, and entertainment:		
a	Travel	24a	
b	Meals and entertainment		
c	Enter 20% of line 24b subject to limitations (see Instructions)		
d	Subtract line 24c from line 24b	24d	
25	Utilities	25	
26	Wages (less jobs credit)	26	
27a	Other expenses (**list type and amount**):		
27b	Total other expenses	27b	

Figure 7.1 IRS Schedule C, Expenses Section, for Reporting Profit or Loss When You Own Your Own Business

LEONARDO MEETS THE I.R.S.

Drawing by Mort Gerberg; © 1988 The New Yorker Magazine, Inc.

I'm not recommending that you start a business in order to show a loss—far from it! But if you apply all of the legally available deductions, then it is very likely that your business will show a loss for the first one or two years. These losses can be deducted from your combined income, and the net effect will be that you keep more of the money you earn.

Suppose both Beth and her husband have salaried jobs, each of them earning $24,000 per year. Their combined income of $48,000 puts them in the 28 percent tax bracket. (This is always subject to change. Carefully check your tax bracket each year.) Beth starts her color consulting business, setting up an office in a room of her rented home. Assuming that she shows a loss in her first year of operation (meaning that her business expenses are greater than her business income), for every $1.00 in deductions her business generates, she receives 28 cents back in the form of an income tax refund. If her business losses are $5,000, Beth keeps $1,400 *more* of her salary than she would have been allowed without those deductions.

Your first thought might be: what good does it do me to spend $5,000 in order to save $1,400 in taxes? The answer is that you are probably converting what would have been personal expenses into business expenses that are deductible. The $5,000 (or whatever amount you choose to spend on your business) will be money you would likely spend anyway, only now it has a business purpose. Part of your rent will be deductible; part of your phone bill will be deductible; if you take a potential client to dinner, that's partially deductible; and so on. When you spend money trying to make a profit in a business, the money spent becomes a tax deduction.

Here is what Beth discovered about her color consulting business. She could deduct the costs of trips to Dayton, Ohio (where her mother lived) by setting up several color consulting sessions while she was there. She could also deduct the cost of books, newspapers, magazines, and videos that she used for her business. She could deduct seminars and classes she took to improve her business skills. Telephone calls to her mother were deductible because her mother set up her consulting sessions in Dayton. Lunches with prospective clients became 80 percent deductible. Office supplies, secretarial services, and equipment all became deductions. Beth and her husband now bank a sizable tax return, and they expect to be purchasing their own home next year.

If you are married and not currently working outside your home, then *your* business deductions can save tax dollars on your joint tax return. Here is another example. Mary is an attorney and earns a salary; her husband, Jack, is a writer and works out of their home. They file a joint return, so Mary's salary and Jack's business income and expenses are included together when figuring their taxes. Jack's legitimate tax deductions can serve to offset Mary's income and, at the end of the year, their joint tax refund is bigger.

I said it earlier, but it bears repeating: You *are allowed* more deductions by running a business of your own than if you work for a salary alone.

My first experience with starting a business was in 1969, when I saw an opportunity to earn extra money. Learning center programs—independent study centers designed for students to work at their own pace—were an educational innovation at that time, and there was a need for education professionals who could write them. The school district offered extra pay to teachers willing to develop and write learning center programs. I accepted the challenge.

The first one I wrote was called "Simple Machines, Friction and Physics." When the project was finished and in use, teachers in other school districts began calling me during the evenings and on weekends, requesting information on the materials. The demand for information sparked an idea. I would start a business to fill the need for new learning center materials.

I formed my company, which I called Creative Activities, with three objectives: to provide a valuable service to students and teachers, to make profits, and to generate tax deductions. I packaged the materials and began calling on school principals. I quickly received enough orders to cover the cost of printing, and before long I was making a profit. In addition, all of the business expenses from Creative Activities were deductions against my regular salary, and I was saving thousands of dollars in taxes. Travel was almost always deductible because everywhere I went, even if I was visiting a friend or relative, I always called on a school. In 1969, I saved a bundle on taxes by owning a business and, as Beth and her husband recently learned, the method is still as profitable as ever.

SETTING UP YOUR BUSINESS

Profit is a very important word to the IRS. The IRS requires that *the intent* of your business must be to make a profit. They realize that you may not make a profit at first, but they want proof that you are trying to make a profit, not just setting up a deduction-generating machine. The IRS would like to see a profit in three or more years of a consecutive five-year period. If you can't satisfy the IRS regarding your profitable intent, your deductions may be disallowed.

In the eyes of the IRS, any legitimate business expense is deductible, provided you can demonstrate intent to make a profit. One of the best ways to demonstrate intent is to set up your business as an S Corporation.

If you start a business and are still showing a loss after the second year, there are two things you can do. First, you can discontinue that business and start a new one. You will still be able to deduct the losses accrued while you were trying to get the first business off the ground.

Second, if you want to hold on to your business but are in doubt as to how long it may take you to show a profit, you can file Form 5213, Election to Postpone Determination with Respect to the Presumption That an Activity Is Engaged in for Profit. Once you file this form, the IRS cannot make any determination of your profitable (or unprofitable) status for five years. You will be able to take your deductions and have a full five years to prove that you are actively trying to earn profits from your business.

I believe the very best option is to set up your business as an *S Corporation* with a bank account separate from your own. When you are in business for yourself, in the eyes of the law (and the IRS), *you* are the business. When you set up an

S Corporation, the corporation itself becomes the legal business entity, and you (or you and several others) are the stockholder(s). This organization provides all the tax benefits of owning your own business (plus some more), but it reduces your personal liability. As an added benefit, establishing your business as an S Corporation is a clear indication to the IRS that you are not engaging in a passing whim or a hobby. In addition, the tax laws for S Corporations allow you to operate at a loss for a number of years and still retain your loss deduction. As long as you can clearly show that you have been *trying* to make a profit, you shouldn't have any trouble with the IRS.

Setting up your business as an S Corporation is easy. Just contact the Secretary of State's office in your state and request the forms. There may be a filing fee of about $50, but the process is almost self-explanatory.

The test for whether a business expense is legally deductible is that it must be "ordinary and necessary" for conducting your type of business. This means that when your personal and business expenses overlap, you can take a deduction for the portion used for business. For example, if you use your car for business purposes half the time, you may deduct one half of all your automobile expenses.

Recordkeeping

Contrary to popular belief, recordkeeping for a business enterprise need not be a confusing nightmare of forms and files. All you need is a simple system to track and organize your income and expenses. You can use a few simple techniques that will make the process very easy.

You can organize a system to keep track of your business expenses in about two hours. Set up a filing system using 30 9-inch by 12-inch envelopes or 30 file folders, depending on your preference. Label each envelope or file with the name of one of the expenses allowed as deductions on IRS Schedule C (see Figure 7.1). Every time you spend money for your business, *get a receipt* and put it in the appropriate file. When you balance your checkbook each month, put the canceled checks written for business purposes in their respective folders or files, stapled or paper-clipped to the appropriate receipts. At the end of the year, you need only add up the contents of each envelope, write them down on your ledger, and then store your files in chronological order.

Travel, entertainment, and meal expenses are 80 percent deductible, provided they are business-related. The IRS requires that you keep a travel and entertainment log, so you can prove your expenses were incurred in the active conduct of your business or trade. You can keep all this information in a simple business diary. List the five W's for major expenses: Who, what, when, where, and why. For example, if you take someone to lunch, you need to write down who attended, what was discussed, when the lunch occurred, where it occurred, and why the lunch took place. It is important that you keep track of these kinds of expenses: they can add up quickly. For example, if you take one prospective client to lunch per week and the average bill is $25, you'll be spending $1,300 a year, of which $1,040 (80 percent of $1,300) is tax-deductible. The minute or two that it takes for you to jot down these essentials will allow you to enjoy a meal with a business associate, or a trip that involves some aspect of your business, and deduct all but a fraction of what it would otherwise cost.

Be careful not to overlook travel expenses and fees paid to attend conventions, business-related seminars, and classes that enhance your business skills.

An often overlooked source of deductions is the cost of equipment such as personal computers, VCRs, television sets, tape recorders, cameras, and so forth, that you may use for business purposes. Keep a notebook on these items. Make three columns: Date, Time Used, and Purpose. Every time you use the equipment, fill in the information in each column, indicating whether the use was for business or personal reasons. Keep the log for three months. If the percentages of business and personal use remain consistent—say, 40 percent business, 60 percent personal—then you can use the 40 percent figure for the rest of the year without continuing to keep the log. At the end of the year, you can write off 40 percent of the cost (or depreciation) of the equipment as a business expense.

Deductions for the business use of your home are allowed, provided they do not result in your showing a tax loss against your other income. In other words, you can only use these deductions to offset business *profits,* not to show a loss. These deductions *can,* however be carried forward to offset future income from your business. Home business deductions may include: a portion of mortgage interest and property taxes; a portion of insurance and utilities expenses; and a percentage of the depreciation on your home. If you rent, then a portion of your rent, as well as a percentage of your utilities, phone, and so forth, can be deducted according to the percentage of use for business purposes.

Some consultants advise against taking business deductions from your home because, they say, it flags the interest of the IRS and may bring on an audit. My advice is to keep good records and take the deductions; with good records, you will have no reason to fear an audit. Your deductions are legitimate, and they will save you money. I was audited once, and the net result was that I got a $15 check in the mail for overpayment! It is especially important to take these deductions if your business is profitable. Because business deductions for your home cannot be used to generate a loss, it may not be worth taking them if your business if not making money.

I strongly urge you to combine a good system of recordkeeping with the help and advice of a qualified accountant. Tax laws change so rapidly that it pays to hire someone who makes his or her living by keeping up with the changes. If you do most of the work yourself, then the accountant's services can pay for themselves by helping you avoid errors and by finding allowable deductions you may not be aware of. In addition, the fee you pay to your tax accountant is deductible!

SAVING MONEY ON TAXES THROUGH REAL ESTATE OWNERSHIP

The relationship between real estate ownership and taxes is simple: The more real estate you own, the less taxes you pay. If you own your own home, you can deduct your property taxes and your mortgage interest on your tax return, which can save you thousands of dollars in taxes each year.

Although tax revisions have limited many deductions, real estate ownership still has many tax advantages, especially for the small investor.

Let's say you earn $24,000 a year. You purchase a property, and the mortgage payment is $500 per month. (At current interest rates, that would be a $60,000 home or town house.) The bulk of your mortgage payment is interest, especially in the first few years. In the first year, you will have a tax deduction of almost $6,000, plus your deduction for property taxes. If you pay a 28 percent tax rate, this deduction will save you over $1,700 per year. In effect, you aren't paying $500 per month for your home, but $350! It is almost as if someone is giving you $150 a month! Think of all the things you could do with $1,700 per year. If you invest that money well, you could someday be a millionaire!

Take this idea one step further. You own your home, you have a tax saving of at least $1,700 a year, and you decide to purchase a piece of rental property. Let's say you purchase a town house for $60,000 and you rent it for $500 a month. You are paying out $500 a month in mortgage payments, but you are receiving $500 a month in rent. Without considering the potential return you may get from property appreciation, consider the tax advantages you would enjoy.

The law allows you to take a depreciation deduction on your investment because, the theory goes, the investment will eventually wear out. You are allowed to depreciate the rental property as if it had a life of about 28 years. For tax purposes, you would take the value of the rental property, $60,000 (in this example, no reduction has been made for land value, which is not depreciable), and divide it by 28. This gives you a $2,142 deduction. At a 28 percent tax rate, this saves you another $600 in taxes per year. With the deductions from your own home, the deduction for property taxes on both properties and the depreciation deduction for your rental property, you have almost $2,500 per year in cash coming into your hands! You pay this money to yourself and not to the IRS. In addition, if you use the guidelines outlined in Chapters 11 through 13 when you buy real estate, your properties will be *increasing* in value far beyond these annual savings. Imagine how it would feel to own ten pieces of rental property. Begin now to visualize how *you* could become financially independent.

KISS THE IRS SHORT FORM GOOD-BYE!

No matter what else you do, don't ever fill out the short form because you think you don't have enough deductions. Doing this is like telling a blackjack dealer she has won without ever looking at your hand. Even if you fill out Form 1040 and end up filing the short form (this year only), filling out the long form is a good education. By filling it out, you can identify opportunities to develop deductions that can be applied next year.

Filling out the short form is a sure way to make a charitable contribution to the IRS!

Make a commitment to get at least one good book about saving taxes. I recommend *Beat the IRS Legally* by Andrew J. Ciaramitaro. It is both easy to read and packed with good ideas about saving money by lowering your taxes. Take notes while you read the book. Visualize a large refund check next year. And remember that the cost of the book is tax-deductible!

COMBINING DEDUCTIONS CAN SAVE YOU TAX DOLLARS

If you earn a salary and don't get reimbursed for all of your business expenses, then you need to know about some of the implications of the Tax Reform Act of 1986. Business expenses for which you are not reimbursed are included in the "miscellaneous deductions" category. Your combined business/miscellaneous deductions must be a minimum of 2 percent of your adjusted gross income. Travel and entertainment expenses are 80 percent deductible; seminars, books, and similar items are fully deductible. If you combine your business and miscellaneous deductions and can show appropriate proof of the expenses, you can save yourself money.

For example, if your adjusted gross income is $20,000, you need more than $400 (2 percent of $20,000) to take these deductions. With all of the possible deductions available, this amount shouldn't be difficult to reach. The following are just a few possibilities.:

- *Travel between two jobs* (the cost of traveling from a first to a second job) can be expensed at the rate of 27 cents per mile (for 1991). If you go home first and then travel to your second job, you can deduct the amount of mileage from your home to your second job location *if* the mileage does not exceed the distance between your first job location and your second.
- *Educational expenses* include such things as tuition, books, and transportation costs to the classroom location. You must be taking the courses either to retain your job, salary, or status; or to maintain and/or improve your job skills. The deduction includes expenses incurred to acquire a degree, provided it leads you toward advancement or specialization in your particular trade or profession. Correspondence courses are deductible, but there must be a relationship between the course and your current job skills. Unrelated general education courses are not deductible.
- *Unreimbursed job-related expenses,* such as the cost of transportation to attend a required company picnic, are deductible. These expenses are listed on IRS Form 2106 and include such items as:

Association dues	Musical instruments
Books, journals, magazines	Parking fees
Medical exams	Passport fees

Safety equipment	Tips, tolls, tools
Samples	Uniforms
Tape recorder	Union dues

- *Partial deduction of divorce attorney fees* is possible for the year of a divorce if your attorney gave you tax advice during the legal proceedings. It is also legal to deduct fees paid to a consultant for advice on tax liabilities, tax shelters, applications for refund, tax planning, and related matters. Have your attorney allocate his or her fees between deductible tax matters and the nondeductible services of the divorce. If the law firm you retain has an in-house tax department, have the fees allocated to tax advice billed from that department. You can deduct the costs of a law firm that specializes in taxes and has advised the other spouse regarding the tax consequences of a tentative property settlement involving alimony. The actual divorce may be handled by another law firm.
- *Job-hunting expenses* may be deducted when you seek new employment in the same trade or business. These expenses can include the cost of preparing your résumé and the expenses you incur in traveling to interviews. Job-hunting expenses are deductible even if you do not take new employment. The job you are seeking must be substantially in the same field as the job you have, or your deductions will not be allowed. These deductions provide an excellent means to deduct the cost of travel to places you want to go. All you need to do is set up several interviews *in your field of business* in the place you want to visit. If you are seeking employment for the first time, your expenses are not deductible even if you get a job.
- *Cruise-ship convention* costs may be deducted up to $2,000 ($4,000 for married couples, as long as both are part of the business) per year, for a convention held on a ship flying the U.S. flag. To take this deduction, you need to: (1) establish that the meeting was directly related to the active conduct of your trade or business, (2) verify that the cruise ship is a registered U.S. ship and that all ports of call are located within the United States and/or it possessions, (3) provide a written statement, signed by you, that details the number

of days you spent on the trip, the hours devoted to business activities, and a schedule (usually a formal typed or printed program) of business activities and meetings, and (4) provide a second statement, signed by you and by an officer of the firm sponsoring the convention, that details the schedule of each day's business activities and the number of hours you attended these activities.

DEDUCTIBLE ASSETS PURCHASED FOR BUSINESS

One of the best things to come from tax reform has been the new *asset-expensing* rules. These rules allow you to write off as a business expense the purchase of any asset costing *$10,000 or less.* An asset is any item or piece of equipment purchased for a business and predicted to last for an extended period of time. In the past, the IRS required businesses to depreciate all assets: only a portion of the cost was allowed each year as a deduction. Today, if your business is profitable, you can elect to show the full purchase price ($10,000 or less) as a one-time business expense, thus reducing your taxable income for that year. There are a few rules to follow, but this new regulation can provide a sizable deduction for your business.

According to the IRS's asset-expensing rules, you can deduct, for the year of the purchase, the full amount of any asset costing less than $10,000.

Suppose, for example, that you start a word processing business and do quite well the first year. You do so well, in fact, that you decide to hire someone to help you handle your growing workload. You buy a desk, a computer, a printer, software, and other peripherals, for a total of $7,500. Under the old tax laws, you would have had to depreciate these assets, taking a deduction of $1,500 per year over a five-year period (this assumes a straight-line method of depreciation). Under the new laws, you can deduct the full $7,500 the first year, provided it does not result in showing a business loss. In other words, if you buy $7,500 worth of new equipment but only show $5,000 in business profits, then the maximum deduction you can take for the equipment is $5,000. The balance, $2,500, would then be carried forward to offset future profits.

SHIPWRECKS AND MOVING EXPENSES

Much of the entertainment in watching a mystery program or reading an Agatha Christie novel comes from seeing whether you can "discover" the information that is going to identify and convict the culprit. I have always approached tax information the same way. I know that almost every piece of tax information that relates to me or my life can save me money. Armed with such knowledge, one year, I even deducted losses I incurred in a shipwreck!

A few months after getting married, I decided to work in Southern California for the summer. I was waiting tables and my husband tried to get work on a tuna fishing boat. When the fish were running, jobs and money were easy to come buy. If they weren't, you worked where you could. That summer, the tuna were nowhere to be found, so my husband took a job on a small swordfishing boat as a deck hand. Two days out to sea, a large wave broached the boat and everything was lost. My husband and the captain were picked up in a lifeboat, and the incident was reported in the newspapers.

After we had made a list of our lost items, we proudly took the newspaper article and the list to a tax preparer at a shopping center. He thought we were crazy, *until* he checked the law. The rules are that you can deduct "unreimbursed losses"—the cost of items lost from fire, storm, shipwreck, or other casualty, provided the items are not covered by insurance. Because we had no homeowners' insurance, we were able to deduct the loss.

There are many such unreimbursed losses that you may be able to take. The IRS says the loss must be "sudden, unexpected or unusual." Here are just a few of the many types of casualty losses you can deduct: avalanches, beetle attacks (loss of pine trees), blasting, blizzard, broken water pipe, drought (if the President declares a "drought disaster area"—the IRS considers this "sudden"), landslides, lightning, ordinary negligence (one court case allowed a taxpayer to deduct the cost of a diamond that was inadvertently destroyed in a garbage disposal unit), riots, sonic booms, thin ice, tidal wave, and more.

Moving expenses are deductible if you are moving from an old residence to a new residence in order to begin employment (whether for a company or as a self-employed individual). This expense is not allowed if you are temporarily employed. Your new place of work must be at least 35 miles farther from your old residence than from your new residence, and you must be employed full-time for at least 39 weeks during the 12-month period immediately following the move. There are a few other restrictions, so check the rules if you use this deduction.

START WHERE YOU ARE AND BUILD A FORTUNE

It's not always easy to think positively about money matters, especially when there seems to be too much month at the end of the money. You have the power to change that. It will take effort and action, but you *can* build a stairway to your financial dreams step-by-step. Make a commitment today to set up a business that you *know* will be successful. Challenge yourself.

There are about 100,000 new millionaires in America each year. You have the power to become one. Although starting a business can provide splendid tax savings, it may also be your road to riches. Three-quarters of all millionaires have self-owned businesses. When you already have decided to do something you like, or possibly love, this passion and energy can open up your hidden talent and possibly your genius. The only limitations you have are the ones you place on yourself.

Chapter 8

Stock Market Timing

Few mistakes are as costly as being right at the wrong time.

Many Americans are fascinated by the stock market, but are afraid to invest in it. They think that buying and selling stocks takes expert skill and knowledge, or that making money in the stock market is the province of professionals or of eccentrics who devote their lives to the study of corporate reports. Believe me when I tell you that *you* can make money in the stock market.

It will take some study, but you won't have to pore over countless, seemingly incomprehensible corporate financial statements, and you won't have to subscribe to dozens of financial newsletters or read hundreds of books. Basically, all you need to know is when to buy and sell. You need to understand stock market *timing*—cycles.

The essence of stock market timing was captured in an old hit record by The Byrds, using verses from the book of Ecclesiastes in the Bible:

To every thing, . . .
There is a season . . .
A time to be born, and a time to die;
A time to break down, and a time to build up.
And a time to every purpose under the heaven:

A time to mourn, and a time to dance;
A time to keep silence, and a time to speak
A time to keep, and a time to cast away.

These verses almost perfectly describe cycle movements in the stock market. Stock price movements follow patterns and, like the seasons, the patterns repeat themselves. Upward and downward trends have a death and a birth, "a time to break down, and a time to build up." There are periods of accelerating growth, periods of relative stagnation, and periods of decline. To be profitable, you need to know when to buy, when to keep, and when to cast away. Knowledge of stock market cycles will point you in the direction of profits.

Stock price movements follow patterns and, like the seasons, the patterns repeat themselves.

PROFITS VIA TWO MAJOR CYCLES

Understanding cycles won't guarantee that you'll profit from your stock market investments, but cycles will tell you when the time for investment is good, and when it is not. If you are considering buying stocks, you should first ask yourself this question: "Is the market *as a whole* in a strength phase or a weakness phase?" In other words: "Are stock prices in a long-term uptrend or a long-term downtrend?"

To make this determination, you should become familiar with the market averages: the Dow Jones Industrials, the Dow Jones Transportations, the Standard & Poor's (S&P) 500, the S&P 100, the Value Line index, and so forth. Each of these is an index derived from averaging a number of stocks. For example, the Dow Jones Industrials is an index composed of a weighted average of 30 stocks; the S&P 500 is a weighted average of 500 stocks; and the S&P 100 is a weighted average of 100 stocks. You can follow the movement of the averages in the financial section of your newspaper or in a financial newspaper such as *The Wall Street Journal* or *Investor's Daily.*

By watching the prices of the averages, you can determine the general direction of price movements in the short term. By looking at historical charts of the averages over a period of months or years, you can better determine the long-term direction of price movements. In general, if the long-term price trend is up, then most of the averages should be moving up over a period of months or years. Conversely, if prices are in a down trend, then most of the average indexes should be heading downward. The tough problem is determining the probability that the price trend will change. In other words, if the long-term price trend is up, what are the chances that it will continue moving up? Answering that question is where cycles come in.

There are two main cycles that can help you determine the direction of stock market price movements. One is a 40.68-month stock price cycle, and the other is a 9.2-year stock price cycle.

There are two main cycles that can help you determine the direction of stock market price movements. One is a 40.68-month stock price cycle (Figure 8.1) and the other is a 9.2-year stock price cycle (Figure 8.2). The Foundation for the Study of Cycles has identified other cycles in the stock market, but most of these are so specific as to be of interest only to professional investors or academicians. For the individual investor, the 40.68-month and 9.2-year cycles provide enough information to build a good strategy for timing buys and sells of stocks.

The 40.68-month cycle shows approximately 20 months of strength and 20 months of weakness. This doesn't mean the price trend of every market average will be up for exactly 20 months and then go down for 20 months; it merely indicates the general direction of the trend and an approximation of how long

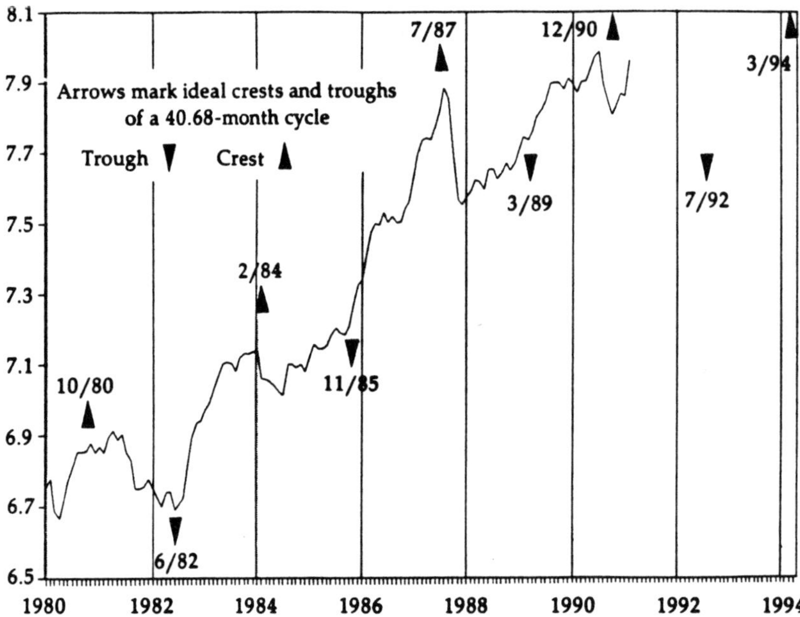

Figure 8.1 The 40.68-Month Cycle in the Prices of Common Stocks (Reprinted courtesy of the Foundation for the Study of Cycles.)

it will last. *You can never use cycles to predict exact highs or lows,* but you might come close!

You also can't use cycles to select specific stocks. In general, the majority of individual stocks move in the same direction as the average indexes, but any given stock price can remain static or even move down when the averages are moving up. Deciding which stock to purchase can depend on any number of factors—company earnings, new technological developments, the debt-to-equity ratio of the company, the stock's price-to-earnings ratio (called the PE), the possibility of a takeover, and many more. Discussion of all of these factors would fill an entire book, and many good books on these topics have already been written. A good starter book might be Peter Lynch's *One Up on Wall Street,* which explains in layman's language the methods Lynch used to pick the stocks that led to his phenomenal performance record as a money manager.

Although cycles won't tell you exact market turning points or what specific stocks to buy and sell, they will give you the basic

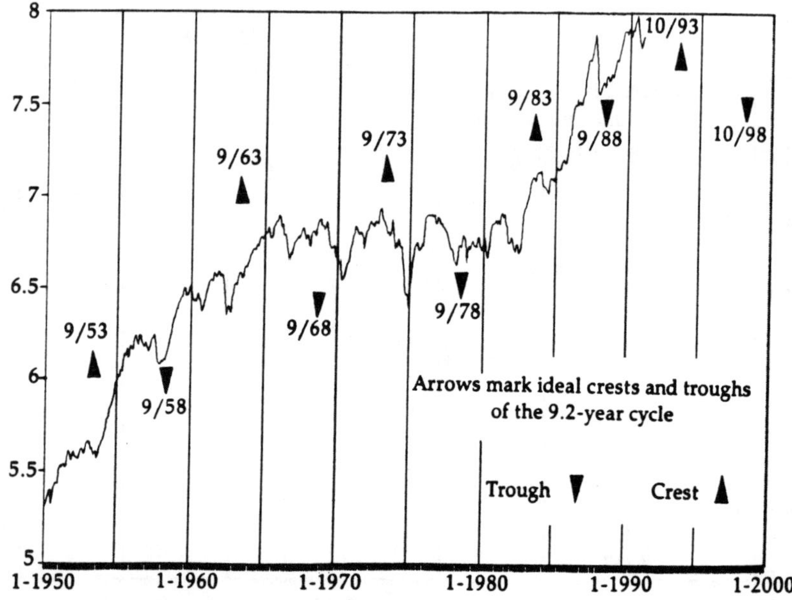

Figure 8.2 The 9.2-Year Stock Price Cycle (Reprinted Courtesy of the Foundation for the Study of Cycles.)

knowledge required to begin your decision-making process. In that light, let's examine the stock market cycles more closely.

The 9.2-year cycle shows approximately 4.5 years of strength and 4.5 years of weakness. Because this is a longer cycle than the 40.68-month stock price cycle, it gives even less indication of exact market turning points. What it *does* provide, however, is additional knowledge with which to evaluate the 40.68-month cycle. The 9.2-year cycle influences the movement of the shorter, 40.68-month cycle.

These two cycle waves interact much like waves coming into a beach. Sometimes, two waves combine to form one larger, more powerful wave. At other times, the backwash from the shore moves against an incoming wave and cancels it out. Body surfers on the Southern California beaches used to talk about the mysterious ninth wave. Supposedly, every ninth wave tended to be bigger than all the others and offered the longest and most perfect ride. Everyone wanted to ride the ninth wave. To this day, I am not sure whether I ever caught the legendary surge, but I did get better at watching for wave combinations. I learned to recognize when the smaller waves would combine with larger ones, and I would get the ride of my life.

Today, I "surf" the stock market. The Dow Jones Industrial Average is the ride, and the 40.68-month and 9.2-year stock price cycles are the waves. When I see these two cycles join, I get on the wave in preparation for an excellent ride. Instead of taking me all the way into the beach, when the 40.68-month and 9.2-year cycles combine, they take me all the way to the bank.

STOCK MARKET CYCLES IN THE 1980s

The best way to get a feel for using cycles to map out the market is to examine cycle movements in history. I started watching the market closely in 1979, shortly after I began my study of cycles. According to what I had learned, stock prices should have been on the rise; instead, the market was lethargic. Was it caused by a nationwide sense of gloom brought on by the American hostage situation in Iran? Or was everyone leery of the double-digit inflation we were experiencing? By January 1980, the market still had not made its move.

Cycles predicted the behavior of the stock market in the 1980s.

I knew that the market rarely stays flat during a strength phase, so I was anticipating an upward price trend in 1980. Like Old Faithful at Yellowstone Park, when the pressure builds up for a long enough period, the stock market erupts. The eruption came in April 1980, and I jumped in. Cycles helped me take a long position in the market within three days of the turning point!

According to both the 40.68-month cycle and the 9.2-year cycle, the market was scheduled to peak in October 1980. True to form, the Dow Industrials rose strongly until October, and only weakly moved higher in November and December. Industrials then sold off and moved marginally higher again in the first four months of 1981, reaching a peak of 1,024.05 in April 1981. But the cycle high *had* occurred in October. The remaining action was a sick market in temporary remission before its death. It didn't matter to me that it went a little higher in November and December. I was out the market and my profits were in the bank. Cycles helped me wait for the right time to buy and for the right time to get out when the up trend was over.

In January 1981, the market took a sizable drop. Some investors were beginning to realize that the bull market had become a bear market (a bull market is a long-term upward price trend, and a bear market is a long-term downward price trend). The Dow Jones Industrials drifted lower and lower before reaching a bottom of 776 in August 1982, less than 22 months after the cycle high in October 1980. Although the market did go to marginally higher levels into April 1981, it was operating on borrowed time. The actual cycle high had occurred in October of the previous year. The 40.68-month cycle had barely missed the mark.

A SIDE TRIP TO SHORT SELLING

Since 1977, when I began my cycles research, I have had a secret desire to short sell the market. Let me explain what that means. In general, if you buy stocks in anticipation of rising prices, you hold a *long* position—you are "long the market," or "bullish." If you think prices are going to go down, then, even if you don't own any stocks, you can instruct your broker to sell stocks for you. In effect, when you short sell, you borrow someone else's stocks, sell them, and buy them back at some later date. If the price of the stock has dropped, then you pocket the difference between the price at which you sold the stocks and the price at which you bought them back.

For example, if I sell 100 shares of XYZ at $20 per share and buy them back at $15 per share, then I make $500! When you sell stocks in this manner, you hold a *short* position—you are "short the market." The danger is that you may be wrong. If the price of the stock goes up—say, to $25 per share—after you sell, and you buy the stock back to avoid losing any more money, you have to pay $500. You lose $500.

I had read how Bernard ("Sell 'em Ben") Smith had effectively shorted the stock market in October 1929, and had made a small fortune. Although the idea of selling short went against my basic optimistic nature, when I saw a shorting opportunity that I knew was a sure thing, I tried my hand at this risky speculative endeavor.

In 1981, I had been purchasing rental property for six years. On each property, I took out a mortgage, usually from a savings and loan institution. The interest rates on these loans ranged from 9 to 10 percent, but, in 1981, savings and loans were paying 12 percent interest on the deposits in their institutions. Simple common sense told me that if they had millions of dollars in outstanding loans at 9 percent and they were paying 12 percent to get more money to loan, then *they simply couldn't be making any money!* Moreover, until interest rates came down, they were going to *lose* a lot of money. Savings and loans looked like a perfect short selling candidate to me! The price of savings and loan stock simply had to drop.

To be profitable at selling the market short, you need at least two things going for you: The stock you are selling must be in trouble, and the market should be in an area of cycle weakness. In 1981, when I sold savings and loan stocks, both factors existed and the stock price dropped by 40 percent. I bought the stock back, and made a 40 percent profit.

Short selling can be a very risky endeavor. If you decide to try it, be sure that your information makes absolute sense, and be doubly sure that the market is in a cycle phase of weakness. If the market turns on you, then you must buy the stock back quickly, even if it means losing money. But if you ever come across an opportunity that seems as obvious to you as this one did to me, go for it!

Armed with knowledge of cycles, your common sense and intuition will provide the information you need to invest and make money.

This brings me to an essential point. Armed with knowledge of cycles, your common sense and intuition will provide the information you need to invest and make money. Never ignore your common sense or your "feelings" about buying or selling stocks. Knowledge of cycles, combined with common sense and a good feeling about a purchase or sale, is worth 100 analysts' or brokers' recommendations.

THE GREAT BULL MARKET OF THE 1980s BEGINS

By June 1982, cycles called for the market to begin a period of strength. By September 6, 1982, the upward movement in prices was so strong that *Time* magazine pictured a huge, charging bull tangled in ticker tape on its front cover. The banner read: "Wall Street, OLÉ!" On October 12, 1982, the *San Jose Mercury News* pushed the World Series aside with the headline: "Wall Street's Raging Bulls Push Dow Average Past 1,000 Mark." The country was coming out of the deepest recession since the Great Depression; the upward movement was gradual, but sustained. By February 1984, the Dow Industrials had moved up to the 1,250 level.

In the spring of 1984, cycles gave a mixed signal. Although the 40.68-month cycle called for a 20-month period of weakness, the 9.2-year cycle called for the beginnings of strength. Not surprisingly, the market zigged and zagged for the next 18 months without moving significantly up or down. This made perfect sense. The 40.68-month cycle was correct: Compared to the previous 20 months, the stock market was definitely weak. But the underlying strength of the long-term cycle kept prices stable.

As you might have already anticipated, the combined movements of the two cycles called for a period of strength toward the middle of the decade. I saw this when I wrote my book, *Investing in the 80s,* in 1981. I am not normally one to brag, but I am proud of the fact that I wrote the following: "Depending on the general strength of the economy after 1981, the next major upturn of the stock market will come around the middle of the decade." In October 1985, the Dow Jones Industrials average was 1,280. By

September 1987, it reached 2,746, more than doubling in two years. This market movement was predicted by cycles some five years before!

BLACK MONDAY, OCTOBER 19, 1987— CYCLES PREDICTED THE CRASH

By June 1987, the market was roaring; everyone was in it. At parties, conversations were about profits from speculation and how high the stock market would go.

In the midst of a raging bull market, cycles predicted a period of weakness in 1987.

Unfortunately, at the height of the speculative activity, many individual investors decided to enter the market for the first time. The 40.68-month cycle predicted a probable peak in market prices by July. Everyone at the Foundation for the Study of Cycles began to look for the cycle weakness to begin. So did I.

The market actually peaked on August 23, 1987, when the Dow hit 2,722. Many forecasters were expecting "a small correction," so not too many people were alarmed when the market began to falter in September. Stockbrokers continued to urge their clients to "buy on weakness."

The downward drift in stock prices continued through September. By October, prices were moving downward in earnest. From October 2 to October 16, the Dow Jones Industrials lost 400 points, dropping to a level 475 points below the high of 2,722 established in the previous August. Disappointing U.S. trade statistics and a declining value of the dollar abroad plunged the market 95 points on Wednesday, October 14. The market rested on Thursday but then dropped 108 horrendous points on Friday, October 16—the largest one-day market decline *in history!* In one week, the Dow had lost 235 points, a retreat of 9.5 percent, the biggest one-week drop since May 1940, when Germany invaded France.

On Sunday, October 18, *The New York Times* reported that the United States was willing to see the dollar drop further against the Deutsche mark. Treasury Secretary James A. Baker let the world know that he was furious with West Germany for reneging on a commitment not to raise interest rates. (When major foreign interest rates rise relative to U.S. interest rates, the value of the dollar falls.)

In Tokyo, Japanese investors scrutinized the U.S. stock market's price action and Baker's comments. In the wee hours of Monday morning, while New York was still asleep, Tokyo stocks were being sold in huge numbers—their market was plunging. When the London Exchange opened a few hours later, traders took Tokyo's cue, and stocks were down 137.1 points at the opening.

At 9:30 Monday morning, when the New York Stock Exchange opened, there were so many sell orders that openings of 20 of the 30 stocks that make up the Dow Industrials average were delayed. Even so, the market opened down 70 points.

By 10:00 AM, two things were clear. The market was in free fall, and something besides investor panic was taking place. Computerized stock-trading programs were kicking in and automatically driving the market down like a sledgehammer. *"Bang, bang, bang;* the things just kept sending off sell orders," said a senior vice president who oversaw program trading at a major investment bank.

The Dow seemed to steady by late morning; around midday, it collapsed again. At 12:46 PM, it was down 191 points. Traders in brokerage houses across the country watched in terror as the stock market continued its death march. "It was the ultimate video experience for a generation that has been screwing around with Donkey Kong for years," said P. J. Johnson, a vice president at Nomaura Securities in New York. "People just stood by their CRTs and watched."

By 2:00 PM, the market was down 295 points, and price quotes released on the tape were running almost two hours late. This turned out to be a major problem for many small investors who made buy-and-sell decisions based on the ticker tape displayed in brokerage offices and on cable television. At 2:30, the ticker quote displayed IBM at 125$^1/_2$; the real price was 119. At 3:00,

IBM was displayed at 125¼, a drop of only ¼ point; the real price for IBM at that hour was 116. By 4:00, the ticker acknowledged that IBM had dropped to 121, but the actual price at 4:00 was 103¼. Sellers were quoted at the close a price that was $17.75 more than the real one. The number of transactions taking place on the Exchange floor created absolute chaos.

Not until two hours after the market closed were totals official: The Dow had dropped 508 points and more than 600 million shares of stock had changed hands—more than double the previous record for most shares traded in a single session. Everyone went home to rest.

That night, markets in Europe and Japan slumped again. Officials in Hong Kong halted trading for a week. On Tuesday morning, October 20, Alan Greenspan, Chairman of the Federal Reserve Board, announced that, if needed, the Federal Reserve would open its lending window to preserve the financial system's soundness. This crucial announcement was later credited with helping to restore confidence and avoiding more panic.

Nevertheless, on Tuesday, more sell orders than buy orders were waiting when the market opened. On this day, many of the sell orders were the result of margin calls. Because of the huge losses incurred on Monday, brokerage houses demanded that investors who bought stock on margin (the investors had put down a deposit on the stock and borrowed the remaining funds from the brokerage house), had to either put up more money or sell their stock. When the market opened, 60 major stocks listed on the New York Stock Exchange couldn't trade because there weren't enough buyers to match sellers.

Several blue-chip companies, such as Ford, brought some much-needed cash to the market by buying their own stock. The market enjoyed a brief rally that lasted until 10:30 AM. Then came the second crash.

The Exchange limited computer-launched trading by sending out letters to brokerage houses asking them to suspend or limit computer trading activity, and by introducing several other stopgap measures. None of them helped. By 11:00 AM, the market was falling and the volume of trading was tremendous. The Big Board's own computer system became overloaded and went blank, halting computer trades altogether. That overload may have kept the market from going down another 500 points. From being down at the opening, the Dow Industrials rallied to

+200 points, then dropped to −26, and then rebounded to finish +102 points on the day. Another crash had been avoided.

From Tokyo to Zurich to London to New York, the bear had knocked down investors with its giant paw. By the week's end, the totals were devastating. The slump in prices on New York's exchanges had been worse than the crash of 1929. The Dow Jones Industrials average lost 13 percent of its value and closed at 1,950.76, nearly 800 points below its August high. In Chicago, traders desperate for cash drew numbers and waited in line to sell their seats on the exchange. The final estimate was that a trillion dollars in stock assets had been wiped out in about one week.

BEWARE THE ADVICE OF BROKERS!

The market crash taught many small American investors the hard-earned lesson that stockbrokers aren't necessarily experts on the market. Cumulatively, individual investors lost millions of dollars because they had followed their brokers' advice.

A retiree in Gulf Shores, Alabama, lost $100,000 and owed the brokerage firm another $72,000. On his broker's advice, he had been selling naked options—one of the riskiest forms of speculation. An option is a contract giving you the right to buy (a "call") or sell (a "put") a specific stock (100 shares is standard) at a specified time, for a specified price. One way to take a long position in the market is to sell put contracts.

For example, if IBM is at $125 per share, and you think it is going to $130, then you could write (sell) $125 puts on IBM, expiring at some future date, for, say, $200 per contract. If you do this without owning the stock, you are said to be selling naked options (options that are not covered by your stock ownership). If the price of IBM goes up as you expected, then the contract expires, and you keep the $200 for each contract you sell. But if the price of IBM goes down to $120 per share and the put contract is executed, then you have to buy the stock at the market price and sell it to the person holding the put at $125 per share. If you sold ten $125 IBM puts, then you have to buy 1,000 shares of IBM $5.00 above the market, and you lose $5,000. If you held enough naked puts going into the crash, you could be wiped out.

That's exactly what happened to the man from Gulf Shores, Alabama. Before the crash, he enjoyed $7,000 in annual income from stock dividends. After the crash, he had to sell all of his stock, he owed the brokerage another $72,000, and he was left with nothing but income from social security. He was financially devastated.

There are many similar cases. Geraldine Herrell, a 54-year-old quadriplegic from Carrollton, Texas, who had no job and no income other than a small monthly disability check, said her broker encouraged her to trade stock options. She lost all but $2,700 of her savings. Robert O'Connor, a 46-year-old owner of a small medical X-ray printing company in Grand Rapids, Michigan, got involved in stock-index options, hoping that his profits would put his children through college. O'Connor said that his broker told him "we would make about $1,000 a month, and if our losses got to $2,000 to $3,000, he would close out the account." On October 19, he lost everything in his account plus an additional $91,000.

Many people—brokers included—made mistakes in the heady days leading to the crash of 1987. As in all groups of professionals, there are good brokers and bad brokers, honest brokers and dishonest brokers. The majority of them are probably well-intentioned. Still, my advice, is, *never* follow the recommendations of your broker unless they fit with your knowledge of cycles and your own common sense and intuition. At best, a broker's advice is no better than your own good judgment.

THE LURE OF THE LBO

Once again, cycles had been correct. They had predicted the area of weakness that had led to the devastating October crash. The stock market was no longer easy money. Individual investors were washed out. Trading volume dried up. Young brokers who had never seen anything but an up market were in a state of shock and feared for their jobs. As the market traced another lackluster sideways pattern, the financial industry laid off some 17,000 workers.

The next upward turning point for the 40.68-month stock price cycle was due in March 1989. The instability of the dollar, the foreign trade deficit, and the budget deficit continued to worry investors. Individual investors had been disillusioned so thoroughly in October 1987 that even good news wouldn't induce them to participate in stock investments. For a while, prices moved sideways.

Leveraged buyouts (LBOs), the one bright spot during this period, were the leading source of strength in the stock market during 1988 and 1989. When Ross Johnson of RJR Nabisco, Inc. proposed a $17.6 billion leveraged buyout that was topped in four days by a $3 billion *higher* offer from Kohlberg Kravis Roberts and Company, ownership of stock shares took on new meaning. Instead of looking for dividends or ordinary gains from stock appreciation, investors looked for stocks whose values could double, triple, or quadruple during the bidding wars that ensued during LBOs.

From March 1989 to October 1990, the market had a period of tremendous uncertainty. Rather than another bull market, this cycle period of strength represented market support counteracted by the growing problem of corporate debt. Junk bonds became the new avenue for instant wealth. Before, only fledgling companies that were too tiny to qualify for debt ratings funded their growth with bonds designated from the outset as "junk." During this period, high-yield junk bonds became the weapon used by corporate raiders and leveraged buyout artists in what had become the LBO craze.

The next scheduled pivot point predicted by the 40.68-month stock price cycle was October 1990. It was on this basis, that, as narrated in the Introduction, I told my friend at the convention in July to sell his stock. True to form, we suffered a marked sell-off that bottomed in mid-October.

As for the current market and the future, the 40.68-month stock price cycle was supported in 1991 by a shorter cycle of 24 months. A base of support was built in 1991 and the market looks good for an area of strength in 1992.

WHY YOU CAN PLAN BETTER THAN YOUR BROKER CAN

I mentioned earlier that you are more capable in planning your financial future than many market "professionals," brokers included. Here are a few reasons why. Unlike your broker, you *always* have your own best interests at heart. A broker's judgment is often tainted with conflicts of interest. I have talked about this problem with more than one broker, and a few were candid with their remarks. They admitted that their very livelihood depends on commission business. It is in their vested interest to have people buy and sell stocks. In other words, many brokers are salespeople, not professional advisers.

It is in the broker's vested interest to have people buy and sell stocks. In other words, many brokers are salespeople, not professional advisers.

Recently, I spoke with a young broker who is one of the top producers at a midwestern brokerage firm and who was willing to tell the truth about his profession. He knew I was writing this book, and he felt compelled to give the public some not-so-public information about stockbrokers. In our interview, here is how he described their world:

> I am not going to sacrifice my integrity for money. It's not that things are always cut and dried, but anyone can figure out that our job is to produce commissions. I mean, that's how we live, that's how we make our money. And people—it's funny—people measure the success of a stockbroker by his car, his clothes, his house. Well, that's not a successful stockbroker, it's a successful salesman.
>
> A broker's financial success doesn't necessarily correlate with his success in terms of getting a good return for his clients at all. That's a gripe I have. They should set up incentives not just for moving stocks, but for making returns for your clients. But, in this business, that has nothing to do with anything. It's terrible.
>
> I sometimes wonder why I am in this business. As a broker, your only success is cashing a larger check at the end of each month. And all the while, your clients come to you as if you were some form of father figure. They sit there and look at you and say, "What are we doing?" You have people that are seventy years old, investing their life savings. They have to live on their savings or the income from their investments, and they're just looking at you saying, "What do we do? What do we do?"

Here is an example. Someone gives me a $100,000 account. I can put that $100,000 into a limited partnership and make an $8,000 gross commission. I can do that, or I can say things are kind of iffy right now, let's put it in a six-month or a one-year CD and wait a while. My gross commission on that would be $500, so we're talking a big difference. The limited partnership might make money, and I could make fifteen times the commission as I would playing it safe.

Don't get me wrong, there are brokers—there's one in my office—when people come to him with a lot of money, he says he will not touch their money until they have insurance. Then there are those who will say, "Sure, come on in. Have a seat. You're a very nice person . . . today, I'll let you in on a little something here, this deal we have . . .," and $8,000 goes in his pocket. You have all types; that's true in any business. But the temptation arises because you are seen as more knowledgeable in the public's eye, and they will listen to anything you say.

Small accounts can't get the attention they deserve. I mean I have six hundred, eight hundred, accounts. Now, not all of those are daily, active accounts, but it's too many for me to watch. The bottom line is that it's absolutely impossible, physically impossible, no matter how many computers you've got, no matter how many buttons you can push, there's no way that a broker can sit and manage your portfolio unless it's big, and one of ten that he manages.

When you come back from New York after training, you sit at a phone and you are penniless. They have you on salary for a year, but basically, you are on straight commissions. You have to call complete strangers saying, "Hello, give me your life savings," or, "Give me your money. You don't know me but you're going to love me when you do."

You see the pressure we're under . . . to produce commissions, to keep our jobs, to support our families or ourselves, and do well for clients. Almost everyone tries to do well for the clients, almost everyone. But we have 25 people in our office, and everyone is commission-oriented, and some more so than others. Let's face it, the ideal is to do well for your clients, so they keep coming back and giving you more money.

Let's say the commission month ends on the 21st. It's the 15th, you've only made $1,200 this month, and all of a sudden someone comes to you with $100,000 or $200,000. Are you going to put them in a six-month CD? You've got mouths to feed. You've got rent to pay. So a lot of times, no . . . no, you won't. And I think I am going to get out of the business. I am agonizing because my manager wants me to do that. I just can't.

You can't rely on an unbiased opinion when you ask a broker, "Well, what do you think?" It's like going into an auto dealership and saying, "I have some money to spend. Do you think I should buy a car from you? And by the way, how much do you think I should spend on a car?" You would never do that.

The best idea is to have your own informed plan, based on your own short-term and long-term goals, your knowledge of cycles, and your own intuition. You determine when you want to buy and when you want to sell. It all boils down to *telling* a broker what you want, not asking.

FINE-TUNING YOUR TIMING DECISIONS: A LOOK AT WHAT'S AHEAD

The stock market should be in an area of strength for most of 1992.

The stock market should be in an area of strength for most of 1992. In addition to the 40.68-month cycle's support of this trend, 1992 is an election year. If politicians are true to form, they will go to many lengths to "assure" the public that the economy is healthy while they are trying to get reelected. This usually means good news for stock prices.

1993 is another matter entirely. Besides the fact that the major upward move will, I believe, already have occurred, years following presidential elections are not usually good for the market. In addition, I believe that interest rates will begin to rise. This brings me to the single most important signal for a change in direction in the stock market—interest rates.

When interest rates go up, the stock market usually goes down; when interest rates fall, the stock market usually goes up. *Usually* is the key word here. Slight fluctuations in interest rates normally won't affect the price trend. The important thing to remember is that, when interest rates change several times in the same direction, it is time for you to reevaluate your own market strategy.

When changes in interest rates occur, look at the changes in the context of cycle phases of strength and weakness. If interest rates drop significantly, it will likely mean the stock market is ready to move upward. If interest rates start to rise, it is time to be very cautious. High interest rates do not usually attract the stock market bull.

You may ask yourself: "If interest rates make this much difference, why do I need cycles?" The answer is simple. Cycles provide the broad framework within which to time your decisions. Interest rates will help you fine-tune those decisions. If you expect weakness, be cautious. If, based on cycles, you expect weakness and interest rates are on the rise, get out of the market! If you expect strength, look for an opportunity to be aggressive. If you expect strength and interest rates start to drop, then it is most likely a time to buy. Changes in interest rates help you identify when the trend changes. They can also help you to find the top and the bottom of a cycle phase more precisely.

1994 may be one of those difficult years. If interest rates have started to drop, then the market could begin to move up. If not, it may be 1995 before we see the next major upward trend. The year 1995 will no doubt be a good year for the stock market. The year 1996 could be a good year because of the November presidential election; however, national and international events will need to be monitored.

The year 1995 will no doubt be a good year for the stock market.

Both the 40.68-month stock price cycle and the 9.2-year stock price cycle will move into an area of strength in 1995. *This will be a major stock market upward move. If stocks are part of your financial plan, don't miss this trend.*

YOU HAVE WHAT IT TAKES

You have all the attributes you need to make successful stock market investments. You may want to supplement your knowledge by subscribing to *The Wall Street Journal* and reading about particular stocks. Cycles give you a basis for using your own intuitive ability. If you are anticipating an upward movement, you will trust your own guidance for action when that trend arrives. It won't matter whether the trend arrives slightly earlier or later than predicted by cycles. By the time everyone else realizes the market is moving up, most of the best profits will have been made—by you and those like you who knew of the trend *in advance.*

The same is true when you are anticipating a market peak. After a cycle has completed an upward trend, you know that the market is destined to start down. You may miss a few percentage points of further increase, but when it finally does fall, you won't be caught like people were in 1929 and 1987.

You are a wonderful source of information. You have a life full of experiences, and this background enables you to recognize good stocks and good stock market timing. The best way to get started is to simply *do it.* Take a few hundred dollars, when you think the time is right, and invest in some stock you have a good feeling about. This may be the stock of a company where you work and where you have seen business increase day after day, or it might be a company where a friend works and where you know the staff has been almost doubled in the past year. You might buy stock in a company that produces something that you and others like a lot, or that seems particularly innovative, or that just opened several new stores in a growing and prosperous area.

When Liz Claiborne's first designs hit the streets, they were an instant success. Why? Because they fit! They were not made for a fourteen-year-old boy or a size 8 model; they were made for women, and women bought the clothes. The price of the stock soared. You see this type of "information" every day. Combine your experience with the knowledge of cycles and you will be successful. You have absolutely everything it takes to make money in the stock market.

Chapter

9

Painting a Rich Financial Canvas with Bonds and Cash

The nice thing about cash is that it never clashes with what you're wearing.

Creating a successful financial life is like creating a painting: You begin with a vision, a thought. You give the image form by sketching out ideas, visualizing the ultimate creation, and evaluating various ways to create the finished product. Just as a painter experiments with different media and hues, you study and explore different investment techniques, keeping and employing only those that enrich the work. Finally, the goal is achieved—a uniquely designed, finished work with unity and balance. As in art, balance is a crucial component of financial planning. Creating balance in your financial plan means integrating individual short-term and long-term goals into your ultimate objective: financial security and independence. One of the hallmarks of a balanced approach is the distribution of your investment risk in such a way that, no matter what happens, you will always have enough money left to continue building your financial future.

DIVERSIFICATION AND ASSET ALLOCATION

One of the best ways to distribute your risk is to diversify your investments. Diversification, in itself, is not a guarantee of success—you can make five bad investments in five different areas as easily as you can make one bad investment in one area. But if you pick each investment carefully, employ your knowledge of cycles, and time your purchases and sales accordingly, then diversification will give your financial plans a broader base of support and you will have a better chance to realize your financial goals.

Deciding how much of your money to put where is a process called *asset allocation.* If you have no idea where to begin in making your asset allocation decisions, begin with "the 25 percent rule" illustrated in Figure 9.1. Assume that you will keep 25 percent of your money in cash (checking accounts, certificates of deposit, U.S. Treasury bills (T-bills), or money market accounts), 25 percent in high-grade corporate or government bonds, 25 percent in the stock market (equities), and 25 percent in real estate. This will give you a starting point for considering how to diversify your investments.

Using the 25 percent rule as your reference point, you can then refine your asset allocation decisions by balancing your knowledge of cycles in each market, weighing the relative risks

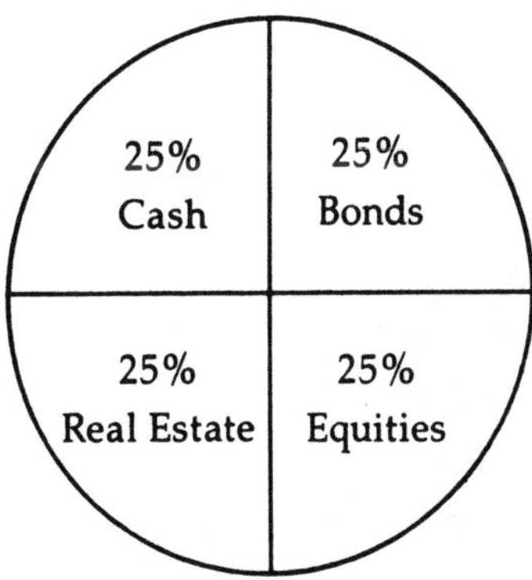

Figure 9.1 The 25 Percent Rule—A Simple Diversification Strategy for Investments

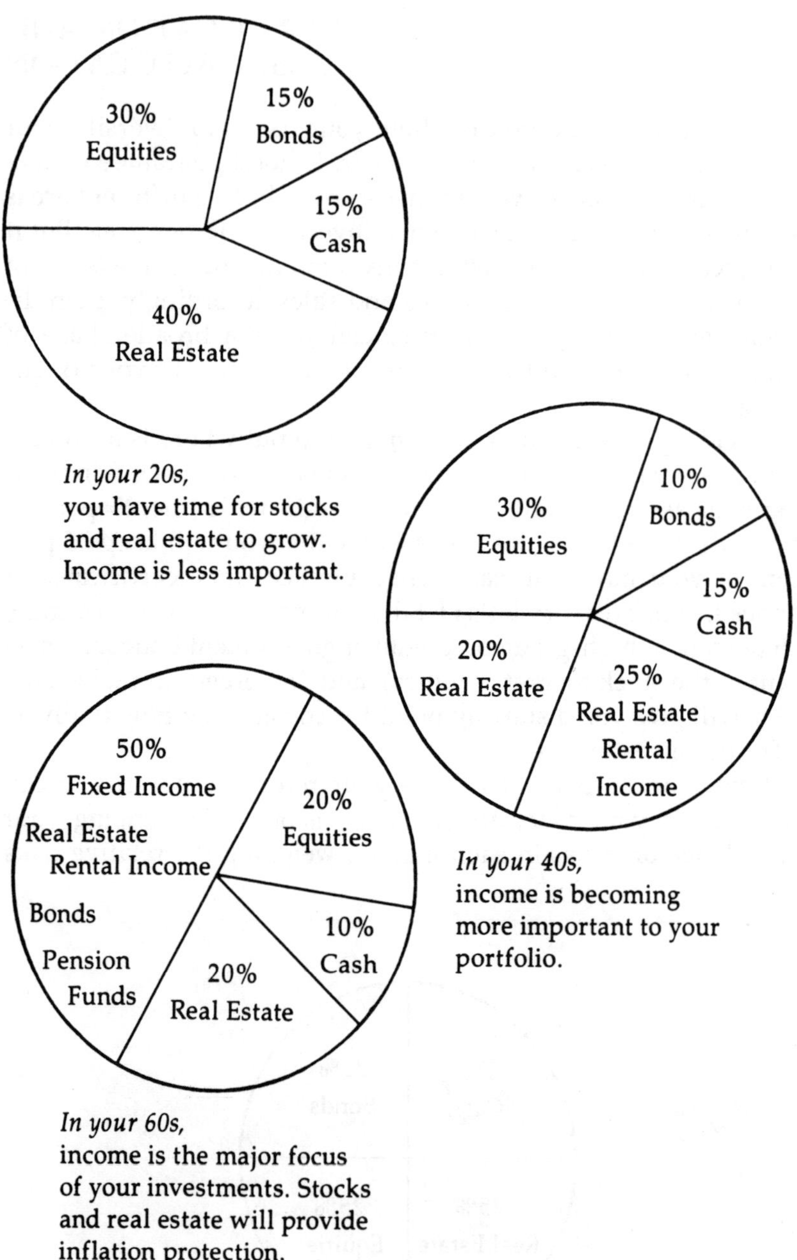

Figure 9.2 Defining Your Diversification Strategy According to Your Age

of different vehicles within each market, and integrating into your decision-making process such important personal considerations as your age, your affinity for risk, your financial condition, and your financial goals. For example, on the basis of your age alone, your asset allocation "pie" might be portioned like one of those shown in Figure 9.2.

BALANCING RISK–REWARD CONSIDERATIONS

In determining the size of the pieces of your unique investment pie, risk should be one of your prime concerns. *Every investment involves some degree of risk.* In discussing the investment vehicle risk pyramid in Chapter 2, I pointed out that the safest investments involved little risk but also offered smaller potential rewards than other investments. When deciding how to diversify your investments, you should consider this risk-to-reward ratio (typically called risk–reward) within the broadest context of your goals, your personality, your age, and your financial condition.

If you refer back to the investment vehicle risk pyramid (Figure 2.1), you will see how, by diversifying your investments into cash, bonds, stocks, and real estate, you are spanning nearly the full range of the risk–reward pyramid, from the lowest risk of holding cash to the relatively high risk of investing in real estate.

Cash, held as CDs or T-bills, presents virtually no risk, but offers returns only slightly above the inflation rate. U.S. government bonds and high-grade corporate bonds offer higher returns, but there is a greater chance you will lose money, especially if you cash them in before maturity. The stock market offers higher returns than bonds, but, as pointed out in Chapter 8, the chance of losing money on any specific stock issue is always present. Real estate, while generally an outstanding long-term investment, presents problems of illiquidity or even loss of equity if you are forced to sell during a cycle phase of weakness. By knowing how to pick and choose your investments within each area, you can increase your odds of success, minimize your risks, and maximize your rewards.

There is always a strong personal element involved in evaluating risk and making asset allocation decisions.

There is always a strong personal element involved in evaluating risk and making asset allocation decisions. For example, suppose someone offered you $10,000 to walk across a six-inch-wide, 12-foot-long board that was four feet off the ground. Would you do it? Most likely you would. The reward would be high and there would be very little risk to the average person. Suppose the same deal required you to walk on the board 300 feet in the air. Would you do it? Maybe those of you who are gymnasts or acrobats would, but few others would be willing to try. The reward is still high but the risk is much greater—the risk–reward ratio has increased to a point where the risk is not worth taking.

There are at least three personal factors to consider with respect the evaluating risk–reward: your emotional makeup, your age, and your current financial condition. For example, a person who is afraid of *any* height may not be willing to walk across a board four feet off the ground, not even for $10,000; neither would someone who is in poor physical condition. Someone who is in desperate financial condition might try the walk across the 300-foot-high board, even though disaster might result.

As for the effects of age on investment, consider your own life. When you were young, everything was an adventure because you had your whole life ahead of you. If someone said pack your bags and move everything you own (which probably wasn't much), you most likely didn't give it a second thought. If you invested money, you didn't mind trying some way-out long shots, because you had your whole life to make up for any mistakes.

Then a few years passed. Perhaps you got married and had children. The financial scene changed almost overnight. You could no longer risk everything on a single venture. Your priorities were different because others were depending on you.

That valuable commodity called "time" was also greatly reduced. The mundane demands of everyday were so great that planning for your financial future was all but impossible. You were lucky to get the laundry washed, the baby changed, the lawn mowed, the car pool organized, the bills paid, and food on the table. If you were fortunate, you were able to buy your own home, but most other financial plans were left to fend for themselves.

A few more years passed. You saw your children grow and knew that soon you would thinking about college. If your life did not involve children, you may have begun to envision your retirement. Now it was time to begin serious financial planning for the kind of expenses that need advance preparation.

In investments, as in most decisions, age often makes us more cautious and more concerned with security and solid returns.

Every investment is unique and so is every person's situation and frame of mind. There is no single strategy or formula that will fit every person's life and financial goals. That is why intuitive financial planning is so important. You are your own best source of information on what is best for you. Only you know intimately your situation, personality, goals and dreams, and tolerance for risk, and only you can properly weigh the personality factors in your asset allocation process. Every person, and that includes you, has what it takes to make his or her own successful financial decisions.

Before you can plan your asset allocation decisions, it is necessary to understand the investment vehicles in more detail. In Chapter 8, we discussed the stock market. In this chapter, let's learn more about bonds and cash.

BONDS DON'T HAVE TO PUT YOU TO SLEEP

In Chapter 2, I pointed out that bonds are an excellent means of saving for the future. I grew up thinking that bonds (U.S. Savings Bonds) were a gift rich people gave to each other on Christmas, birthdays, and graduation days. As a young adult, I was in a fog about bonds and the bond market. The only type of bonds I knew anything about were the "bearer bonds" stolen in James Bond movies. I knew these mysterious certificates were somehow as good as cash and had something to do with interest rates, but that's about all I knew.

High-grade corporate and government bonds are a safe and effective vehicle to help you reach your financial goals.

Today, I know that the bond market is a diverse and interesting area that can be an integral part of a sound financial plan for anyone. High-grade corporate and government bonds are a safe and effective vehicle to help you reach your financial goals. Some types of bonds offer a steady stream of income; others offer the potential for capital appreciation (profit you can realize if the value of your bonds increases). In addition, bonds don't require maintenance. If you buy the right bonds and hold them until maturity, they are nearly worry-free and almost risk-free. These are very attractive features to many investors.

How Bonds Work

When you purchase a bond, you become a lender, just like a bank. You lend your money to the government or a corporation and are given an IOU—the bond certificate. The bond certificate spells out the terms and conditions of your loan contract: when you will receive your principal back, how much interest you will earn, how the interest will be paid, whether the borrower can pay you back early or not, and so forth.

The bonds I will be discussing in this chapter are negotiable; that is, they are traded on the open market. The process works like this. Suppose a corporation such as IBM wants to raise some capital to market a new product. IBM would go to an investment banker, such as Merrill Lynch or Prudential, and make a proposal to raise $20 million by selling a specific number of 20-year bonds at the current market coupon rate (the interest rate carried on the bond). Knowing that IBM is financially sound and has a high rating (to be discussed shortly), the investment banker decides to go ahead with the deal, and guarantees IBM a minimum amount of income from the sale of a large percentage of the bond issue.

Next, the investment banker prices the bonds at, say, a $1,000 face value with a coupon rate at current market value, say, 8.5 percent payable annually. This means that the banker wants to sell the bonds for $1,000 each, in return for a promise to pay back to the purchasers in 20 years the full amount plus an annual 8.5 percent interest payment. The banker issues a prospectus and prints up the bond certificates; the bank's brokers prepare to sell the bonds to the public.

From the time the coupon rate is established to the time the bonds are actually offered for sale (usually a period of several weeks), coupon rates, or interest rates, on competitive bonds and other investments can change. For example, if the interest rate drops to 8 percent during the interim period, then the higher coupon rate on IBM's new bonds would make buyers willing to pay more than face value for the bonds—the bonds would be sold at a *premium* to face value. If interest rates rise during the interim period, then buyers would purchase the bonds at some level below face value—at a *discount* to face value.

After the investment bank sells the entire new bond issue, the bonds continue to trade, usually on a daily basis. As time passes and interest rates fluctuate, the bonds trade at different prices, according to the time–interest rate relationship. The bonds' price will rise and fall in proportion to the amount of time remaining to maturity and the current market interest rate—the bonds' price will be higher when interest rates drop and/or the maturity date draws near, and lower as interest rates increase and/or the maturity date is still in the distant future. The maturity date and the coupon rate do not change, but the price the market is willing to pay for the bonds changes almost constantly, according to both actual and anticipated changes in interest rates relative to the maturity date.

Often, an institution or investment bank will buy huge quantities of bonds, place them in a trust, and then issue new bond-related instruments such as *zero-coupon bonds,* using the bonds held in trust as collateral. For example, the coupon may be "stripped" from the bond and sold separately as an income-producing investment. The principal, or face value, portion of the bond may also be sold separately as a zero-coupon bond. In effect, one bond is converted into two bonds (or more than two, in more complex issues).

The zero-coupon portion of the bond is sold at a discount; the effective interest rate from the time of purchase to the time of maturity closely approximates competitive interest rates. For example, if the prevailing annual interest rate on bonds maturing in five years is 7 percent, then a $1,000, zero-coupon bond maturing in five years would trade somewhere close to $700. (If you deposited $700 into a savings account yielding 7 percent annually, your account would be worth approximately $1,000 in five years.) Although the zero-coupon bond is sold at a discount to face value, the coupon (the interest-bearing portion) is sold for its cash value plus a premium or discount, depending on whether the prevailing market interest rate is higher or lower than the coupon rate.

For example, if a coupon expiring in five years was issued at 8.5 percent, then it will yield approximately $500 in income over the next five years. If the prevailing interest rate for bonds maturing in five years is 7 percent, then the coupon would probably trade somewhere close to $350. In other words, because the coupon rate is higher than the prevailing interest rate, you have to pay more money up front for the privilege of making a higher yield.

There is a wide variety of bonds and bond-related instruments that you can consider using in your financial plan. I personally prefer to use high-grade corporate and government bonds as a source of stable financial growth at higher yields than are available in savings accounts. Picking high-grade bonds is fairly easy.

Companies such as Moody's and Standard & Poor's rate or grade bonds. AAA bonds are the highest quality, meaning that the chances of being repaid the full amount at the stated interest rate is very high. AAA bonds are liquid, that is, you can convert them to cash easily. AA bonds are good quality, but not quite as good as AAA bonds. A bonds are slightly less good and may carry a slightly higher yield, to entice purchasers. A BBB bond isn't as good as an A bond, and so on down the list of grades. The lower the grade of the bond, the higher the risk of holding them. "Junk bonds," which get no grade at all, represent bonds associated with the highest degree of risk. My advice is to stay away from junk bonds.

To keep things simple, purchase either government or AAA corporate bonds. Leave the more complex and risky instruments to the professionals.

To keep things simple, purchase either government or AAA corporate bonds. Leave the more complex and risky instruments to the professionals.

Your personal plan will provide many opportunities for creativity. You may decide to try to take advantage of market fluctuations by buying and selling bonds for profit. Or, you may want to buy bonds solely for the purpose of holding them until maturity. In any case, it is important that you understand the relationship of bond prices to interest rates in more detail.

Bond Prices and Interest Rates

The relationship between bond prices and interest rates may seem a bit confusing, but it is really quite simple if you understand a few basic concepts about the time value of money. Money is like an other commodity: It changes in value according to supply and demand. Unfortunately, because inflation is virtually a way of life these days, a dollar today is almost always worth more than a dollar tomorrow. In deciding whether a bond is a good investment, you should have an idea of what your total return on investment will be. By investing in a bond, you will receive returns that preserve or expand the value of the cash you invest today.

When you put your money into a savings account, you deposit a specific amount and you earn interest on it, say, 5 percent per year. In the simplest terms (without considering compound interest or the declining value of your deposit because of inflation), if you deposit $1,000 in a savings account paying 5 percent interest, then at the end of one year you will have $1,050 in your account. If you are in a 28 percent tax bracket, you will pay about $14 of that income back in taxes. If inflation is 5 percent per year, then approximately another $2.50 of your interest income will be consumed by declining purchasing power. That makes your net return on investment $33.50 divided by $1,000 or just over 3 percent per year.

To figure your net return, or yield, on a bond purchase, instead of working from the present to the future, as you would when considering your return on a savings account, you have to work backward from the future. If, for example, you purchase for $700 a $1,000 zero-coupon bond maturing in five years, that would be equivalent to putting $700 in a savings account at the fixed annual interest rate of about 7.4 percent. In other words, the current yield on the bond is 7.4 percent. If you plan to hold the bond until maturity, your return is higher than that of a savings account.

The relationship between bond yields and interest rates is quite simple: They are virtually the same thing in different forms!

The relationship between bond yields and interest rates is therefore quite simple: They are virtually the same thing in different forms! There are many interest rates in the market, never just one. Bonds generally pay higher interest rates than bank deposits because they carry more risk. A savings account is completely liquid and (theoretically) totally safe. You can pull your money out at any time, including all of your accrued interest. Even if your bank fails, the FDIC (Federal Deposit Insurance Corporation) will pay you your money (up to their $100,000 limit). When you invest in a bond, however, if you sell before maturity, you may either make or lose money, according to the market value of the bond at the time.

In general, if you buy a bond and interest rates go up, then the current market value of your bonds is apt to decline. If interest rates decline, then the market value of your bonds is likely to go up. No matter what the current market interest rate, if you buy high-grade corporate or government bonds, you will virtually always achieve your projected return if you hold them until maturity.

Whether you want to buy bonds as a long-term investment or with the intent to trade them for profit before they mature, it is essential that you bear in mind the future trend in interest rates. If you buy a 15-year bond yielding 8.5 percent and anticipate that interest rates will be declining during most of the period you hold the bond, then you are making an excellent investment. On the other hand, if you buy a 15-year bond at 6 percent and hold it while interest rates rise to 10 percent or more, than you are virtually giving away some of your investment money.

If you buy bonds for the purpose of trading them for profit before maturity, then you want to buy bonds near the interest rate cycle's high and sell them near the interest rate cycle's low. If you are buying bonds to hold until maturity, then you should buy when the interest rate cycle is near a peak in a strength phase (when interest rates are high) and pick maturity dates that will allow you to cash in your bonds after taking advantage of the interest rate cycle's weakness phase.

TWO MAJOR INTEREST RATE CYCLES AND GOOD BUYS IN BONDS

Just as there are two major cycles in buying and selling stocks, there are two major interest-rate cycles for buying and selling bonds. The first, a cycle of approximately 3 1/3 years (Figure 9.3), is similar in length to the 3 1/3-year (40.68-month) cycle in stocks. The second is a 12-year cycle (Figure 9.4). The biggest difference between the 40.68-month stock price cycle and the 3 1/3-year (178-week) cycle in interest rates is that the stock market cycle peaks just about six months before the interest rate cycle peaks.

Just as there are two major cycles in buying and selling stocks, there are two major interest-rate cycles for buying and selling bonds.

You can use this information in your asset allocation decisions. From Figures 9.3 and 9.4, you can see that the 178-week cycle predicts a peak in interest rates in April 1993 and the 12-year cycle predicts a peak somewhere in the latter half of 1993. Another interest rate cycle—the 54-year interest rate cycle discussed in Chapter 11—indicates that interest rates will be in a long-term downward trend until shortly after the turn of the century.

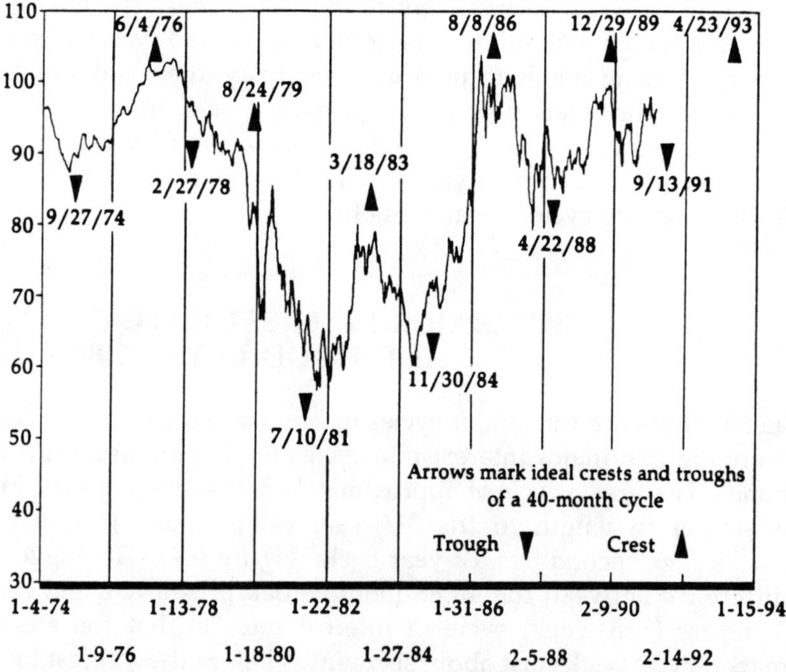

Figure 9.3 Cycle in Interest Rates for Bonds: 3⅓ Years (40 Months) (Reprinted courtesy of the Foundation for the Study of Cycles.)

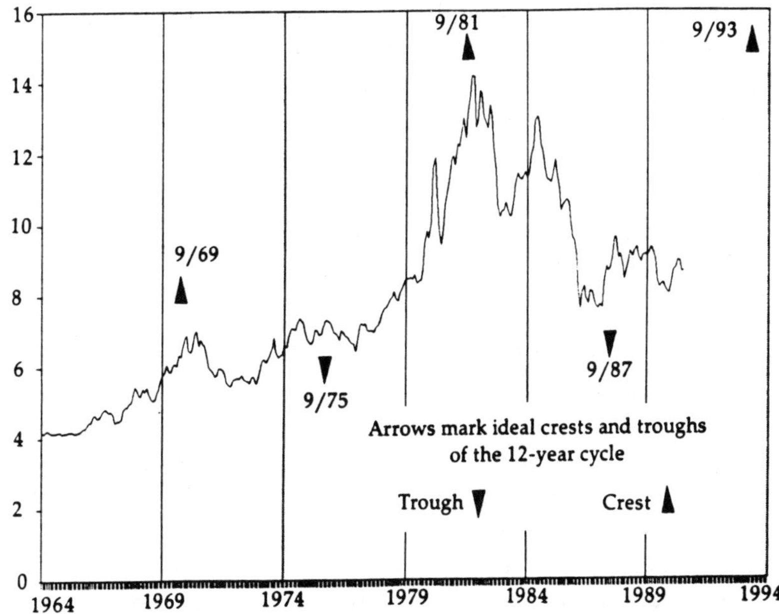

Figure 9.4 Cycle in Interest Rates for Bonds: 12 Years

The downward trend of the 54-year cycle tells you not to expect each peak of the shorter cycle to reach its last high or to go higher still. Instead, you will see interest rates rise in the short term, only to fall to lower levels over the long term. Some people get caught up in trying to pick market turns by looking for specific interest rate levels (some people also try to do this with the stock market, and it is folly). With your knowledge of cycles, you will expect peaks and troughs to occur but you will not be looking for an exact interest rate level to be reached.

Assume that you decide to follow a bond-purchasing schedule in your intuitive financial plan. On the basis of this information alone, the time to become aggressive in your bond purchases is near the cycle high in 1993. Until then, you may decide to purchase bonds on a more moderate basis, making them, say, 10 or 15 percent of your asset allocations. In the interim, you could balance your asset allocations to be more heavily weighted in stocks which, according to the cycles presented in Chapter 8, are due to be in an area of relative strength until sometime in 1993. Or you may want to put more of your money into CDs, T-bills, or some other cash equivalent.

When considering asset allocations between stocks and bonds, there are two important factors to consider. The first is the six-month time lag between cycle highs in the 40-month stock market cycle and the 178-week interest rate cycle. Knowing that the stock market is apt to reach its peak six months before bonds, you can use this lag to your benefit by moving into bonds when cycles tell you that the peak of the stock market is approaching. The second consideration is the relationship between interest rates and election years, especially presidential election years.

Interest rates, especially shorter-term interest rates, are dramatically influenced by actions of the Federal Reserve Board—the "Fed." The Federal Reserve Board and the Federal Open Market Committee (a group comprised of the Federal Reserve Board members plus 7 of the 12 presidents of the Federal Reserve District Banks) influence interest rates by two means: (1) raising or lowering the discount rate (the interest rate charged to member banks by district banks for short-term borrowing), and (2) open market operations (the purchase and sale of government securities to raise or lower the cash reserves of member banks). A discussion of the way these processes work is beyond the scope of this book, but it is enough to know that the Fed has enormous power when it comes to short-term interest rates.

Because Federal Reserve Board members obtain their jobs by political appointment, it is not surprising that the interest-rate policies established by the Fed are often politically motivated. Usually, in the 12- to 18-month period preceding a presidential election, the Fed lowers interest rates to stimulate lending, which tends to boost the economy and give voters confidence in the ability of the current Administration. The months immediately after a presidential election are the best political period to raise interest rates, or "tighten" credit. Any weakness in the economy will then appear long before the next election approaches. Historically, interest rates tend to drop before presidential elections and to rise after them.

1993 will be an ideal time to buy bonds.

This factor points to 1993 as an ideal time to buy bonds. Until then, because interest rates are in a intermediate-term upward trend but a long-term downward trend, it is not a terribly bad time to buy bonds for the purpose of holding them until maturity, but your buying should probably be moderate. When the 178-week cycle high approaches its peak in 1993, that is the time to buy more aggressively. By waiting, you will get more bonds for your dollars.

Personally, as of this writing, I am moving into real estate aggressively in select areas (see Chapters 11, 12, and 13). With respect to bonds and the stock market, I am in stocks to take advantage of the 1992 area of cycle strength, and I'm waiting to purchase bonds sometime in 1993. I will definitely be in stocks in 1995.

Before making your first bond purchase, it is advisable to spend a few hours reading a good book on bonds. Different bonds have different provisions, and it is important to understand any pitfalls you might face.

For example, some bonds can be called in before maturity. "Early calls" work like this. Suppose you purchase a bond with a coupon rate of 10 percent. By the provisions outlined in the prospectus, the company that borrowed your money agrees to pay you 10 percent for 30 years. In the fine print, however, you discover that the company has the right to "call in" the bond in three years or any number of years it chooses, *at the company's option.* If interest rates go down, the company can pay you off and sell new bonds at a lower interest rate. You lose the 10 percent per year income that you had anticipated. If interest rates go up, the company is borrowing your money at a low rate and will not exercise the call provision. Call provisions turn the bond into a very lopsided bet in favor of the company issuing them. The early call provision basically says, "Heads I win, tails we start over."

There are a few things you can do to protect yourself from call provisions and similar pitfalls. First, ask your broker whether the bonds you are interested in have call provisions or any other special provisions. If the bonds can be called, have your broker show you the stipulations in writing. Follow up by stating your understanding of the provisions in a letter to your broker. This will offer you some protection, in case your broker intentionally or unwittingly misrepresents the nature of the bonds he or she sells to you. Your best bet is probably to stick with bonds that have no call provisions whatsoever. You may get a slightly lower return, but you won't get sold out when interest rates drop. Almost all U.S. Treasury Bonds are noncallable.

When purchasing bonds, as with all investments, take *nothing* for granted. Bonds should be a sound, safe investment; but there are bonds, and then there are bonds—some of them didn't get the nickname "junk" for nothing. Be as careful with bonds as you would with any other investment.

CASH AND LIQUIDITY

Not too many of us need to be reminded about the merits of cash and liquidity. Cash is what we use to buy groceries, pay the rent (or mortgage), and, if you don't use your credit card, purchase VCRs and vacations in the Caribbean. A special sense of security comes with having plenty of cash in the bank. We use cash to consume goods and services, and we use cash to play.

Properly considered, cash is an important part of any financial plan. You have probably heard the rule: "Have six months' salary in the bank at all times." Like "Keep your feet dry," this is one of those rules of thumb that keeps on making sense year after year. During the recession the early 1990s, many people had wished they had heeded it. Maintaining a healthy cash balance is important.

"Cash" is a widely used term. When the financial press refers to "cash," the understood meaning is T-bills (short-term U.S. Treasury issues that are less volatile in price than notes and bonds and can be converted to cash literally overnight), and short-term money market funds. To the individual investor, "cash" refers not only to T-bills and short-term money market funds, but also to demand deposits (checking and savings accounts that can be converted to cash on demand) and short-term CD (certificates of deposit that can be converted to cash, although usually with a penalty for early withdrawal).

All of these different forms of cash and cash equivalents have two things in common: (1) they are highly liquid, and (2) they are not as volatile as other investment vehicles. Liquidity is a measure of the ease with which an asset can be converted to cash of equivalent value. Stocks, bonds, T-bills, mutual funds, and CDs are all highly liquid—almost as liquid as the funds in your checking account—but you may need several days to convert them into cash. In addition, at any given time, stocks and bonds may be worth less than when you bought them, whereas the deposits in your checking or savings account will retain their cash value over time. T-bills, CDs, and short-term money market funds are considered cash equivalents because they are far more likely to retain their original cash value than are instruments such as stocks and longer-term bonds.

There are four basic motivations to hold cash: for transactions, as a reserve for unforeseen expenses, for financing a future purchase (savings), or for speculation. Cash for transactions is held to carry on day-to-day activities. Reserve cash held as a precaution is money set aside to cover emergencies such as an unexpected medical bill, a car repair, or temporary unemployment. Money held for savings is accumulated to finance a particular goal, such as purchase of a home or a car. Cash for speculative purposes would be held in the unlikely event that the purchasing power of money will increase over time. About the only way to apply this motivation in our modern, inflationary environment is to hold foreign currency that is declining in value relative to the dollar.

OBTAINING THE BEST INTEREST RATES FOR YOUR "CASH" HOLDINGS

Because many "cash" assets are interest-bearing, it makes good sense to get the best interest rates available. What you want is nearly instant liquidity paying the optimum interest rate. Analysts estimate that individual savers cumulatively lose $40 million a day because they place their money in low-paying, interest-bearing accounts instead of using other higher-yielding money market accounts and certificates of deposit.

Passbook accounts and interest-bearing checking accounts are at the lowest end of the interest rate spectrum. It is fine to keep small amounts in these accounts for day-to-day needs, but, as a general rule, they pay lower interest rates than any other cash options. Unless you know you will need your money in the very near future, you should minimize the amount of cash you keep in passbook and checking accounts.

Money markets are one effective way to hold cash and earn interest at the same time.

Most of your cash should be kept where you can earn more interest. Money market accounts are one such alternative. Available through banks, savings and loan institutions, and the larger brokerage firms, money market accounts pay a variable rate of interest that is generally higher than passbook accounts. They provide almost the same convenience as a checking account and the accounts offered by banks and S&Ls are insured by the federal government. Money markets are a good place to keep cash for which you want easy access.

Certificates of deposit (CDs) may be advisable for cash that you know you will hold for a period of 30 days or longer. CDs offer a fixed interest rate in return for your promise to keep the money deposited for a specified amount of time. The time period for CDs can be as short as 30 days or as long as 10 years or more. Usually, longer-period CDs pay higher rates than shorter ones. If you want to buy a CD, be sure to shop around—rates vary substantially both within states and throughout the country. Search for the best available rates.

One way to find the highest rates is to subscribe to a service like *100 Highest Yields* (P.O. Box 088888, North Palm Beach, FL 33408-8888; telephone: 800-327-7717). Although there is a fee for the service (a one-year subscription for the weekly publication is $98; an eight-week trial membership is $34), it can save you time and money by helping you find CDs paying much higher rates than those you can get locally. If you have a sizable amount of cash, the cost of this service may pay for itself many times over.

Another way is to find brokerage firms that handle out-of-state CDs. Many brokerage houses commit to $25 or $30 million worth of CDs offered by a specific institution for a good rate. They offer the CDs to their customers in smaller amounts, making money by taking a fee from the institution or by keeping a small percentage of the yield (the percentage of interest paid on the CD) as their fee.

T-bills are an excellent cash option, but they require a minimum investment of $10,000, plus any commission attached to the purchase or sale. It is possible to purchase T-bills directly from the U.S. government, but most people go through a broker or bond dealer. The government sells T-bills with three- and six-month maturities at an auction held every Monday (except bank holidays). Treasury bills pay higher interest rates than money market or passbook accounts, similar rates to CDs of the same duration, and lower rates than longer-term government notes and bonds. T-bills are a highly favored cash instrument for portfolio and institutional money managers because of their absolute safety.

SAFETY AND INSURED DEPOSITS

During the Great Depression, people lost thousands or even hundreds of thousands of dollars of savings when banks closed. As a result, the government established an insurance program that protects you from losing all your money in a bank failure.

Wherever you decide to deposit your money, make sure the institution is covered by the FDIC or the FSLIC. Many depository institutions are not.

Wherever you decide to deposit your money, make sure the institution is covered by the FDIC (Federal Deposit Insurance Corporation) or the FSLIC (Federal Savings and Loan Insurance Corporation). The FDIC and FSLIC insure deposits up to $100,000 *per account.* If you are fortunate enough to have more than $100,000, be sure to place your money in various accounts and/or institutions so that the amount on deposit in any one institution doesn't exceed the $100,000 limit. Your bank or depository institution should have a booklet explaining various account combinations that will keep all of your money safely insured.

As we have seen in the past several years, the fact that bank deposits are insured doesn't prevent depository institutions from failing. If your bank or savings and loan fails, it may take several weeks or even months before the FDIC or FSLIC returns your money to you. If you miss installment payments or fail to pay bills on time during this period, you may damage your credit rating. Therefore, be sure to verify the health of a financial institution before placing your money there.

One way to do this is to contact a service called Veribanc (P.O. Box 2963, Woburn, MA 01888). For $20, Veribanc will provide a short analysis of any depository institution, based on the most recent federal financial reports. The color-coded rating system used is simple: green is the best, yellow is for caution, and red is for a troubled institution. Veribanc also provides instant ratings by phone (1-800-44-BANKS). For each call, the cost is $10 for the first institution and $2 for each additional report. A similar service is the Shesshunoff Information Service (P.O. Box 13201, Austin, TX 78711).

THE ART OF FINANCIAL INDEPENDENCE

Most great artists are noted for their individualism. They have a vision, and no one can sway them from their path. Your financial life is your own creation; it is up to you and you alone to make it a great work of art. With your knowledge of cycles, your ability to save money on taxes, your detailed knowledge of the financial instruments available, and your intuitive capabilities, you have all the raw materials you need to create your own unique and successful financial future.

Studies have shown that the majority of people who fail to accumulate money are easily influenced by others. Belittling their own ability, many people assume that "the experts" know more than they do, and they let "professionals" make decisions for them. The problem is, there are as many opinions as there are professionals—there will always be someone to "tell" you what is best for you.

Listening to and learning from others is beneficial, but it is one thing to listen, and another to relinquish your own judgment. If you let your own knowledge and intuition be heavily influenced by the opinions of others, you will most likely fail in your goals. You will create bits and pieces of everyone else's vision, not riches of your own. Instead of feasting on gourmet meals that you create, you will pick at everyone else's stew.

Keep your own counsel. Accept the joy and responsibility of making your own decisions. Share your plans openly only with those whose energy is as positive as your own. Even close friends and relatives, while not meaning to, can send you negative "signals" that may cloud and distort your optimism and creative vision. The easiest way to prevent this is to let your dreams be your own private province. Like a great artist, show the world your dream by making it into a concrete reality.

Use both your intellect and your intuitive abilities to design your own financial strategies. If you need facts or information, then acquire them by reading, asking, and listening. Read, but don't be led. Ask for information, not solutions. Listen more than you speak. Above all, maintain your vision and your dreams. Think of them and renew them every day. You are the artist, the creator of your life. Create your financial future and your happiness, for your life is your greatest work of art.

Chapter

10

Mutual Funds and Mental Ecology

> **Do what you can, with what you have, where you are.**
>
> **THEODORE ROOSEVELT**

The relationship between the words "ecology" and "economics" goes far beyond their closeness in the dictionary. Ecology concerns the interrelationship of an organism and its environment; economics concerns the utilization of resources and the production and distribution of wealth. On an individual level, economics is the ecology of finance; it concerns your relationship to your financial environment.

In any ecosystem, balance and harmony among the interrelated components of the system are crucial to sustaining and nurturing growth. The same is true of your financial ecosystem. As pointed out in Chapter 9, to build your personal fortune you have to find the right balance of investments within the context of your knowledge, risk, goals, personality, financial status, age, health, and a variety of other factors. When you diversify your funds into cash, bonds, stocks, and real estate, you are making a major step in the direction of balance.

One way to conveniently and effectively invest in bonds, stocks, and cash is by investing in mutual funds.

One way to conveniently and effectively invest in bonds, stocks, and cash is by investing in mutual funds. A mutual fund is a pool of money, obtained from both individuals and institutional investors, that is invested in securities (stocks, bonds, T-bills, CDs, and other market instruments). When you invest in a mutual fund, you are investing in the fund, not in the securities themselves. Your money is turned over to professionals for management, and in return you are issued shares in the fund. If the fund is profitable, the value of your shares increases proportionally. If the fund loses money, then the value of your shares falls. In effect, you have an equity interest in an investment company.

In the current environment, where 3,500 mutual funds now manage approximately $1.2 trillion, selecting funds that are compatible with your financial goals can be a challenge. *Business Week's* "Mutual Fund Scoreboard" (published in February 1992) reported that out of 760 funds evaluated, only 41 demonstrated a superior risk-adjusted performance for the past five years. Even so, if you know the facts about mutual funds, they could be the right investment vehicle for you.

DIFFERENT FUNDS FOR DIFFERENT INVESTMENT GOALS

The most familiar type of mutual fund is the money market fund. As discussed in Chapter 9, these near-cash equivalents have assets consisting of highly liquid, large-denomination, short-term debts such as T-bills, CDs, and some commercial paper (commercial loans or money borrowed by corporations whose debts are rated AAA by established rating services). By pooling the resources of both small and large investors, the money market mutual fund is able to secure for all of its depositors higher interest rates than would be attainable for investors with small deposits. For example, if you invest $1,000 in a money market mutual fund, you will most likely receive an interest rate at least equal to the current T-bill yield, without needing to invest the $10,000 it would otherwise take to purchase a T-bill.

Other types of mutual funds are designed with different objectives and different levels of risk. Some mutual funds concentrate on blue-chip stocks (capital funds), looking for value appreciation (an increase in the price of the stock); others focus on stocks in smaller, faster growing, but usually riskier companies (growth funds). Some funds target income (interest-bearing bonds, plus government and commercial loans); others want appreciation of the cash value of bond holdings. Specialized funds, called industry or sector funds, invest in specific economic sectors such as high-tech (computer company) stocks, gold stocks, health industry stocks, drug stocks, or international stocks. The Investment Company Institute, the trade association for mutual funds, lists some 22 major categories of investment objectives for mutual funds.

Often, mutual funds are offered in groups called families. A family of funds consists of a group of funds, offered by the same fund management company, in which each fund has a different investment objective. Just as a cereal company offers many different types of cereal to suit various tastes and preferences in an attempt to increase its share of the cereal market, mutual fund companies offer a variety of different mutual funds to increase their share of the mutual funds market. By offering a wide variety of "products," mutual fund companies compete for your investment dollars.

A savvy investor like yourself, with knowledge of cycles, can use mutual fund families to your advantage. Many fund management companies will allow you to switch your money between different funds with no charge. This will allow you to maintain your diversification strategy while optimizing returns by switching to different funds according to cycle phases of strength and weakness. Using the 25 percent rule, you could begin by placing 25 percent of your money into a money market fund, 25 percent into a capital fund (stocks), and 25 percent into an income fund (bonds and other debt), and keeping the last (or first!) 25 percent in real estate. If the bond market is in a cycle phase of strength and the stock market is approaching a cycle high, you may want to switch all or a portion of the money you have placed in the capital fund into the income fund or money market account. Switching your money within a family of funds allows you to diversify your investments and to change your asset allocations without paying a commission each time. The mutual fund is your agent for each transaction.

MUTUAL FUNDS: A CONVENIENT INVESTMENT

No other investment provides the convenience and potential for diversification that are available from mutual fund shares. Mutual funds provide a number of other features that make investing in them relatively easy, even for someone with modest investment assets.

No other investment provides the convenience and potential for diversification that are available from mutual fund shares.

For example, after making your initial deposit (usually, $300 to $500 is the minimum requirement), deposits can be made at any time and for any amount. Unlike stocks, which have to be purchased on a share-by-share basis, mutual funds allow you to purchase fractional shares, so you can invest whatever amount you choose. This may seem like a small advantage, but the convenience of being able to invest a small, fixed dollar amount, on a regular basis, keeps your personal bookkeeping simple, thus encouraging you to invest regularly.

Dividends, interest, and capital gains can usually be automatically reinvested, which allows your earnings to be immediately placed back in the fund so you can profit from your profits. No decisions on reinvestment are needed, and you will be less likely to spend your profits on tempting but unnecessary items.

With mutual funds, your investment capital can be easily withdrawn. Most money market accounts offer limited check-writing privileges. If you write and sign a letter requesting withdrawal of your funds, you will usually receive a check within seven days. An even faster means of withdrawal is by wire transfer. If you make arrangements for wire transfer to the bank of your choice when you first open your account, your funds may be deposited on the same day you request them. With this arrangement, your mutual fund becomes more liquid than your stocks or bonds. Usually, it takes five business days to receive the proceeds from a stock or bond sell order.

FINE-TUNING YOUR MUTUAL FUND TIMING

As with other investments, you can use cycles as the basis for selecting when to place what amount of your investment assets in stock funds, income funds, or money market accounts. When it comes to fine-tuning your timing, however, you may want to enlist the assistance of one or more timing services before deciding exactly when and how to switch. In several investment newsletters and services that are available, you will find lists of top-performing no-load funds (more on no-load funds later) and advice to subscribers on when to get into the stock funds and when to switch back to money market funds or income funds. One of these services, *The Telephone Switch Newsletter* (800-950-8765), boasts an annualized compounded growth rate of 18.43 percent. This service was one of the few that issued a sell signal on October 15, 1987, getting its subscribers out of stocks before the big crash. It also switched subscribers back into funds in December 1988, when the stock market entered another period of strength.

USING CYCLES FOR FUND SWITCHING

Before you can use cycles for fund switching, the mutual fund family you choose must meet several criteria. First, the family must include a fund in each of the three basic categories: stocks, bonds, and money market. Second, your selection of funds should be limited to those having more than $30 million but less than $3 billion in assets under management. Third, you should avoid closed-end funds (funds that have a fixed, limited number of shares outstanding) because they generally perform poorly.

Suppose you find a family of funds meeting these criteria—let's call it the Columbus Family. The three funds of interest to you are the Nina fund (a capital stock fund), the Pinta fund (a bond fund), and the Santa Maria (a money market fund). You know from reading the prospectus (more on prospectuses later) that your money can be switched among these funds without limit and without a sales or service fee to you.

Based on the stock and bond cycles presented in Chapters 8 and 9, the following might be a good strategy for the next five years. Because the 40-month stock price cycle has projected the probability of strength in the stock market during 1992, place the bulk of your funds in the Nina fund (stocks). In late 1992 or early 1993 (following your own intuition) switch your money into the money market fund, the Santa Maria. (Although cycles call for strength in the stock market well into 1993, I personally believe it will weaken shortly after the presidential election in 1992.) In 1994, you can consider investing in the Pinta fund (bonds) near the 178-week interest-rate cycle high. During 1995 and possibly 1996, you would consider switching your money back into the stock fund, the Nina, as stocks enter a major cycle phase of strength.

Although necessarily general, this example should give you an idea of how to employ cycles in fund switching. If the strategy suits you, you can go beyond the simple diversification plan of stocks, bonds, and money markets by investing in other funds within the family. For example, because 1995 should be an ideal time to enter the stock market, it might be a good time to put a portion of your assets into an aggressive stock growth fund. Although the risk of growth funds is generally higher than some other stock funds, if you enter during the early stages of a period of stock market strength, you may substantially reduce your risks.

By offering switching as a strategy, I do not mean to imply that you should switch your money from fund to fund, always chasing the new "hot" group. Quite the contrary; by using financial trends as a guideline for moving your money from one fund to another, you won't be *chasing* anything. Rather, you will be entering the particular fund *in anticipation* of coming strength.

By using your knowledge of cycles to allocate your investment assets, you improve the probabilities that you will be in at least one top-winning strategy *most* of the time.

By using your knowledge of cycles to allocate your investment assets among several different funds in order to fulfill different investment objectives, you improve the probability that you will be involved in at least one top-winning strategy *most* of the time. Your overall rate of return will increase more than if you simply bought shares in one fund each year for the next five years.

THE PROSPECTUS: EVERYTHING YOU EVER WANTED TO KNOW AND MORE

The single most important action you can take in selecting the right fund to meet your objectives is to read the prospectus of the fund. This little booklet of information, standardized by the Securities and Exchange Commission, *must be* presented to prospective investors. Most mutual funds have toll-free (800) numbers and will send you a prospectus if you request it. When you read a prospectus, you will learn the following: important information:

- *Investment objectives and policies.* In my opinion, this is the most important information—whether the fund is investing for growth, income, or both, and what kind of investments the fund will make to accomplish these objectives.
- *Who runs the mutual fund operation.* The directors and officers of the fund are listed, along with information on their other business connections. You will be told whether the fund employs an advisory service. The stars of mutual fund management come and go—and move around a lot. (We will discuss this later, when we take a look at "red flags" in mutual fund selection.)

- *Who manages the portfolio.* You will learn who decides what securities to buy and sell for the fund (the fund manager), as well as who carries out the transactions, who receives the brokerage commissions, and what the fees for research are. The custodial bank (the bank that holds the cash and securities) will be named.
- *How to purchase shares.* This section of the prospectus will spell out how to purchase shares and will indicate acceptable means of payment. In the case of a load fund (to be discussed later), you will be informed of the percentage of the total purchase that goes to the broker or the salesperson.
- *Shareholder services.* This section describes any special services that the fund provides, such as the ability to switch to other mutual funds within a family of funds without incurring sales charges. If the fund is a money market fund, check-writing privileges and other benefits are detailed.
- *How to redeem shares.* This includes instructions on how you can redeem your money by phone, by letter, or by wire. You will also learn about any redemption fees (rear-end loads) that may be charged.
- *Accounting and financial statements.* The fund's investments, as well as other assets and liabilities, are listed here. There is also a financial statement for the previous fiscal year and a statement showing the changes in the asset values for the past several years. You should be alert for any notice of pending litigation against the fund.

Just as you should read a contract before you purchase real estate or read the most recent issue of *Consumer Reports* before you buy a car or major appliance, reading the prospectus of a mutual fund is a must. It will help you match the right fund to your financial goals and maximize your profits.

MUTUAL FUNDS AND FEES

Mutual funds make money by charging a management and expense fee, typically 0.75 to 1.25 percent of the assets under management. This provides an incentive for the fund to be profitable—the more money it makes, the more new investors it will attract, and the more fees it will accrue.

Other costs may be involved. Some funds levy a sales charge, called a front-end load, when an investor first purchases shares. This fee can be as high as 6.8 percent of the entire investment amount—a hefty fee! It means that when you sell your shares, you must have received a 6.8 percent increase just to break even, and this is in addition to the management and advisory fees. Such mutual funds are called "load funds."

If you are considering investing in a load fund, you should feel confident that you will be receiving outstanding investment advice and management of your money, because you *will* be paying for it.

If you are considering investing in a load fund, be sure you will be receiving outstanding investment advice and money management.

No-load funds are funds that do not charge a load or sales fee. In a no-load fund, every dollar you spend for stock in the fund goes directly to work as investment dollars, and nothing is taken out to pay a broker or salesperson. The benefit of these funds is obvious. If you purchase one day and sell the next, assuming the net asset value of the fund does not change, you will be able to get all of your money back.

Some no-load funds have "rear-end loads," also called "exit charges" or "redemption fees." In many cases, the redemption fee is charged only if your funds are withdrawn within six months after you first purchase shares. Although I like to avoid paying fees whenever possible, I can understand a fund wanting to charge an investor who is unwilling to leave his or her money in place for a reasonable period of time. To plan an effective strategy, a fund manager needs to be confident that total assets won't be going in and out of the fund like the tides.

Most research indicates that the track record for good load funds is no better than the track record for good no-load (or no-fee) funds. In my opinion, unless you find an exceptionally good load fund, you should probably stick to no-load funds.

RED FLAGS IN MUTUAL FUND SELECTION

There are a number of specific warning signs to look for when choosing the right mutual fund for your needs.

First, as a general rule, avoid new funds. Having attended horse races, I understand the importance of knowing a track record before placing your bets on a potential winner. The same holds true of mutual funds: Don't bet on a fund without a record. Limit your selection to funds that have at least a five-year record of success, or you may be taking an unnecessary risk. If a younger, successful fund is managed by someone whose established and successful record is well known, then that is tantamount to the same thing.

When analyzing a fund's track record, be sure to look at performance during bear market years we well as bull market years. It is good to know how the fund you are considering held up under adverse conditions. There are a number of good sources to use when comparing the track records of different funds. One is *Money* magazine. In almost every issue, you will find information on the performance of various mutual funds. Another good source, the *Wiesenberger Investment Company Service,* is most likely available at your public library.

In narrowing down the field, pick about 20 potential funds from lists of top performers. As a further test, make sure that the companies you look at offer a family of funds that includes both growth and balanced stock strategies, a fixed-income fund, and a money market mutual fund.

As a general rule, eliminate funds that charge commissions. This criterion will probably slim down your selection list a great deal—and help you keep more of your money. Some funds won't charge for a purchase, but they may charge you a great deal for redemption of your funds. Know exactly how much your costs will be in both directions, getting in and getting out.

If you are working with a broker and he or she suggests a fund that charges commissions, don't buy. On the other hand, if a fund doesn't charge commissions, keep asking questions. A broker once told me there was "no commission" on the purchase of a fund, except that paid by the fund company. Technically, he was correct. What he didn't tell me was that for every $10 I gave the fund, it was going to invest only $9.20—the fund company paid the commissions with *my* money, at a rate of 8 percent!

Any fund that reports a loss greater than 15 percent in a single year is sending you a red flag.

Any fund that reports a loss greater than 15 percent in a single year is sending you a red flag, except perhaps in periods when nearly all funds are down 15 percent. Protecting yourself from such general losses is largely your own responsibility. With your knowledge of cycles, you will most likely be in cash or a money market fund while stock funds are trying to make money during a cycle phase of weakness.

Another good rule is to avoid funds with a new fund manager, unless it is someone whose record you are familiar with and whom you trust. You are paying for professional money management; don't risk your cash unless the fund manager has an excellent record. If you have a very good "feeling" about the person who has managed your money in a mutual fund, you may wish to follow this manager if he or she moves to another fund.

Avoid highly leveraged funds. Leverage can be good in real estate, but, except for the most aggressive investors, borrowing money to invest in securities of any kind is too risky. In general, mutual funds borrow against their own assets to obtain cash for redemptions. If they didn't, they would have to sell their own stock to pay you. This borrowing usually amounts to a debt of about 5 percent of assets under management. If the fund you are considering borrows more than this, then the fund likely carries a good deal of risk. (A few dollars in a very aggressive fund, during a strong cycle upward trend, can be fun. Like the long shot at the race track, however, it is not the basis for a balanced investment strategy.)

ECOLOGY OF THE MIND

Mutual funds can be an integral part of your financial ecosystem, but not without a more important element—what I call "mental ecology," the relationship of your mental environment to your life, including your financial life. There is a direct connection between the mental environment you construct for yourself and making money.

GIGO, *G*arbage *I*n, *G*arbage *O*ut, is computer jargon used to explain that no matter how good the programming of your computer is, if you put bad information in, you'll get bad information or garbage out. This same idea can be used to describe your subconscious mind. If you feed your mind with negative thoughts and emotions, you will end up with negative results in life. GIGO.

Because positive experiences are what we truly desire, we need to keep our minds full of positive ideas and images to get positive returns.

Because positive experiences are what we truly desire, we need to keep our minds full of positive ideas and images to get positive returns. Being positive is often very difficult when we try something new. There is something about those first plans, that first step, which brings up every negative emotion we have ever experienced, especially fear. Getting past fear can be accomplished by changing our way of looking at things.

In the study of physical science, you can create interesting designs with iron filings and a magnet. However, your designs can instantly become chaotic when other magnets are put in the middle of your design. This same concept holds true with positive and negative thoughts. You can create harmonious, balanced, positive experiences with your thoughts, or introduce chaos and disruption with the magnets of negative thinking. Just as one piece of bad data can ruin the output of an otherwise perfect computer program, allowing fear to dominate your mind can ruin the results you seek in your investments.

A prosperous life is a worthy goal. Prosperity, which is created with positive thoughts and positive expectations, is difficult to produce in a chaotic environment. If you "make an attempt" to invest but the entire experience is surrounded with fear, you are less likely to find success. Like a magnet drawing metal filings, negative expectations and fears can attract negative experiences. When you are skeptical and fearful about investing but proceed anyway, things are more likely to "go wrong," and you may find yourself confirming the negative experience with words like, "I knew this was going to happen."

You can change this pattern by building on your successes one step at a time. Start with a small amount of money—money you don't expect to lose, but money that won't be deeply missed if you do lose it. Invest this amount, *knowing* that someday you will add many zeros to your original investment amount. Visualize yourself successfully investing larger and larger amounts of money and receiving better and better returns.

Don't expect your outcome to happen overnight; make it a part of your long-term financial plan. Cycles show you how to see future probabilities in financial trends. See your own future success in those same cycles. Picture yourself participating in and receiving profits from the next stock market or bond market upturn.

Your first successes do not have to be with thousands of dollars. Success is success. Your subconscious mind will respond just as positively to a success with two zeros as it will to one with five zeros. Once you have the feeling of success in your mind and spirit, adding the zeros will become easier and easier. Then you can confirm your own success with those same words, "I knew this was going to happen!"

If there is mental garbage in your world, call it BFI—Before Financial Independence. Recycle what you can by allowing it to change into some useful form. Get rid of anything that has absolutely no positive purpose—fear, jealousy, hate, revenge, greed, or anger. Recycle your negative thoughts into positive ones and you will create the prosperity and financial success you desire.

Chapter 11

Real Estate: The Foundation for Wealth

Every improvement in the circumstances of the society tends either directly or indirectly to raise the real rent of land, to increase the real wealth of the landlord.

ADAM SMITH, *THE WEALTH OF NATIONS*

Real estate is the foundation for wealth. Beyond the world where real estate tycoons make millions of dollars on a single venture, there is a different world in which thousands of people just like you are quietly building fortunes. At the base of all lasting wealth is real estate.

I was not born into wealth. I realized very early that I would have "the opportunity" to acquire it on my own. I did so primarily through buying, developing, and selling real estate at the right time and in the right place. I started modestly, finding the first home for my young family. From then on, real estate became the basis for my financial future. It can be the basis for yours as well.

TRIAL BY FIRE

My experience in real estate started in 1969, after I had been teaching school for several years. I truly enjoyed teaching but, like most people, I grew up yearning for financial independence. It didn't take long to realize that I would never find my financial freedom by relying on my income as a teacher. All around me, people were making money by buying and selling property, so I delved into the world of real estate.

The first step was to buy a home. The timing was great as far as the real estate cycle was concerned. (We'll discuss real estate and other cycles later.) For $27,750, we purchased a lovely three-bedroom, two-bath home that had a family room. The builder had gone bankrupt, and we bought the home from the bank for construction costs. It had a great floor plan, and it was on the side of a hill with a lovely view of the entire Santa Clara valley. It needed landscaping and decorating, but it was a great buy.

The biggest problem was coming up with the down payment we needed—$1,000. We put together all of our savings, but it wasn't quite enough. I ended up borrowing money from the realtor who was selling the house, and we moved in.

Once nestled safely in my room with a view, I started looking for other real estate opportunities. At a party, I overheard several engineers from Silicon Valley talking about a land deal. From the sound of it, they were making money hand-over-fist. They were buying the land for $500 an acre, dividing it into smaller parcels, and selling the parcels for what amounted to $2,000 an acre. Why couldn't I do the same thing?

I discussed the idea with the realtor who had helped out with the loan to buy my home. Not only was he interested, he already had in mind a parcel of land just south of San Jose, and the numbers sounded great. By this time, I had quit teaching to raise my first daughter. I took out my accumulated teacher's retirement, $2,300, and invested it in Lake Estates, our newly-formed land development partnership.

Mine was a one-sixth interest. Half of the land was owned by one man and his wife, and I shared the other half with my husband, the realtor and his wife, and another couple. After all, if the realtor had put his money on the line, it must be a good deal, right? WRONG! I soon learned that the realtor got *paid* for selling me, the other couple, and *himself* our interest in the property, and then applied what we paid him to the purchase price of his share. He essentially got one-sixth interest free, so what did he have to lose!

At first, things seemed to go perfectly. The first five parcels sold immediately. We had paid $500 an acre for the land and were successfully selling it for $2,000 an acre. With another 180 acres to sell, I was mentally spending the profit. I dreamed of overnight fortunes, but then my real education in the world of land deals began.

Our mortgage was carried by the previous owner, and something called a "release clause" was in our contract. I didn't know what that meant then, but I know now that release clauses are one of the biggest red flags you will ever see in real estate transactions. They are an agreement to pay the mortgage holder a sum of money to release the parcels of land after you sell them.

For every parcel we sold after the first four, not only didn't I receive any money, but I had to *pay* money to finalize the sale! With one small daughter to take care of and another one on the way, I found this agreement very annoying. I had some income from a company I had founded, called Creative Activities, but it wasn't enough to cover the mortgage payments on the investment *and* the release fees.

The Lake Estates Partnership turned into my trial by fire. I learned the good, the bad, and the ugly about real estate. Beyond learning about release clauses, I also learned what it means not to be in control of an investment. Buying a one-sixth interest in land wasn't a smart move. At the best of times, getting my eight associates to agree on anything was challenging. As the partnership evolved, it became next to impossible.

Imagine trying to shoot arrows at snowflakes. Just when you think you have hit one, it bursts into oblivion. Within 18 months of the birth of the venture, the realtor and his wife got divorced and so did the other couple. Now I was dealing with people who not only didn't live together, but didn't even want to speak to each other!

Every time a parcel sold, we needed eight signatures. With the leadership of the realtor gone, I took on the responsibility of promoting the land and trying to get all the signatures together when a parcel sold. I can remember the day I decided I'd had enough. It was a Sunday afternoon, at a wedding. One of my partners was marrying a girl some 30 years his junior. In the hippie fashion of the times, the wedding was held outdoors in the mountains. It was hot, so everyone in the wedding party decided to take off their shoes. I remember thinking, "What am I doing at this hippie wedding? I'm trying to get my partner's signature, so I can sell a piece of land, and pay money to the mortgagor out of my pocket to satisfy the release clauses. Enough of this madness!"

What a learning experience! I came face-to-face with an immortal real estate saying: "Behind every real estate bargain there is a sale screaming to get out." I decided that the Lake Estates Partnership was not going to reach its objective. To reach mine, I would have to find a new course of action: I would sell my one-sixth interest. I advertised. I waited by the phone. But people weren't interested in buying a one-sixth interest in a land partnership. I can't imagine why.

I was a sale screaming to get out. My interest had to be a bargain for someone. But who and how? Thinking back to my expertise in real estate board games, I realized that if no one would buy my interest, then someone might *trade* for it, and that someone would have to be as desperate as I was.

After an eight-month search, I found a desperate builder. He had a home that he'd been trying to sell for over nine months. When I looked at it, I saw two basic flaws. It was located on the side of a hill, but you could only enjoy the view from the kitchen window. It also had a truly *ugly* breezeway. I decided that if I enclosed the breezeway and installed patio doors toward the view, the house would be quite marketable. Over the phone, I pitched the builder the deal of the century: "How would you like to trade the house for a one-sixth interest in a partnership called Lake Estates?"

Funny thing, he didn't hang up the phone. In fact, he even expressed a mild interest. I went into my spiel about the property's potential, especially because he was a builder, and we set up an appointment to talk. To complete the deal, I traded my interest in the partnership to my other partners in return for 29 acres of the partnership land and a building site in Clear Lake that I'd never seen. I traded the 29 acres to the builder for a $20,000 credit for his home and kept the lot in Clear Lake.

Then I sold my home in San Jose for a $35,000 profit and moved into the new home. I put almost nothing down, and I had $35,000 in cash to boot. After 18 more months and a lot of hard work, I sold my new home, netting another $35,000 from it, which *finally* included the cash from the Lake Estates Partnership. Although it took six years, I ended up doubling my total investment in Lake Estates. I made it through my trial by fire without getting burned.

I knew nothing about cycles in those early days, but I did learn many lessons about the do's and don'ts of real estate investing. What I learned can be summarized in a few simple rules:

- Avoid real estate purchases and partnerships that require you to relinquish control over your investment.
- Always thoroughly read and understand real estate contracts before you sign them. Consult with an attorney if there is any doubt about the meaning and terms of the contract.
- Never assume that the "experts" know more than you do.
- If you are considering entering a partnership, scrutinize your partners before you sign anything. Understand what your partners will have at stake in the deal—what they can make and what they can lose. If your partner has nothing to lose, you probably won't be able to count on him or her during tough times.
- If you realize you have made a bad investment, look for a way out of the deal that will bring you out on top. Let your imagination guide you to innovative ways of turning your loser into a winner. Somewhere, someone else needs to trade out of what, for them, is also a bad deal. By exchanging your interests, you may both be better off. It worked for me.

If you remember these simple guidelines, you will minimize your mistakes as you enter the world of real estate investment. They will enable you to begin the process of building your financial foundation in real estate without going through your own trial by fire.

No other consideration approaches the importance of timing real estate purchases and sales correctly.

Although these guidelines are important, none of them approaches the importance of timing your purchases and sales of real estate correctly. When I started in real estate, I intuitively knew that the real estate market was in a period of strength. Since then, I have learned much more about real estate investment timing.

When I talk about timing, what I am really talking about is being able to move into the market when you know it will be strong and out of the market when you know it will be weak. In other words, you have to be aware of the real estate cycle. Real estate markets have a cycle that moves within a broader cycle of general economic activity.

THE 18-YEAR RHYTHM IN GENERAL ECONOMIC ACTIVITY

The cycle rhythm in the general economy lasts about 18 years and is very similar to the real estate cycle of $18^1/_3$ years (discussed in detail in the next chapter). As shown in Figure 11.1, the general economic cycle was first discovered as early as 1885. To date, it has predicted business cycles with remarkable accuracy.

The figure shows an M-shaped cycle pattern. It indicates a strong upward trend lasting six to eight years, followed by a period of weakness. After this weakness comes another area of strength and then a steep but shorter period of weakness. Then the cycle begins anew.

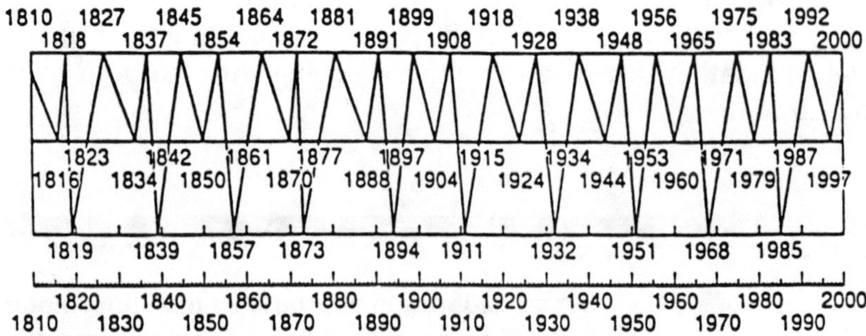

Figure 11.1 A Chart of Cycles Found in 1885, More Than a Hundred Years Ago (Reprinted courtesy of the Foundation for the Study of Cycles.)

If you look very closely at the figure, you'll see that the components of each cycle are *similar,* but they're not exactly the same. The phases of strength and weakness are not always of equal length. Alfred Frost and Robert Prechter pointed out that longer cycles in the stock market are always influenced by the nature of the shorter cycles that precede them.

Skeptics might criticize the usefulness of cycles as a predictive tool because of their variability, but these critics would be missing an essential point. Cycles as broad as this patterning of the general economy act as general guidelines, the way the season of the year guides the choice of clothing for a particular day. In many areas that experience the four seasons, a 70- or 80-degree day may occur in December and a frost warning may be posted in June, but *in general,* the climate will be predictably cold or warm according to the season. The 18-year economic cycle tells the general nature of what is going to occur; it gives a broad framework within which to analyze specific events.

The peak that was projected for 1983 actually came in 1981. The major recession of 1982 followed. The economy was sluggish during the weakness phase that followed this recession, and it took massive tax cuts by the Reagan Administration to get the economy moving. These tax cuts, which bloated the federal deficit and turned us into a debtor nation, also kept the economy from sinking into what could have been a depression. The real strength came during the middle of the decade, when the cycle moved from weakness to strength.

The recession that arrived in 1990 was exactly as cycles had theorized.

The recession that arrived in 1990 was exactly as cycles had theorized. I predicted this recession in 1988, and participants in my Money Cycles seminars have been thanking me ever since. The crest of that recession will have passed by the time this book is published in late 1992. We will be in another area of strength by the middle of the decade. Not until late in the decade will we see the next major downturn, a time for a defensive real estate strategy. Until then, the prospects for discriminating real estate investors are splendid.

REAL ESTATE: A STOREHOUSE OF WEALTH

In 1917, Morton F. Plant, a man born into a railroad fortune, sold his Fifth Avenue mansion in New York for $1,200,000. Rather than take cash from the purchaser, the jewelry firm of Cartier, Plant took the payment out in trade. In exchange for his mansion, Morton received a "two-strand, Oriental pearl necklace."

At the time, it seemed like a fair transaction. The mansion and the necklace were of equal value, at least as far as buyer and seller were concerned. In the 75 years since, however, the value of each has changed.

The real estate is now a New York City registered landmark. Located on the southeast corner of Fifth Avenue and 52nd Street, the mansion remains Cartier's foremost American location and is one of the most desirable properties in the world. It is difficult to even place a value on the property, although it is known that the air rights (the rights to build above the actual property) recently sold for tens of millions of dollars.

As for the pearls, the value of a two-strand Oriental pearl necklace today would be in the $200,000 range. The mansion is worth at least a hundred times that much. Although the purchasing power of the dollar has diminished since 1917, not every asset has increased in value to keep pace with the change. Not all properties have the value of the corner of Fifth Avenue and 52nd Street, but across the country and throughout the decades, real estate has remained a consistent means to preserve and expand wealth.

INFLATION AND REAL ESTATE PROFITS

Inflation is now a way of life for Americans, and it is here to stay. In 1971, President Nixon introduced his disastrous wage and price controls when inflation was at the "dangerously high" level of 3.1 percent. At that time, a 5 percent inflation rate would have been political suicide. Now, after the double-digit inflation in the 1970s, 5 percent inflation is considered acceptable, if not downright good.

As a long-term investment, real estate tends to at least keep pace with inflation and usually appreciates faster.

As a long-term investment, real estate tends to keep pace with inflation. In some areas of high demand, the rate of increase in real estate prices not only keeps up with but actually outstrips the general inflation rate. No matter how much you hear about methods for wringing inflation out of the economy, you can anticipate and even expect that most residential real estate in areas of general economic growth will appreciate at a rate of about 3 to 5 percent.

At first glance, a 5 percent annual appreciation rate may not seem very good when compared to the 10 or 12 percent that is potentially available on some other investments. It is important to remember, however, that if you borrow money to buy a property, you get the benefit of a 5 percent return on the full value of the property while paying only a fraction of the market price as a down payment.

For example, if you buy a $100,000 house for $20,000 (20 percent) down and an $80,000 mortgage, and if you live in the house for several years during a period of real estate strength, then your effective rate of return on your home is much, much higher than 5 percent. To live in your home, you invest $20,000 in cash plus closing costs, loan origination fees, and so forth, amounting to, say, another $5,000. Your total cash investment is $25,000. If the price of the house keeps up with a 5 percent inflation rate, then at the end of the first year, you have an asset worth $105,000. Your house has appreciated 5 percent in value, but your return on investment is much higher.

Assuming that you are paying toward your mortgage what you otherwise would have been paying in rent. At the end of the first year, you have $5,000 more in net worth than you otherwise would have had. For an investment of $25,000, you are $5,000 richer—a 20 percent return on your cash investment. If you have bought at the right time, the size of this return will grow each year. If you buy a rental property, the equation becomes a little more complicated, but the returns are as good or better. When you add in the tax advantages derived from the depreciation of rental property and the tax-deductible interest expense for the homeowner, real estate investment remains one of the best ways available to make money above and beyond the inflation rate.

The most commonly used measure of inflation is the Consumer Price Index (CPI), an index of the general price level of consumer goods. The CPI is obtained by evaluating the market prices of a representative "basket" of currently produced consumer goods and services. When the CPI goes up, it means that the general price level is going up, or inflating. When it goes down, it means that prices are going down or deflating.

Other than the notorious deflationary years of the 1930s (the Great Depression years) and two single years, 1949 and 1955, the CPI has risen every year. During the inflationary 1970s, the CPI almost doubled from 1970 to 1979, rising from 116.3 to 217.4. The growth rate of inflation slowed in the 1980s, but it still increased from 246.8 in 1980 to 390.4 in 1987. Prices increased more slowly than they did in the 1970s, but the increase has been consistent and dramatic. Sooner or later, real estate prices will reflect this creeping inflation in almost every region of the nation.

Alan Greenspan, the chairman of the Federal Reserve Board, has stated that the Fed's ultimate goal is to achieve 0 percent inflation. With all due respect, I don't believe that we will see zero inflation in our lifetimes. Inflation is a hidden tax system. Prices rise because the physical supply of money grows faster than the supply of goods and services. Guess who is primarily responsible for the rate of growth of the money supply? The government. When it overspends, the government pays its expenses by creating more money. Prices rise because the market is flooded with currency without producing much of anything. When prices rise, your real income falls.

Inflation is a subtle form of taxation.

The way this actually occurs in our economic system is very complex, but the principle is simple: The government keeps printing a "little more" money each year so it can pay its bills. Each of your dollars is then worth a "little less" in terms of what it can purchase, so your real income falls. You may even get a raise, but then you will probably pay more taxes. In principle, inflation is a subtle form of taxation.

Price inflation has been a continuous economic problem for centuries. Adam Smith, in *Wealth of Nations,* discussed the practice of writing leases based partially on "corn rent," or the price of corn; the remaining part of the long-term lease was based on currency. If inflation ate up the value of the currency, then at least the landlord would be partially protected by the rising price of corn. The practice was born of necessity, a protection against inflation developed over 200 years ago.

Our managed economy has built-in inflation. New tax bills come and go, but few politicians seem willing to cut federal spending in their districts. Because our government seems incapable of significantly reducing spending, inflating the currency will continue to be the most viable political option.

If you understand how this process works, you can create an opportunity. Rather than sit paralyzed with fear because your money is losing value each day, you can invest so that the system will work for you instead of against you. You can do this with investments in real estate. In Chapters 12 and 13, I'll show you how.

THE INTEREST RATE CYCLE AND PROFITS

One of the single most important factors affecting the real estate cycle, and therefore the timing of buying and selling, is interest rates. If you borrow money to purchase real estate, changes of just a few percentage points in the interest rate can have a huge impact on your cash flow. For example, borrowing $80,000 at 11 percent interest for 30 years requires you to pay $755 monthly; borrowing $80,000 at 9 percent interest requires a monthly payment of $638—a difference of $117 per month!

Fortunately, there is a cycle that will tell you the general trend of long-term interest rates. Like the long economic cycle, which points to a period of strength toward the end of the decade, this cycle (along with the knowledge that inflation will most likely continue) can point you toward real estate profits in the 1990s.

Figure 11.2 shows 54-year cycles in railroad bond yields. There is a direct correlation between the 54-year cycle and long-term interest rates in general. As interest rates rise, yields rise on the new bonds issued. (This also means that bonds you own at lower rates will drop in value because investors can get higher yields, as discussed in Chapter 9.) As tracked by the Foundation for the Study of Cycles, Figure 11.2 shows that

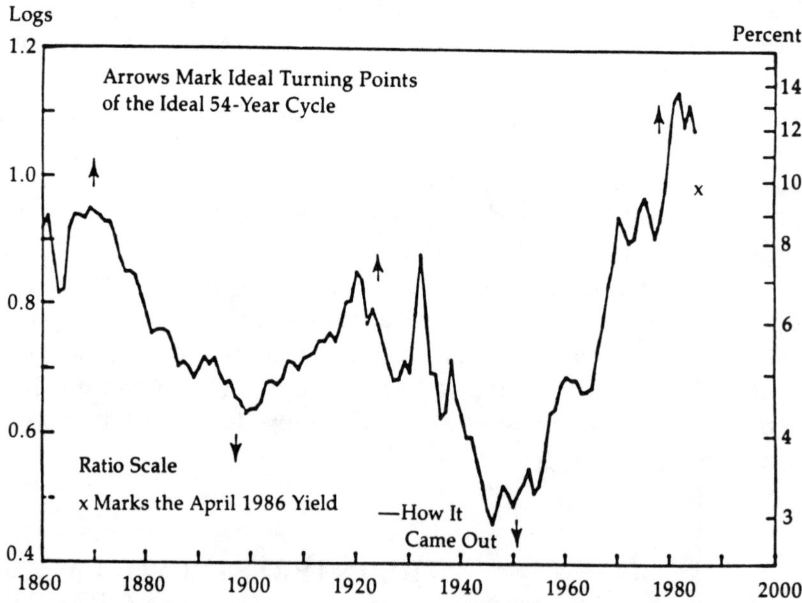

Figure 11.2 Railroad Bond Yields, 54-Year Cycle, Yearly Average (Moody's), 1857–1985. (Reprinted courtesy of the Foundation for the Study of Cycles.)

bond yields from 1857 to 1985 have had a significant repeating pattern—a cycle—that has been quite accurate with respect to the direction of interest rates. Even with the spike in interest rates that occurred in 1931–1932, the trend of the long cycle has been accurate.

Long-term interest rates peaked in 1980; most of us can remember mortgage rates of 18 percent and a prime lending rate of 21 percent. Since then, rates have been declining. This doesn't mean that we will see 6 percent fixed-rate mortgage money again; it means that there is a trend toward lower rates, downward from previous highs. Most people today feel that a low interest rate is one that is less than 10 percent. Based on the cycle, this is a reasonable assumption, but trying to predict an exact interest rate in the future is almost impossible.

The effect of the long-term interest rate cycle on the real estate market is quite significant. We will look at specific decades of real estate activity in the next chapter, but it is safe to say that very high interest rates correlate to a depressed real estate market. When interest rates are lower, the real estate market is stronger. Lower interest rates usually stimulate demand and push prices up, especially in areas where supply is restricted. After the real estate market completes its shakeout in the early 1990s, lower interest rates, as predicted by this cycle, will contribute to a healthy and active real estate market in many areas of the country.

In the real estate market of the 1990s, there will be areas of strength and weakness. Analyzing individual communities will be more important than ever before.

Unlike the 1970s, when real estate throughout the country went up in price, in the 1990s there will be certain areas of strength and others of relative weakness. Analyzing the economic environment of individual communities will be more important than ever before—and so will using your own intuition.

Have you ever entered a community and been surprised at how good you felt there? You may have sensed vitality, creative energy, growth, vigor, spirit, and good planning. Perhaps buildings were being built or revitalized, or new businesses were relocating in that community because the price of housing was affordable and commute times were reasonable.

When you find such places and real estate diversification is on your financial agenda, you should begin to analyze the economic condition of the area. Apply the law of supply and demand. Look for areas where there are plenty of jobs and where new land for development is scarce. Areas with a strong economic base will likely stay ahead of the rate of inflation. Check out the want ads in the local newspaper to see what positions are available. Find out whether local schools are gaining or losing students. Evaluate the strength of major employers. People are attracted by employment opportunities and this will positively affect real estate markets. These important steps will back up your feelings, your intuitive insight, with serious economic data. These steps will also keep you from wanting to invest in vacation resorts just because it feels good to be on vacation.

In the next few years, take your time with real estate investments. There's no need to hurry. Look for the very best deals. You will know when they occur because by then you will thoroughly understand the marketplace. Because the real estate activity cycle was just beginning to move into an area of strength when it was flogged by the recession of the early 1990s, there are some areas that may not recover for another three or four years. There is plenty of time to invest. If you miss one opportunity, there will be others. Because of our present position in the long economic cycle of the Kondratieff wave, we will not see an inflationary spiral like that of the 1970s.

Examine carefully the communities in which you invest. Some specific attractive investment areas are considered in Chapter 13.

REAL ESTATE INVESTMENTS AND CHANGING TAX LAWS

Tax laws can dramatically affect the profitability of real estate investments. Prior to the Tax Reform Act of 1986, the tax deductions allowed on real estate investments created a positive cash flow for many investments that today would be losing propositions. Many limited partnerships survived and were profitable almost purely because of tax advantages. Now, the incentives are different. Investors can show paper losses (called depreciation) in real estate, but only up to certain limits. Tax laws now confine the loss deduction to $25,000, which is allowed only to taxpayers who are active in the management of property and whose income is under $100,000.

What do these changes mean for individual investors? In most cases, they mean that investors need to be more selective. Specifically, the best investments will be income-producing properties that have a positive cash flow *before* taxes. Before the tax laws were revised, many properties that showed a negative cash flow before taxes showed a positive cash flow after tax considerations. New restrictions have altered that strategy. The best real estate investments will be those in which rental income at least covers the payments due (mortgage, taxes, and insurance).

To decide whether a real estate investment is right for you, you need only do a simple calculation. For example, if the rental income doesn't immediately cover the payments, you need to analyze how many years it will be before the rents can be expected to rise. Project a cash flow on your investment, for the next three to five years. Be sure to include out-of-pocket expenses for maintenance and other items. With the help of your accountant, factor in the tax advantages of depreciation. Finally, add in expected appreciation. You will then know how much money you can expect your property to earn for you. Your earnings are your projected return on investment.

For example, assume you are trying to decide whether to purchase a $100,000 home as a rental property. You find out that you can qualify for a 30-year loan at a 10 percent fixed annual interest rate; your monthly payment would be approximately $700. Taxes and insurance on the home will cost $2,400 per year

($200 per month); comparable homes in the area are currently renting for about $875 per month; and rents are increasing at a rate of 5 percent per year. For the first year, your cash flow would look something like this:

Cash Flow Summary—Year 1

Initial investment		$20,000
Expenses or cash out:		
Financing and closing costs	$ 2,500	
Mortgage, taxes, insurance (12 × $900)	10,800	
Repairs and maintenance	$ 500	
Total cash out		(13,800)
Cash in:		
Rental income		10,500
Cash flow before taxes	– $(3,300)	$(3,300)

At first, this may not look like a good investment, but if you are making less than $100,000 per year and are active in managing the property, then you can deduct interest expenses, property depreciation, closing costs, and any other expenses associated with your property. This dramatically changes your cash flow as follows:

After Tax Cash Flow Summary—Year 1

Assumption: 33% Tax bracket		
Cash flow before tax considerations	$(3,300)	
Major tax deductions:		
Interest	7,980	
Property depreciation	2,963	
Financing and closing costs	2,500	
Repairs and maintenance	500	
Taxes and insurance	2,400	
Total major tax deductions	16,343	
Less: Rental income	(10,500)	
Investment loss on your tax return	$ 5,843	
Tax savings (33% × $5,843 =	$ 1,923)	(savings in taxes by owning this property)

Net cash flow after taxes:

$ 3,300	(actually spent; see cash flow before taxes)
(1,923)	(savings in taxes)
$1,372	

Actual loss for the year: $1,372

At the end of the first year, you have spent $1,372 to own a property that has appreciated approximately 5 percent or $5,000:

$$(\$5{,}000 - \$1{,}372/\$20{,}000) \times 100\% = 18\%$$

Not bad, if you can afford a small negative cash flow during the first year. The next year, things will look much better (remember, your rental income is going to increase by 5 percent) and you won't have financing and closing costs during the second year.

Cash Flow Summary—Year 2

Expenses:	
Mortgage, taxes, insurance (12 × $900)	$ 10,800
Repairs and maintenance	500
Total cash out	11,300
Cash in:	
Rental income	11,025
Cash flow before taxes	$(275)

After taxes, your cash flow would look like this:

After Tax Cash Flow Summary—Year 2

Assumption: 33% Tax bracket	
Cash flow before taxes	$(275)
Major tax deductions:	
Interest	$ 7,934
Property depreciaiton	2,963
Repairs and maintenance	500
Taxes and insurance	2,400
Total major deductions	$ 13,797
Less rental income	(11,025)
Investment loss on your tax return	$ 2,772

Tax savings (33% × $2,772)	$914	(savings in taxes by owning this property)

Net cash flow after taxes:

$275	(actually spent: see cash flow before taxes)
914	(savings in taxes)
$639	(money in your pocket by owning this property)

After the second year, you will have an income-producing property. In addition, your house will have appreciated another 5 percent in value ($105,000 × 105% = $110,250). By the end of year 2, you will have spent for the two years a total of $733. Your property appreciation will total $10,250. At the end of year 3, your positive cash flow for that year (after-tax savings) will be $1,008 and you will have $15,762 in additional equity in the property.

You have already made an excellent investment, and your returns will keep growing in the future! Perhaps these numbers will help you realize why I prefer real estate investments over virtually any other kind. If you time your purchases well, the returns can be phenomenal! Please realize, however, that these numbers are only for purposes of illustration. If you are considering purchasing a rental property for investment, enlist the assistance of a qualified tax accountant to discuss the financial impact your investment will have on your cash flow.

REAL ESTATE AND THE INTUITIVE CONNECTION

Real estate is the foundation for a *long-term* financial strategy, which makes it an ideal area in which to apply your intuitive abilities. At each step of the process, you have ample time to connect to your inner abilities and make sound judgments. The process of making contract offers and negotiating prices sometimes takes a month or more. When the contract is accepted, additional time passes before you close on the deal. Realizing the return on your investment takes time.

You should never have to rush. You can be guided by your inner voice during each step of the process. Acting on the guidance of your intuition will consistently increase the success of your decisions.

I am fond of the saying, "If it doesn't *feel* good, it isn't!" If you are in the process of a real estate purchase or sale and the process is not going smoothly, perhaps there is information you are overlooking. When I feel a door shut or even close substantially, my experience tells me to look for another door. Invariably, when I look for other doors, I recognize as time passes that had I forced the transaction I was involved in, it would have been a mistake. That is what I mean by listening to your inner voice. Often, you know more than you may realize.

I often think of Donald Trump's bidding war against Merv Griffin over what is now the Trump Castle in Atlantic City. Because of the emotion involved and The Donald's desire to "win," he seems to have overlooked some crucial facts. As an outside observer, it seemed obvious to me that unusually profuse revenues would be needed for the Castle to support itself at the prices that were shooting back and forth during the bidding. Trump was so highly leveraged that there would be no escape if his highly optimistic projections proved faulty. As of this writing, The Donald has not gone down for the count, but the Castle is in deep trouble, as are the holders of its bonds. It remains to be seen whether the Trump Castle will bring down the Trump empire.

Donald Trump has made a number of excellent real estate investments. In the process, I am sure he often relied on his intuition. I believe, however, that strong emotions of unbridled competition or greed obstruct the intuitive connection. Intuition is a sensitive connection to an inner power. Negative emotions of any kind impede that link. Perhaps Trump's fierce desire to "win" at all costs caused him to disrupt the connection to his own source of intuitive power.

Optimism promotes the intuitive connection, and real estate can promote optimism. Besides being something that you can hold onto long-term, real estate is tangible. You have been around it since you were born; you can see it, feel it, touch it. You can also improve it, which is not true with many other investments. Unlike other investment vehicles, there is nothing that seems mysterious about real estate. Because there is less mystery, you will feel more capable, and your confidence will generate optimism. Optimism shuts out fear of failure. When you eliminate fear, you have a greater bond with your intuitive self. With intuition as your guide, you will not be tossed about in an economic storm. You will be connected to the source of your own power. Success will surely follow.

Chapter

12

Cycles in Real Estate: Cycles in Life

I know of no way of judging the future but by the past.

PATRICK HENRY

Optimism, enthusiasm, and hope—these important and powerful attitudes can be difficult to maintain in today's world. The media bombard us with negative information. News programs fill our minds with true-life horror stories. Television sitcoms often trivialize or degrade human life, and violence is so typical in movies that it has all but lost its impact. In this environment, creating a positive world for yourself takes determination, and more: It takes the expectation of a positive outcome.

One factor that separates winners from losers in real estate investments, and in life, is the expectation of a positive outcome.

This same concept is true in your financial world. Creating a positive investment strategy takes determination, optimism, action, AND the expectation of a positive outcome.

I'm not advocating that you should sit on your couch expecting to win the Publishers' Clearinghouse Sweepstakes or waiting to inherit a fortune. These things may occur, but a life spent waiting is no life at all. Successful people know that life is a self-fulfilling prophecy, that you usually get exactly what you *truly* expect. The challenge is to learn to expect and believe in a positive outcome in a world often filled with harsh, unexpected, realities.

How can we do this? Do we just close our eyes and hope? No. We can, in fact, use the knowledge of cycles. When the winter weather is cold, we may be uncomfortable, but we know that spring will soon blossom forth. We can use this information to remain hopeful and positive, even in the face of current discomfort. With knowledge of cycles, we can adjust our positive expectations for investment success to fit with the natural flow and rhythm of cycles in investment probabilities. Our optimism can remain intact when we understand cycle trends.

A POSITIVE APPROACH TO REAL ESTATE

The 18-year cycle in real estate activity supports positive expectations for real estate investments. As shown in Figure 12.1, from 1795 until about 1945, this cycle operated with remarkable accuracy. Unfortunately, no one has updated Dewey's work, but assuming that the cycle has continued to remain relatively accurate,

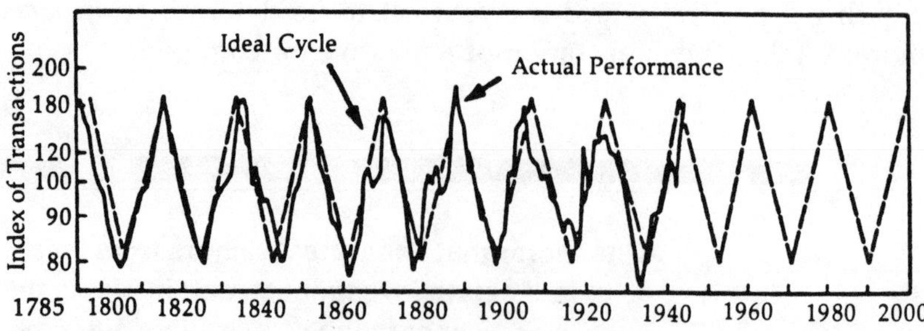

Figure 12.1 The 18⅓-Year Cycle in Real Estate Activity (Reprinted courtesy of the Foundation for the Study of Cycles.)

it points to a bottom in the early 1990s and a relative boom later in the decade. This fits the long economic wave discussed in Chapter 4. Perhaps even more important, the cycle demonstrates that bad times will always be followed by good times.

The cycle is, more precisely, 18 1/3 years—although the trends are more easily thought of as nine-year spans—one of strength and one of weakness. Another cycle, the 18 1/3-year rhythm in building construction, confirms it, but the two are not identical (see Figure 12.2). The peak in real estate activity appears to precede the peak in building construction by about six months.

Although these cycle studies only carry us through about 1950, they provide strong evidence of a cycle pattern in real estate activity. Remember, however, that cycles aren't perfect. In every area of science, theories are invariably imperfect. In physics, Boyle's Law correlates the volume, temperature, and pressure of a gas in a simple equation. The equation is based on the assumption that individual molecules of gas behave as if they were perfectly elastic, tiny billiard balls. Physicists today know that gas molecules don't always behave like this, especially under extremes of temperature and pressure; yet, Boyle's Law is still taught in virtually every introductory chemistry class. It still does an excellent job of predicting the pressure–volume–temperature relationship of most gases under certain conditions. In the same way, real estate cycles may not be perfect, but they are still an excellent tool for timing your real estate investments. Dewey's work brought us to about 1950. An examination of the past four decades provides convincing empirical evidence that both of these cycles are continuing in their

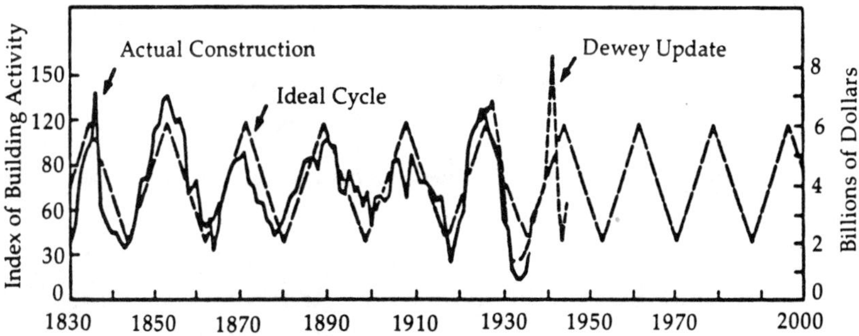

Figure 12.2 The 18 1/3-Year Building Construction Cycle (Reprinted courtesy of Foundation for the Study of Cycles.)

nearly 200-year-old pattern. By looking at real estate trends over the past 40 years, you can not only affirm the value of cycles, but also begin to get a feel for the natural ebbs and flows of the real estate rhythm.

REAL ESTATE ACTIVITY IN THE 1950s

I was a young girl in the 1950s, and I was aware of real estate because we moved so much. I noticed that each place was different. Our rent money bought us a little more or a little less; the closer we were to town or to school, the more rent money my parents paid. The neighborhoods in which most of the people owned their homes were always nicer than those that consisted predominantly of rental homes.

With each move, we seemed to have fewer possessions as a family. It seemed to me that if we could just stay in one place for a while, we might be better off. Evidently, my mother felt the same way. In the late 1950s, we found a home to purchase—a three-bedroom, one-bath house in Torrance, California. The woman who owned the home sold it to my mother for $500 down. I think that's about all the money we had.

I was in heaven. I had my own room and could feel secure that I would be in Torrance for a while. I didn't know it then, but we were buying as the cycle high of the real estate market was approaching. These were my high school years, and it was great fun to be able to spend all four of them at the same school!

As predicted by cycles, the real-estate market started to take off in the mid-1950s.

In the mid-1950s, the real estate market was taking off throughout the country. Florida, in particular, was experiencing a true land-sales boom. The Florida market was so outrageous that most properties sold by mail! Venice, Florida, was one of the many "paradise properties" that promoters were offering to would-be landowners. One extensive development consisted of 13,000 lots that sold for $200 each. Customers could get in for as little as $10 down, but were required to purchase a minimum of two lots. The land sold like popcorn in a movie theater. No one seemed to mind that there was no mortgage money available for home building.

In November 1955, *U.S. News and World Report* gave coverage to the strong housing market. It reported a firm, grass-roots strength supported not by sight-unseen land buying, but by young couples with children, who were buying homes. In spite of tight credit, the market for houses was brisk and housing prices were stable, if not on the rise.

In Denver, Colorado, unimproved land sold for as much as $6,000 an acre. Investors who had bought land just three years before were selling lots and doubling their money.

As the real estate cycle continued its upward trend (as predicted by the 18 1/3-year cycle), the market evolved and changed. Brokers and builders began to identify how families moved from home to home. Before, most young couples had bought their homes and stayed in them for a lifetime. Now, they were trading houses as their needs changed. Those who purchased two-bedroom homes after World War II were now moving into larger, more expensive homes.

Qualifying for a loan was no easier than it is today; it might even have been more difficult. Some brokers had to sell a house two or three times before a deal would stick. Lenders carefully scrutinized the loan applicant's debt load, especially if it included a car loan. As a real estate broker from El Paso, Texas, put it, "A man who is making payments on a car just can't get a mortgage down our way. The auto salesman is our biggest competitor."

In December 1958, after a small slowdown for 18 months, Florida land sales were booming again. Few promoters had either the intention or the capability to develop the land, but it didn't matter. The speculative atmosphere heated up to the point where land was bought on credit and resold before the first payment came due. One piece of property in northern Florida first sold for $75 an acre and then almost immediately passed through three more sets of hands until it sold for $300 an acre. The original owner commented, "It wasn't worth $75."

In addition to speculation, there was exaggeration. With 40,000 Florida real estate hawkers trying to sell 3 million homesites to the 7 million tourists and 3,000 new residents who arrived every week, who was minding the store? The Florida legislature caught the fever. In its 1959 session, acting with nothing more substantial than developers' plans, it chartered cities that didn't even exist. At the end of the summer of 1959, not one family lived in the new "towns" of Royal Palm Beach or Lauderhill.

Developers of low-lying inland properties unabashedly described them with terms such as "heights" and "mountains," in a state where the highest point is 345 feet above sea level. Names like Mount Dora and Mount Pleasant popped up without apology or visible embarrassment to their originators. One developer went so far as to describe Iron Mountain as "the pinnacle between New Jersey and Mexico." The pinnacle crested at 325 feet above sea level. The National Better Business Bureau found that Baldwin Heights was literally under water.

Florida wasn't the only spot in the nation with a booming real estate market. While developers in Florida were promoting land that was under water, 70-year-old Marion Philips was making a fortune selling parcels of land in the barren and forbidding deserts of California. Operating on his simple principle, "You can't buy a poor piece of California land; you can only pay too much for it," Philips claimed to have sold more than 100,000 parcels. People paid $2,000 to $4,000 for each one-third-acre lot in his Salton City development. As Los Angeles inhabitants moved to the open spaces under the sun, Philips's settlements prospered. In his Hesperia community, lots that sold for $795 in 1954 were selling for $6,000 in 1959.

In 1959, in Seattle, Washington, minstrels in Norse costumes serenaded guests at a new residential housing development named Valhalla. To promote a proposed 126-acre housing enterprise, K. A. Sanwick, Jr. and his associates staged a lavish outdoor party, complete with spit-roasted pig served by young athletes and fair-skinned blondes in medieval dress. Sanwick was trying to sell his guests on the features of his luxurious planned community—a private golf course, a yacht basin, a year-round gas-heated swimming pool enclosed by an "air house" in the winter, a private club exclusively for residents, tennis courts, and riding stables. Of the 420 home sites available, the least expensive were

$25,000, and the others were expected to reach such phenomenal prices as $70,000 and $80,000.

The 1950s were a decade of astonishing growth for the real estate market. The real estate cycle had been moving up for over seven years. From a cycle low in 1953, the pace of activity increased through boom after boom. From Florida to California and from Denver to Washington, real estate was the darling of the decade.

Cycles accurately predicted a period of weakness in the 1960s.

THE 1960s

Cycle theory had projected that the ideal crest would occur in the real estate market in 1962; it actually occurred a little over a year earlier. In its November 26, 1960 issue, *Business Week* described the national real estate scene as follows:

> Real estate people all over the nation are screaming that their business has gone to pot. They don't have firm material statistics to back their claim, although industry leaders estimate trading in real estate on the whole is off about 25 percent this year. . . . Industry leaders generally concede that New England is down about 30 percent from last year. The West Coast is off about 6 percent and the South is off about 9 percent in real estate transactions of all types—new homes, used homes, industrial and commercial and tract development.

The swift reversal of the market was the subject of discussion at the annual convention of the National Association of Real Estate Boards in Dallas, Texas, in mid-November, 1960. The attitude of participants ranged from mildly worried to genuinely concerned. Almost overnight, the real estate market had turned from a seller's to a buyer's market. Nester Weigand, a realtor from Wichita, observed, "The fellow you meet at the airport says everything is fine, but at the cocktail party, you hear from those whose business is not holding up."

Realtors tried an innovative approach to stimulate sales: they took old homes in exchange for new ones. Lyn E. Davis of Dallas stated that, of the approximately 500 realtors in his area, 50 to 75 were taking in trades. "This is 30 percent or 40 percent more than last year," he said, adding, "in the next couple of years, a fellow who doesn't take a trade won't be doing any business."

People who traded in their old homes were often in for a rude surprise. "People seem to be thinking of the high prices that prevailed through the Korean War," said Clifford A. Zoll of Chicago. "This is the first time people haven't been making a profit on their house when they sell it."

In Florida, the market had dried up (even if some of the $200 lots had not). Signs advertising new cities, happy communities, and prosperous futures stood alone. Dirt roads that were to lead to the new developments trailed off to nowhere. Business analysts discussed the future of the 40 luxury hotels in the area around Miami and The Gold Coast. Generally, they were in financial trouble—two of them were already in bankruptcy. In Dade County, 3,000 homes stood empty, their buyers gone.

In the West, things were as bad or worse. There were more reports of unsold homes or foreclosed mortgages than ever before. By January 1962, the Federal Housing Authority (FHA) was holding 27,375 houses whose owners had defaulted on federally insured mortgages. By July, the FHA reported that foreclosures were at the highest level since the Great Depression era of the 1930s. An official of New York Life Insurance Company, a company that annually invested some $250 million in residential and commercial first mortgages, stated, "There isn't an area in the country where home prices haven't turned down." *U.S. News and World Report* confirmed, saying, "The easy money days may be ending." The real estate activity cycle had peaked and was on the way down.

For the next few years, only the large, well-financed developments prospered. Small hotels, isolated discounted houses, and apartment complexes became distressed merchandise on real estate brokers' shelves. The small developers and investors were shaken out. By June 1963, *Fortune* magazine was describing the downward trend in the real estate construction cycle this way: "The home builders did a lot to transform the style of

American life in the 1950s, and made themselves a pile, just by doing what comes naturally. But in the 1960s, it's plainly not going to be so easy!"

As the demand for single-family homes decreased, repossessions and foreclosures increased. In the 1950s, rising home values insulated sellers from failure. In the 1960s, many people were faced with a choice: stay with a losing proposition or walk away. In areas like Sacramento, California, people who had invested in nearly new tract homes elected to walk away rather than bear the burden of selling at a loss and paying closing costs.

By 1966, real estate had not only lost its glamour, it had become an object of satire. In the following excerpt from a feature section, "The Human Comedy," by John Skow, published in *The Saturday Evening Post,* a grandfather is speaking to his nine-year-old grandson, Henry, by "videophone." Henry is listening from his home in the "Yellowstone Park section of East Los Angeles":

> It's something you young sprouts can't realize, but in my day there were real-estate developers as far as the eye could see. A man couldn't put a number to them, and no one tried, but the dust from their bulldozers could darken the sun. Swampdale! Brackwater Gardens! Freeway Vista! Wilderness Apartments! Ah, the Acre Ranches! All-Plastic Patios! Landscaped in Enduring Orlon! No Down Payment for Vets and Those Willing to Recite the Pledge to the Flag!
>
> Well boy, the country was young and strong then, and thoughtless. No one imagined that there could be an end to the great, slow-moving herds of earthmovers. The developers weren't just a part of our country; for years it seemed that they were our country, driving their Cadillacs and each one of them wearing a 42-short-portly and carrying three ballpoint pens.
>
> But even then there were signs, if a man had known what to look for. In the early Seventies the developers began breaking up the fine old half-acre suburban estates. Then they developed the cloverleaf intersections. A developer named O'Brian got six high-rise apartments into the outfield at Yankee Stadium. Roofing over the national parks helped postpone the inevitable for a while.

Real estate was the subject of ribs and barbs across the country. Interest continued to wane, sentiment for real estate plummeted, and, as the decade marched on, the real estate cycle continued on its downward trend.

The optimism of the 1950s was displaced with talk about the Vietnam War and the draft. Americans mourned the death of

John F. Kennedy, and the free-speech movement hit college campuses. Very few papers even carried a real estate section. The public had other things on its mind.

I wasn't aware of cycles at the time (at least not rigorously), but when the real estate cycle was approaching a bottom at the end of the decade, my interest in real estate was climbing to new heights.

Some people spent their weekends playing tennis, golfing, fishing, going to the beach, or watching television. I spent my weekends with real estate. I could hardly wait for the Saturday paper, to see whether any new housing tracts were opening. I would take tracing paper and draw over the small outlines of the floor plans in the paper. Then I would think, "If I could put a closet here, move out that wall three feet and add a window . . . ," always drawing, designing, forming a plan in my mind for the if-I-could-have-any-floor-plan-in-the-world dream home.

I looked at homes within and beyond my price range. I eagerly studied how wealthy people lived, knowing that part of obtaining wealth was understanding their life-style. I looked in the window of Saks Fifth Avenue, examined the price tags on things I could not yet afford, and went to open houses in expensive homes. Finally, I found my first home two years before the nationwide bottom in the real estate activity cycle.

THE 1970s

Cycles projected a bottom in the real estate market in 1970 and an ensuing upswing for the rest of the decade (see Figure 12.1). In July 1970, *Forbes* ran an article entitled "Real Estate: On the Brink? The public is moving into real estate again."

Cycle theorists expected a strong real estate market in the 1970s, and they were right.

Real estate once again became a sizzling product for investors. In the summer of 1970, a Los Angeles real estate firm was reported to have in its lobby a myna bird with a two-word vocabulary: "Tax shelter, tax shelter." After nearly a decade of a downward trend in the real estate activity cycle, Americans were buying property again.

Recreation property was the new darling. In the early 1970s, it was a status symbol to own a second home for vacations or weekends. Many who couldn't afford a second home bought a lot or a few acres, planning to build "some day." There was a rekindling of the age-old dream of owning a piece of land, and many people seemed to think that this might be their last chance.

Around the nation, property sales picked up. A recreational development in Macon, Georgia, sold 1,200 lots in its first year. In Florida, lots were sold over the phone. In February 1972, *Time* magazine described the new land rush like this:

> At the stroke of noon on April 22, 1889, some 50,000 settlers scrambled into the Oklahoma territory in one of history's most famous land rushes. Today that phenomenon is being repeated. The object of the new American land rush is vacation and retirement property in nearly every part of the country. Developing planned recreational communities has become a billion-dollar business, and property that is often much less desirable than the Oklahoma Territory is being peddled as shamelessly as snake oil.

The new boom wasn't limited to recreational property; the small investor fell in love with the Real Estate Investment Trust (REIT). REITs were like tax-sheltered mutual funds that invested in real estate. They seemed to have all the advantages and none of the disadvantages of other real estate investments.

The new wave of real estate interest carried across the Pacific to Hawaii. The large Hawaiian landowners shifted their interests from agricultural production to land developments not only in Oahu, but also in the relatively unpopulated islands of Maui, Kauai, Lanai, and "The Big Island," Hawaii. Mainland money streamed in. On Maui, the Amfac Corporation and other operators, including Hilton and Sheraton, spent $35 million on five hotels at Kaanapali Beach.

Like unseasonably cold spring storms, the oil embargo, a tight credit policy by the government, and a deep recession cooled the speculative fever in the mid-1970s. Those who had warned that there were too many REITs were vindicated. Many poorly run REITs came tumbling down like the walls of Jericho. Recreational buying also cooled, and there were some 100,000 unsold properties in Florida alone. But for those who bought (with the exception of some recreational developments) during this temporary halt in the upward trend of the real estate cycle, profits were just around the corner. The boom resumed in a big way in 1976.

In 1975 and 1976, the over-built Florida market became a promised land for those with the courage, wisdom, and resources to participate. From September 1974 to August 1976, more than 1,000 projects failed in Dade and Broward counties, the home counties of Miami and Fort Lauderdale. Although many buyers were scared off, those who could look beyond the storm found some of the best buys in the country in Florida in 1976.

By fall of 1976, the upward trend in the cycle was back in full swing. In Santa Clara County, California, prices of new development homes increased at the mercurial rate of $1,000 per week, and demand continued unabated. Entire developments in prime locations sold out before the ground was broken for the first foundation. In some locations, would-be home buyers literally camped out for up to two weeks to put in a reservation for their dream home. In other locations, developers set up lotteries to determine who would be allowed to purchase their homes. Prices kept rising, week by week.

In Southern California, the story was much the same. The Irvine Company, a large Southern California land developer, was selling new condominiums in its Harbor View development at Newport Beach for $87,050. One buyer resold his unit two weeks later for $117,500 while it was still under construction! In an attempt to temper the speculative fever, some builders and lenders imposed restrictions requiring buyers to occupy their homes. It dampened the speculation, but certainly didn't kill the flame.

Compared to the skyrocketing prices of new homes, many considered the prices of used homes a bargain. After a brief lag, prices in the used-home market began to follow the path of new homes. Homes in the low-end price range sold for the full asking price (and more) by 9:00 AM on the day they were listed. Some real estate agents who listed homes would purchase them and then resell them at a profit before they even closed escrow.

I vividly remember the spring of 1977. I had been buying rental properties since I'd closed out my Lake Estates partnership interest, as narrated earlier. In 1975, I purchased my first investment house, a basic three-bedroom, two-bath starter home located in Los Gatos. It needed landscaping, but I had just finished improving my own $2^1/_2$ acres, so improving a standard lot seemed like an afternoon's work. The house also needed painting and decorating but was basically sound.

Better yet, it was part of a development of larger, more expensive homes. The builder had finished off his project by constructing six homes that were smaller than the others, and people had to drive through the area of these larger homes to get to the smaller ones. I knew that people would pay a premium in rent to live in that community, so I bought one of the smaller homes. It rented easily and my career as a landlady began.

Eager to pick up new properties, I drove the streets of Los Gatos as often as I could, looking for other bargains. I called when houses went up for sale or lease, so I could find out the asking price or the rent, and became increasingly knowledgeable about potential profits in Los Gatos.

I also looked for something else as I drove the streets of Los Gatos—the perfect building site for my dream home. With most of the available sites in the hills of Los Gatos already taken, this was no easy task. Hills are wonderful for beautiful views, but they also make good building sites about as difficult to find as winning lottery numbers. I searched and searched, and finally found a prospective site. The day I called the owner to present my offer he told me he had just decided to build a speculation home on the property. I was devastated.

When I searched my mind for another solution, I remembered driving one back road near town. At the end of this road was the most beautiful piece of property I had ever seen. It was covered with California Oak trees and the view was absolutely magnificent. It was also covered with three small shacks and tons of stuff! There were parts from wooden toys, stacks and stacks of boxes filled with marbles, sand, stars, nails, nuts, bolts, wood . . . you name it. Outside the shacks, old cars and plumbing fixtures were scattered about—a virtual junkyard.

Visualizing how beautiful the property would be minus the junk, I drove out and knocked on the door of the house nearest the site. A stylish-looking older woman answered the door. "Do you know who owns the 'estate' next door?" I inquired. "My husband does," she answered. "Would he be interested in selling?" I asked. "I believe so," she said, adding, "I think he applied with the county to separate these parcels." I was ecstatic! My intuition told me my search was complete. This was where I would build my dream home.

I made an appointment to meet the owner of the property. He loved to tell stories about his life. He had been a teacher, a race car driver, and a polo player, and he was currently a toy manufacturer, working in the shacks sitting on the most beautiful building site in Los Gatos.

When his wife told me he had applied to the county to separate the parcels of land, she was absolutely correct. All he had done was *apply,* and I was soon to learn what that meant. After securing the property with a contract, effective when the lot split was complete, I began trying to do what I could do to speed up the process of obtaining building site approval. As soon as I began to "help," the former owner sat back, put his feet up, and watched the action.

Subdividing land within town limits is far more complicated than subdividing land in the way we did at Lake Estates. In the Lake Estates deal, all we really needed was a certified survey and a source of water. On this site, I had to satisfy the local government agencies that I had a water supply, soil strong enough to support construction, utilities to light and heat the home, a good survey, road improvements, fire truck turnarounds and, in the words of the King of Siam, "etcetera, etcetera, etcetera."

I had to contact and get approvals from soil engineers, building departments, utilities companies, the fire department, the county road department, and so on. All approvals needed to be signed, stamped, and inspected. The process took me a full year, working on it almost every day. When all the paperwork was complete, not only did I have building site approval, I had one of my best returns on investment to date.

By taking the property from the point of raw land to an approved building site, the land that I had purchased for $28,000 plus my yet unseen lot in Clear Lake was now worth between $100,000 and $150,000. I had paid the seller less than $13,000 cash and was paying him the balance in small monthly payments. He wanted the income, and I wanted to keep as much cash as possible. Because I owned the lot (my note was secured by a bank deposit), the bank gave me a construction loan for 100 percent of the building costs.

With the construction underway, I returned my attention to the goal of acquiring a number of rental properties. My first rental purchases were doing well. I still had money to invest because I had maneuvered my way in and out of property with as little of my own money as possible. I bought six houses. I painted them, decorated them, landscaped some of them, and then rented all of them.

It is interesting how the focus in our lives changes as we grow. I had not earned a "real salary" (other than a little substitute teaching) for six years. Yet, I was happier than I had ever been in my life. One of my daughters was in the second grade and the other was in preschool a few days a week. When I had those few hours to myself, I would collect supplies to be used at the rental houses. After I picked up the girls from school, we would change clothes and go to the house I was currently improving. Armed with all the necessities—peanut-butter-and-jelly sandwiches, toys, bicycles, games, jackets, fruit, juice, cookies, music, blankets, pillows, and a lot of love—the three of us would work together. For small children, they were a lot of help, and it was a joy to have them with me.

I felt wealthy in so many ways. I was building a solid financial future. I worked long hours, but I was my own boss. I was able to keep my beautiful daughters with me as I worked. I was grateful.

In 1977, I was scrambling with the rest of the speculators, buying houses as fast as I could. At first, I didn't consider the possibility of buying a property and immediately reselling it at a profit. I had always bought properties to fix up, rent, and hold. I changed my tactics. With the market so wild in California, I started turning over properties practically overnight, for substantial profits.

Each morning, I picked up the newspaper and turned immediately to the classified ads. By then, having made the exploration of this area a "hobby" for almost three years, I could almost instinctively tell whether a house was underpriced or overpriced for a particular street. If a home was on a street that I liked, I would get in the car and go have a look. If I liked it, I bought it. I also used to drive up and down the streets I liked, looking for new "For Sale" signs on the front lawn. When they appeared, I would call immediately and ask for the price. If the price was right, I would buy the home, often before it even reached the Realtors' Multiple Listing Service.

One of my biggest thrills was to find a house with an unmown lawn, what real estate expert Albert Lowry would call a "valuable defect." Usually, when the lawn wasn't mowed, there were other small defects that brought the house's market value down but could be remedied with a small investment of time and a little bit of money. For a few hundred dollars, I often added several thousand dollars to the value of the home. In a six-month period, I bought and sold a half-dozen houses, making substantial profits on each one.

By 1978, I had 12 rental homes plus my mansion on the hill. I was feeling good about life. I had come a long way from my first job, waiting on cars at a drive-in.

In 1979, I noticed a "For Sale" sign on a small home on an intriguing street in Los Gatos. The street was unique because it had been subdivided so long ago that each lot was almost half an acre—a lot of lot for a city lot! The particular house that was for sale sat on a lot that was bigger than others in the neighborhood. I checked with the city and found, to my surprise, that the area was zoned for 8,000-square-foot lots. This meant that the property could be subdivided and up to two more houses could be built on the property. I was *very interested.*

The house was part of an estate sale—another new experience for me. Although the contract was written by a realtor, the actual sale took place at the courthouse. At a special hearing, I actually bought the property in court. Even more interesting was the requirement to put up 10 percent of the purchase price, with my own money, that day. If, for any reason, such as a bank's refusing to approve my loan, I couldn't close the deal. I lost the money. Ten percent of $155,000 was $15,500, and it took confidence for me to hand over that check.

One big reason I had the courage to make this investment was my knowledge of cycles. I had been studying cycles for well over a year, and I knew that the real estate activity cycle was still in an area of strength. I could also *predict the probability* that the cycle would remain in an area of strength at least for a while. I felt certain I would have enough time to get the necessary approvals to be able to sell off the lots *before* the time of weakness occurred. Because of some neighborhood opposition, I was able to divide off only one extra lot from my property. The next year, I sold the house for $164,000 and the lot for $100,000 cash.

For me, the decade of the 1970s was a profitable bustle of real estate activity. It ended with a $100,000-plus bang.

THE 1980s

If you look back at Figure 12.1, you'll see that cycle theory projected the boom of the 1970s would end in the fall of 1980. The peaks in activity actually appear to precede the predicted timing by one to four years, depending on the area. Considering the available statistics as a composite, the overall cycle peak occurred in 1979.

One of the greatest gifts of cycles is that you can plan your moves based on probabilities. You can change your strategy before the crowd changes theirs.

As the end of the decade approached, I *knew* the cycle period of strength was coming to an end. For me, this meant a time to stop buying and prepare to "ride through" any weakness phase. I had no intention of selling my properties. They were sound; each mortgage payment was covered by income from rent. I also knew that the early 1980s would not be a time for speculation. This is one of the greatest gifts of cycles! You can plan your moves based on probabilities. You can change your strategy before the crowd changes theirs. Cycles were right on target.

By this time, I was in my dream home. My financial independence was secure. *Cycles provided the knowledge with which to protect my fortune, the touchstone to expand my intuitive abilities, and the courage to act on them.* While builders, realtors, and speculators of all kinds were going under in the early 1980s, I was waiting on the sidelines, enjoying my beautiful view. I was safe. The knowledge of cycles had done all I had hoped it would do and more!

By December 1980, home sales were weak in virtually every area of the country. Even in the vibrant sunbelt states like Texas and California, home sales were anemic. Houston builders prepared for declines in new home construction of 30 to 40 percent from the year before. In Dallas, the huge construction firm, Centex Corporation, was building, said vice chairman Paul R. Seegers, "only as we get orders."

In the declining market, new marketing plays and gimmicks seemed to provide the only hope of stimulating sales. A Cleveland realtor, the Smythe Cramer Company, enjoyed a 23 percent increase in sales of existing homes by pushing creative financing. Lease–purchase deals, which provided renters an option to buy for a fixed period, were used to lure prospective buyers. Some California builders actually started selling the house to one buyer and the underlying land to another. In Pittsburgh, Ryan Homes Inc. began offering factory-built homes, only 50 percent assembled, to buyers willing to finish the job. This tactic was to save buyers up to $10,000 on a $50,000 home.

By mid-March 1981, over a million homes were up for sale nationwide—about 750,000 old or existing units and another 336,000 new models. Ken Kerin, vice president of sales for the National Association of Realtors, stated bluntly, "This is the worst wringer I've been through in the post-World War II period . . . and that includes the '66 credit crunch when mortgage rates went through the roof and savings and loans were forced to shut off the lending faucets."

Scott Biddle, former president of The Building Industry Association of Orange County and a well-respected builder, had 103 people on his payroll in 1979, and employed hundreds of subcontractors. At his peak in earlier years, he was cranking out 400 to 500 homes a year and had sales just short of $50 million. By 1981, only two years later, Biddle employed only 18 people and had drafted his wife to work in the office. All of the projects he had planned to start in 1981 were on the shelf. He was paying out $300,000 a month in interest payments and had income of only about $30,000. In his words, "I've had to sell many of my 'keepers.' I've sold an industrial park and other things I had built up as personal assets. But I'm running out of assets. . . . We are not going broke. We are paying our bills, but it's getting to be serious."

Biddle wasn't alone. In California, the issue of new building permits dropped by 31 percent from 1979 to 1980. The total of 145,000 permits issued in 1980 was 40 percent below 1978 levels and 47 percent below those in 1977. Over 50,000 new homes stood unsold and unoccupied. Shapell Industries of Beverly Hills, the largest new-home builder in California, cut its work force by one-third and was starting no new projects. The Northern California division of Kaufman and Broad Inc., the largest U.S.-based multinational home-building firm, would only start a new tract development if all of the homes were sold in advance.

Data from the 1980 census brought sobering news. There were nearly 4 million more dwelling units in the nation than had been previously thought. Economic forecasters said that housing construction, which had generated more than 10 percent of the gross national product, would remain at suppressed levels through at least 1985.

By April 1982, the sales of new, single-family homes had plummeted to 315,000 units per year, the lowest rate since the Commerce Department began keeping tabs in 1962. As Michael Sumichrast, vice president of the National Association of Home Builders, put it, "Right now, there are 5 million existing homes with for-sale signs in the front yard and few takers. The market for single-family homes is pretty well shot to pieces."

The year 1982 was a time for bargain hunters. Investors who wanted security looked for fully leased properties for which the long-term financing was committed. Risk-oriented investors with staying power looked for half-vacant properties in foreclosure. Smart buyers looked for a desperate seller saddled with debt or facing a loan coming due, and then offered cash, for a discount. William H. Elliott, president of Angeles Corp., a real estate investment syndicator, said, "We don't even want to look for a seller. We want to find him bleeding in our lobby with a deed in his hand."

As the decade rolled inexorably forward, real estate prices in some parts of the country seemed mired in quicksand. In some cases, values dropped in a way that, for most of us, was reminiscent of the Great Depression. For example, in 1984, a successful investment banker, whom I interviewed at a convention, purchased a two-bedroom, one-bath condominium located on the outskirts of Denver for $42,000. He moved in, pleased to be in the first home he could really call his own. By 1988, he wasn't pleased at all. A condo like his was being sold by HUD (the Department of Housing and Urban Development) for $13,000!

The banker described what happened:

> The people who owned them started to move out and rent them and then the market got soft. Finally, they just let their properties go. It's a vicious circle. There is no way to sell a property like I have legitimately except to an equity skimmer. What these people do is find a condo with a loan that's nonqualifying. They say, "You give me a thousand dollars to take over your payments." He signs because he doesn't have to qualify. He takes the money, never makes any payments. Maybe he will let someone move in until the property is foreclosed on. They make out with pure cash. There must be, conservatively, 25 percent of the place being sold like that.

Weakness in the real estate activity cycle hit the agricultural sectors as well as the residential and commercial sectors. During the 1970s, when land prices were appreciating at rates of up to 22 percent per year, farmers borrowed money against their property to build homes, buy equipment, expand their cultivation, and perhaps even buy more land. In addition to farmers, outside investors put their money in farms and farmland. In the 1980s, farmland prices hit bedrock.

"He bought the farm!" This morbid wisecrack was never intended to be a commentary on agricultural real estate. But as an article in *Barron's* on May 6, 1985, observed, "Nowadays it seems to serve that purpose—and the folks who sunk their cash into farms aren't laughing." The 1970s had sent farm prices up an average of 15 percent a year. The article went on to say that the market peaked in 1981. Market prices were adjusted for inflation. "The top actually came a year earlier, and blew apart in 1982 and 1983 with the ferocity of a tornado carving through a field of wheat."

By the end of 1984, farmland values had dropped a calamitous $64 billion, or 20 percent in real prices. As 1985 began, the Department of Agriculture estimated that 46 percent of all family farms had "serious financial problems." They held $98.2 billion in debt they had undertaken thinking that the rising values of their property would keep them secure. The bankers, who had so willingly loaned farmers money when land prices were on the rise, now found their loans undercollateralized. Thousands of farmers and ranchers faced foreclosures. Tracts once worth hundreds of millions of dollars were sold off at pennies on the dollar. It was truly pathetic.

In any area of weakness, there are pockets of strength, and the 1980s were no different. Throughout most of the decade, real estate activity and prices in Boston, New York City, Los Angeles, and scattered other areas continued in an upward spiral. I expected there to be exceptions, and there were. However, an overzealous, largely unregulated savings and loan industry artificially contributed to higher prices in many areas. Without this distortion, the downward trend in the real estate activity cycle would have been more apparent in many areas.

The next five to seven years will provide steady growth in real estate prices in many parts of the country.

CONCLUSION

We live now in the decade of the 1990s. The cycle of weakness is behind us. Cycles have stood the test of time for almost 200 years, and they predict a solid decade ahead. The next five to seven years will provide steady growth in real estate prices in many parts of the country.

You'll make your best profits when your timing is right. The time for real estate purchases is now, at the beginning of an uptrend that is supported by several cycles. The greater the number of supporting cycles, the stronger the trend. This trend should last at least into 1996 or 1998. The trend won't be confirmed until well into the next decade, but I am confident.

If real estate is your investment area of choice, begin *now* to plan your profitable future. You have every reason to expect a positive outcome for real estate investments in the 1990s. Real estate is, and will remain, the real basis for lasting wealth.

Chapter 13

Real Estate Today and Tomorrow

Adopt the peace of nature, her secret is patience.

Ralph Waldo Emerson

Real estate is on the threshold of a major upward move. Several areas that saw price devastation in the 1980s or a prolonged slump in 1990 and 1991 are already bouncing back. Those who thought that Houston and Denver would never hit bottom have seen these areas turn around and start growing again. The 18-year cycle in real estate activity has nearly bottomed, and we are moving into an area of strength.

The coming period won't be a wild, inflationary boom like the 1970s, when prices in residential, commercial, and agricultural real estate rose dramatically in every area of the country. Instead, it will be characterized by an underlying strength, that will accelerate in pace as the decade proceeds. For you, this means the odds are with you that carefully selected purchases today will mean profits tomorrow.

Both the real estate activity cycle and the building construction cycle point to a coming period of strength. In addition, several fundamental economic and demographic factors also support future profits in real estate. Specifically, long-term interest rates are on the decline, American life-style preferences are changing, and foreign capital is coming into the real estate market.

The long-term interest rate cycle is down, supporting probable strength in many real estate markets.

Money has become less expensive to borrow. The long-term interest rate cycle is down and will remain in a downward trend for most of the 1990s (see Chapter 9). With current rates on variable home mortgages historically low in some areas, more people will purchase homes. More home purchases will mean stronger demand and higher prices. For the individual American investor, this will mean opportunity.

A change in the pattern of life-style preferences is beginning to emerge. The hard-driving young professionals of the 1980s are beginning to nest. Young people who spent much of the past decade in pursuit of the ultimate job are now becoming more aware of the rewards of family life. The upwardly ambitious group that had an insatiable appetite for high-tech, high-performance products is stopping to reevaluate "life in the fast lane."

A report commissioned by Chivas Regal, entitled "Working Americans: Emerging Values for the 1990s," suggests that many Americans are questioning their former focus on material success. This survey of working Americans between the ages of 25 and 49 showed that 75 percent of those who responded would like to see a return to a simpler society and more emphasis on down-to-earth values like family, community, and job loyalty.

There is a definite correlation between a yearning for a simpler, more family-oriented life-style and an increased desire for real estate. As people center more of their social and recreational life around their family and children, their home becomes a focal point for family activities. As couples marry and have children, the need for homes with outdoor areas, nearby parks, abundant community activities, and good schools becomes more imperative. These factors will combine to increase demand in specific areas, therefore putting upward pressure on prices.

In addition to changing family needs, there are an increasing number of people choosing to live alone. Single life is a choice for many, not a regret. This translates into a need for more houses, and more demand puts pressure on prices.

In addition to a lower cost of money and a shift in life-style aspirations, there is an increasing amount of foreign capital flowing into the United States for real estate purchases. British, German, and Canadian investors have long been visible participants in the purchase of real estate in the United States. Lately, Dutch and Australian buyers have become very active. The Japanese, however, are rapidly becoming the major foreign real estate force. They are buying major hotels and resorts, malls, office buildings, and individual homes. Foreign investors with deep reservoirs of cash have bought up property on the beaches of Hawaii and the Florida coast, as well as in downtown areas of Los Angeles, Seattle, and New York.

Foreign investors are not just buying, they are building. The largest Japanese construction firm, Kumagai Gumi, is a partner on both U.S. coasts, with a 62-story, $225-million office building called Gateway Tower, in the heart of Seattle, and a massive development called Worldwide Plaza in Manhattan. Two other major Japanese companies, the Aoki Corporation and the Tokyo Corporation, are members of separate partnerships planning or building six major hotels as well as condominiums and residential communities in Hawaii. Japanese companies already own most of the major existing hotels in that state. Downtown Los Angeles has, for the most part, already been purchased. "Downtown L.A. is 70 percent owned by non-U.S. owners," said David Shulman of Salomon Brothers. Foreign capital will help keep the real estate activity and building cycles dynamic.

TIMING REAL ESTATE PURCHASES FOR PROFITS

Lessons from the past are the best indicators of the importance of timing. The most successful real estate investors of the past were usually those who built or purchased real estate at or near building construction troughs. One of the most notable of these investors was John Jacob Astor.

Successful real estate investors of the past realized the importance of timing.

Although poor when he emigrated from Germany, Astor began acquiring land at an early age and eventually amassed a fortune from real estate. In 1809, using a combination of unscrupulous practice and correct timing (his uncanny timing ability was to become his trademark), Astor laid the groundwork for making a fortune.

An energetic young lawyer told Astor that there were 51,012 acres in Putnam County, New York, that did not legally belong to the more than 700 families (mostly farmers) who lived there. The farms had been purchased from the State of New York, and most of the families had been there since shortly after the end of the Revolutionary War.

The land had originally been in the estate of Roger Morris, who had held a life lease on it. The state had confiscated the property, but without the legal right to do so. When the young lawyer informed Astor that no state could legally confiscate a life lease, Astor saw an opportunity. After satisfying himself on this legal point, Astor set off to England to buy-off the heirs of Roger Morris. It cost him a little over $100,000.

The day after he returned to New York, Astor notified the residents of the Putnam County land that they were trespassers. The farmers, in a state of shock, appealed to the state. At first it was a stalemate—the state refused to recognize Astor's title, and Astor refused to recognize the state's title. After a lengthy court battle, the state compromised and granted Astor $500,000 in 1827.

Armed with half a million dollars (a *huge* amount of money in 1827), Astor was fully prepared to take advantage of the next down trend in real estate activity, which took place in the 1830s. After a boom cycle had peaked in 1833, a number of landowners were not prepared to ride through a period of real estate sluggishness. It was on these people that Astor preyed.

His favorite investments were purchases of heavily mortgaged farms on Manhattan Island. One such parcel, the Eden Farm, now makes up a portion of Times Square. During the panic of 1837, Astor foreclosed on some 60 farms or parcels of land on Manhattan.

Although Astor's methods were often ruthless, his timing was exemplary. The best way to increase wealth is to buy at the beginning of a real estate activity cycle area of strength. That is the position we are in today. Purchasing at the beginning of an area of strength, as close to the turning point as possible, enables buyers to reap the highest profits.

Many other successful investments of the past were timed during a real estate cycle trough. The Wrigley Building, which was built in Chicago after the cycle bottom in 1916, was a dramatic success during the strong market of the 1920s. The Rockefellers built their seven-building Rockefeller Center in New York at almost the exact bottom of the building cycle in 1933, and cashed in on the rising demand for space during the recovery from the Great Depression in the late 1930s and early 1940s.

You don't have to be a Rockefeller or an Astor to secure your financial future with real estate. For example, in the 1950s, a novice real estate investor named William Nickerson turned himself into a millionaire. His success story is a real estate version of "The Ugly Duckling." His approach was to find an ugly, well-built house in a good area, but with peeling paint or other small problems—and buy it under very favorable conditions. He would then make the home attractive with simple touches like paint, wallpaper, and landscaping. Finally, he would sell his beautiful new swan to a young couple for a handsome profit. His simple concept was incredibly profitable.

There is no doubt that Nickerson worked hard on his investments. Starting with a $1,000 down payment on his first home, he maneuvered his way into a half-million-dollar estate in just 14 years. In the 1950s, that was a lot of money. Nickerson's timing was next to perfect—his biggest and most profitable real estate investments were made during the real estate activity cycle uptrend of the 1950s.

TAKE ADVANTAGE OF THE COMING BUILDING CYCLE

The necessity for correct timing becomes even more important when you realize the length of the complete building cycle. As George Warren and Frank Pearson point out in their book, *World Prices and the Building Industry,* "The building cycle is so long that few people experience two complete cycles in their business life."

If you have the opportunity to invest in real estate and capitalize on the strength phase of the complete building cycle, then it may be the best opportunity of your lifetime.

In other words, if you have the opportunity to invest in real estate and capitalize on the strength phase of the complete building cycle, then it may be the best opportunity of your lifetime. You may *live through* the next cycle, but you will then be older, less aggressive, and more inclined to reduce your real estate investments rather than increase them. The time to act is *now.* If you don't, you will have to wait until the next century to find an equivalent opportunity for success.

Remember that real estate is a long-term investment. Be prepared to leave your money invested for seven to ten years. This will allow you to take full advantage of the real estate activity cycle's uptrend. It will also allow you to ride through any rough spots or soft prices that may develop during the strength phase of the cycle.

What to Buy

Small residential properties, especially single-family dwellings, offer the most potential for profit for small investors. Not only are single-family residences the easiest for small investors to purchase, but they also have an inherent resistance to economic slumps.

The price structure of the housing market is less sensitive to recessions than commercial real estate or other investments. If you have to sell, your price will be affected, but because housing is a basic need, its built-in stability forms a foundation of financial security. Statistics support this conclusion. According to the Census Bureau, during the recessions of 1893–1894, 1913–1914, and 1920–1921, housing prices were not significantly affected. Housing prices did fall after 1929, but, against an 89 percent drop in the price of common stocks, the approximately 21 percent drop in the prices of existing homes made them a comparatively safe shelter. House prices remained stable through the 1930s and single-family homes have been unparalleled assets ever since.

A truly remarkable example of housing's resistance to price declines occurred during the particularly deep recession of 1973–1975. During this period, the percentage of unemployed people seeking work rose from 4.9 to 8.5 percent. The price of common stocks dropped 49 percent. Numerous commercial real estate investment trusts collapsed, and some builders went bankrupt. *But the price of homes continued to increase* (1973–1975 was part of the strength phase of the last real estate activity cycle).

According to the National Association of Realtors, the average selling price for existing homes was $30,000 in 1972, $32,900 in 1973, $35,800 in 1974, and $39,000 in 1975. The Commerce Department listed the average price of new homes as $30,500 in 1972, $35,600 in 1973, $38,000 in 1974, and $42,600 in 1975. Looking at house prices today, with the average price in the $125,000 range, it is easy to see why single-family homes are a good investment.

It is true that during the past decade prices dropped in places like Denver, Houston, and the farm belt. These price reductions were caused by a tremendous drop in the price of oil, and by the effects of the weakness phase of the real estate activity cycle. Prices have also dropped in areas where prices had been inflated by poorly managed Savings and Loan operations. Once these prices stabilize, it will be time to buy.

If you still worry about putting your dollars into the right home, consider these other factors supporting single-family home prices:

- Unlike investments such as stocks, limited partnerships, and commercial real estate ventures, investor psychology plays only a limited role in home purchases. Most people purchase a home as a place to live, not as an investment. If people want a home and can afford the down payment, they will probably buy. Very few people who are looking for homes refuse to buy because their down payment would bring them better returns in another investment.
- Housing possesses a great deal of intrinsic value; that is, the prices of the components of a home—land, building materials, labor costs, appliances, and so forth—are not likely to drop substantially. Restrictive zoning, building codes, and environmental regulations will continue to add costs to new-home construction. The scarcity of good land to build on in desirable areas will also tend to support higher, firmer prices.
- Houses don't wear out like other assets do. The only limit on the life of a house is how much time, effort, and resources the owners put into maintaining and upgrading it. Many buyers prefer remodeled old homes to newly constructed ones.
- Inflation is here to stay, probably at a minimum level of about 5 percent per year. Continuing inflation will push up the price of houses. In 1982, who expected that houses in Santa Monica, California, would reach prices between $900,000 and $1.5 million in a single decade? Someday, those prices will be the norm across the country. It is only a matter of time.

Am I trying to talk you into buying a home? Yes, because I'm excited about the prospects in the coming decade. I'll be in the real estate market-buying, fixing up, renting, and eventually selling—and I'd like you to join me in this coming cycle of prosperity.

Let's look now at some more specific trends and characteristics of the real estate market to come.

MAKE WAY FOR THE HOME OFFICE

As the next millennium approaches, there will be some trends in American life that may look more like the past than the future. One of the most visible trends will result from the growing desire of many Americans to work at home. To accommodate this need, many floor plans will change—the guest room will be abandoned to make way for the home office.

As the next millennium approaches, there will be some trends in American life that may look more like the past than the future.

Actually, this trend is already in progress. For example, in Cupertino, California, a builder called the Gregory Group faced a problem. A group of city planners who were "sensitive to growth" had imposed a limit on the number of bedrooms that could be included in homes in the Gregory Group's new project, Seven Springs. Because the target market at Seven Springs was the dual-income family with kids, the builder was faced with a dilemma—how to provide the desired space and still adhere to the demands of the city planners. The Gregory Group opted to build extra rooms and merchandise them as dens and home offices.

The architect for the project designed the first-floor offices so buyers could easily convert them into bedrooms. The city planners wouldn't allow closets in these rooms, so built-in desks were installed in closet-sized nooks. The intent was to make it easy for buyers to convert the offices to bedrooms after the homes were purchased. The design was a runaway hit. What came as a surprise, however, was that buyers did not want to convert the offices into bedrooms. They wanted to use them as home offices.

Follow-up studies showed that about 80 percent of the buyers worked in Silicon Valley. The idea of a home office appealed to them not only as a place to keep and organize their personal paperwork, but also as a place to set up their home computers. A home computer becomes a file cabinet, a learning and game center for the children, and a tool for doing extra work at home. Many Silicon Valley professionals hook up to their company's computer through a modem. This allows them to capture those essential periods of creativity that come when they are musing in the comfort of their homes. They have all of the necessary work tools in their home office—computer, software, books, desks, and files for keeping track of everything. The home office is ideal.

A growing number of people are also deriving some or all of their income from work in their home. About 28 million people nationwide worked full- or part-time at home in 1990 (about 10 million more than in 1985), and that number could reach 40 million by the year 2000. According to the American Home Business Association, located in Darien, Connecticut, one out of every seven businesses in the country is entirely home-based.

Home offices are a future trend for all segments of the population, including those who are past mid-life. In a 66-unit town-house development in Northbrook, Illinois, Red Seal Development effectively merchandised a home office for affluent couples whose children were out on their own. In Myrtle Beach, South Carolina, one builder, designing for retirees, decorated one bedroom in his two-bedroom condos as a combination office–guest room. It was a hit. When people retire, they may no longer have a job, but that doesn't mean they don't work. Many retirees want to follow their investments on a computer, write letters, and pursue hobbies. The home office creates an environment for these activities. It is a place for feeling and being productive while still being at leisure.

OTHER TRENDS TO LOOK FOR

Another trend that began over a decade ago and shows no signs of abating is the desire for a large master bath, and, if possible, a master bedroom suite. In a recent survey of the deluxe category in the top 25 housing markets nationwide, would-be buyers mentioned large master bedrooms and baths the most.

In less luxurious homes, the kitchen is the key feature. "The kitchen is becoming the focal point of the house, where people entertain and the family gets together," according to Seattle builder Jim Merrill.

The quality of a community will likely be a primary consideration for real estate purchases in the coming decade.

Aside from specific architectural features, another trend is the growing concern for the design of the community itself. "Sometime during the past half-century," said Amy Saltzman in the April 9, 1990, issue of *U.S. News and World Report,* "the American Dream of a home in the suburbs turned into the American Nightmare of social and economic isolation, traffic clogged commutes and pervasive sexism." In response to this, a number of "neotraditionalists" believe it's time for an overhaul. Their goal is to recreate the small-town atmosphere of the past while addressing the needs of the 1990s.

"The neotraditionalists are taking a giant step backward in order to move forward," says Todd Zimmerman, a Clinton, New Jersey, housing consultant. "They are going against every conceivable trend in housing since the end of World War II." Andres Duany, a Miami architect, and his wife, Elizabeth Plater-Zyberk, are considered the founders of neotraditional town planning. Duany feels the suburbs simply don't work anymore. The suburb is designed for the car, thus creating social isolation. "The suburb is a profoundly sexist development pattern," says Duany. "It assumes that the woman will always be there to play chauffeur."

The goal of the neotraditional community plan is to make life more convenient and less isolated while simultaneously nurturing a sense of community in residents. A number of these communities are currently being developed, but there is only one functioning model, the resort community of Seaside, located in the Florida Panhandle. Seaside's approximately 150 homes are within a few blocks of the local post office, the gourmet-food market, the bookstore, and the neighborhood pool. All family members can walk or bike to most of the places they want to go.

If this type of community becomes a growing trend in the 1990s, it could provide an excellent investment opportunity. While home prices in Seaside's surrounding areas flattened or dropped during the latter part of the 1980s, sales of Seaside's simple, tin-roofed homes skyrocketed.

The need to belong, a desire for a sense of community, is a strong underlying factor that will support the growth of more communities like Seaside. I have experienced the needs these communities fulfill and remember the year we moved from our home in San Jose to a two-acre site in Gilroy, California. The country was quiet, the air was clean, and the land was beautiful. There was plenty of room for my girls to play and no worry about busy streets. We could ride horses and let the pets roam freely. Even to this day, it *sounds* so nice, but now I know better.

Not long after we moved in, I realized it had been a good investment move (providing an exit from the Lake Estates partnership) but it was not where I wanted to *live.* The problem was the isolation: it took 20 minutes to get to the next point of civilization. San Jose was 30 to 40 minutes away, so when I went to town I tried to run as many errands as possible. The worst aspect was the complete lack of community. People were so spread out that it was difficult to get to know anyone. I did become friendly with one neighbor, but when she moved, there was absolutely no one.

From that home, I moved to Los Gatos, California. I picked Los Gatos for its pervasive sense of community. Its population was only 25,000. The road sign at the entrance to the community read, "*Town* of Los Gatos," not *city* of Los Gatos. There was a town square, a town post office, a main street, and a town library. When you *walked* to town, the clerk in each store knew your name. I went to town council meetings and voiced my opinion on community matters. In short, I belonged!

It is this feeling of community that people will increasingly search for in the 1990s; more and more, they will seek out areas that offer privacy without isolation. Doesn't this make intuitive sense? Would you rather leave your home in the suburbs, get into the car, fight the traffic and crowds of strangers at the supermarket, and then return to your home two hours later; or, walk to town, stopping to chat with familiar passers-by, be greeted on a first-name basis at the grocer's, buy some stamps from Martha at the Post Office, and walk back home feeling restored and ready to get back to work? The changing values of America will create a new demand for the community atmosphere. The trend toward community will continue because a home with a sense of community fills more human needs than just shelter.

GREAT STRENGTH IN THE LOS ANGELES/LONG BEACH AREA

There are several locations that remain at the top of everyone's list. Whether you would want to live there is an individual choice, but as far as potential profits go, things look good for Los Angeles and Long Beach, California. From a city that used to be called "tinsel town," Los Angeles has grown to be one of the nation's dominant metropolises. It is seizing political, economic, and cultural superiority from the declining cities of the East and Midwest.

Much of Los Angeles's strength comes from its base of high-technology and service-oriented industries. Massive industrial development that was sparked by military buildup during and after World War II provides ever-increasing jobs in aircraft, military equipment, and electronics factories. There are more manufacturing jobs in Los Angeles than in any other metropolitan area, including greater New York. If it were an independent country, Los Angeles would rank at least twelfth in the world in terms of gross national product.

The sectors of economic growth are not confined to military and high-technology products. New York's dominance in the garment industry is gradually slipping, and Los Angeles is picking up the slack. While 50,000 garment industry jobs were being lost in New York during the 1970s, nearly 30,000 were being added in Los Angeles. This trend continued through the 1980s; California styles became the leading edge, and new lines boasted their "California chic." California-based Hang Ten and L.A. Gear promote a life-style as much as a clothing style.

Hollywood, as the epicenter of the entertainment industry, adds not only glamour but solid economic structure to the area. With the American family now watching a minimum of five hours of television daily, Hollywood is in demand. In addition, the movie industry continues to find new means of promotion, and international distribution provides an ever increasing source of revenue. With VCRs in almost every household, movie rentals and sales will remain solid. The entertainment industry will continue to grow.

Adding to its long list of assets, Los Angeles boasts an enviable location on the Pacific Ocean. With its ability to service the trading ships of the fast-growing economies of Asia, Los Angeles is a lucrative center for import-export businesses. Although Los Angeles lacks a fine natural harbor, its manmade port has been expanding.

Before you pack your bags for Los Angeles, understand that there are problems in this land of profits. Real estate prices are high, and finding rental properties where rents cover mortgage payments will not be easy. The crowded freeways and long commutes can be exasperating, and many feel the general quality of life is poor. On June 12, 1989, Frederick Rose described Los Angeles in *The Wall Street Journal* as a "mecca of culture and economic energy, a wilderness of crime and poverty." The cultural diversity that produces a Korean-owned lunch counter specializing in "kosher" burritos creates challenges for schools and public institutions, as well as culture shock for older, long-resident citizens who remember when Orange County was filled with orange groves.

Problems, yes; but the area will maintain an important edge that may more than counteract its dark side. It will offer jobs for many years to come. Less and less land is available in the areas where people want to live, so real estate prices are likely to continue to escalate. According to *Money* magazine, in June 1989, the National Association of Realtors, based on data from the WEFA Group, an economic research firm located outside Philadelphia, listed Los Angeles/Long Beach as one of ten areas in the country where prices of homes could greatly exceed inflation in the foreseeable future.

SMALLER CITIES OFFER PROFITS

If cities like Los Angeles are not compatible with your life-style, finances, and other interests, you can consider second- and third-tier cities for your real estate investments. These are the midsize cities that combine the best of a city with a feeling of space. Many Americans will seek out and migrate to cities that are small enough to avoid big-city problems, yet large enough to be economically and culturally alive.

High on the list of winners in this category is Boulder/Longmont, Colorado. Its population is educated and sophisticated. In addition, the revenue, research applications, and academic quality of the University of Colorado provide a stable foundation for this area. The Woods and Poole Economics Group, based in Washington, DC, forecasts Boulder/Longmont to be a big winner during the 1990s, with the population expanding from 263,000 in 1990 to 364,000 in the year 2000. Total employment will increase from 170,000 in 1990 to 236,000 in the year 2000. Per-capita income is expected to nearly double, from $21,352 in 1990 to $40,467 in 2000. All of these factors mean more homes and higher prices for homes.

An important criterion for growth and quality of life in any area in the 1990s and beyond will be the availability of cultural events. A resurgence of interest in the arts is dawning, consistent with the Kondratieff economic long wave revival (see Chapter 4), and in this category Boulder is tops. The Boulder Philharmonic performs from September through April, and the Boulder Repertory Company produces contemporary and classic plays in the fall and summer. The University of Colorado annually hosts the Colorado Shakespeare Festival, and the Boulder Dinner Theater operates six nights a week and specializes in Broadway productions. According to the Chamber of Commerce, there is "so much open space that no one need live more than half-a-mile from a recreation site." There are a lot of things to like about Boulder.

Whenever real estate hot spots are mentioned, locations in California are always on the list. Orange County (home of Disneyland), Riverside (not *too* far from Los Angeles), San Jose, and San Diego are likely to see housing-price appreciation that continues to exceed inflation. Keep in mind, however, that housing prices in these areas are already so high that rents may come nowhere near covering the payments, making the properties unsuitable for most individual investors. If you buy a home and have to pay more out than you receive in rent, it may still be possible to make money, but why put yourself at such risk? If there is a downturn in the area, you may have trouble selling your property.

Sacramento, on the other hand, may still make economic sense. With a population of 330,000 people, the size of the city is manageable. Its location, within a few hours' drive of San Francisco, makes it an obvious expansion area for Bay Area growth. The median family income is a respectable $22,000, and the median home price is $100,000. If you make a 20 percent down payment, there is a strong possibility that rental income will support the mortgage payment. Unemployment in the area is a low 5 percent, and there is a strong chance that price appreciation will exceed the inflation rate.

Sacramento has a number of other notable features. Lake Tahoe, with its sapphire-blue water and magnificent forested shoreline, is just a little more than a two-hour drive away. One of the premier skiing capitals of the world, the Lake Tahoe area contains Squaw Valley (home of the 1960 Olympic Winter Games), Heavenly Valley, North Star, and numerous other small resorts. On the Nevada side of Lake Tahoe you can find gambling, entertainment, lavish shows, and big-name stars. Reno, Nevada, another gambling and resort center, is less than a three-hour drive away.

The opportunities for outdoor sporting activities are also abundant. The area is surrounded by numerous lakes for fishing and water skiing. The city itself has 120 tree-rich parks, many of which are equipped with softball fields, soccer fields, and tennis courts.

Arts and cultural resources rank almost as high as the natural resources. There are numerous art galleries, two symphony orchestras, an opera house, and a ballet company. Jazz clubs and coffeehouses flourish. The NBA's Sacramento Kings play basketball to sell-out crowds, and city leaders hope to attract professional baseball and football teams. "Sacramento doesn't fire you up," says land developer Phil Angelides, "It seduces you."

Numerous other towns and cities will provide solid real estate profits in the 1990s. Orlando, Florida, has been labeled "Hollywood, the Sequel." With 64,000 hotel rooms (topped only by New York City), its flourishing tourist industry provides a solid economic base in the service sector. Downtown Lake Eola Park features swan boats, a lighted fountain, and a red pagoda. The Orlando area has good potential. The median home price is currently around $80,000, and the prospects of covering mortgage payments with rental income are good.

The Carolinas, which experienced significant growth in the 1980s, are likely to continue to outpace many areas of the country. Noteworthy are Hickory and Greensboro, in North Carolina; and the Charlotte/Gastonia–Rock Hill area in South Carolina.

The Woods and Poole Economics Group estimates that by the year 2010, per-capita income in Hickory will rank it 38th in the country, up from 227th in 1984. Mean household income is estimated to reach $42,200 by 2010, an increase of 46 percent from the median of $28,900 in 1988. Greensboro will also see significant gains in these areas. Charlotte/Gastonia–Rock Hill can expect a 44.2 percent increase in mean household income, from $31,400 in 1988 to $45,300 in 2010.

There are too many good areas to cover them all in detail, but you might want to investigate Albuquerque, New Mexico; Columbus, Ohio; Portland, Oregon; and Seattle, Washington. Also look for growth in New Bedford, Massachusetts, where household income is slated to rise from $32,300 to over $45,000 by 2010. Significant growth is also likely to occur in Sherman–Denison, Texas.

If you think your financial future might include real estate investments, then start taking steps immediately to find out more about properties in these areas or in other areas of economic strength around the country. Begin by contacting the Chamber of Commerce in the area of interest, to pick up the essential demographic information—population, employment, industry, growth rates, and so forth. Contact The National Association of Realtors to get the names of several Realtors in the area. Call and ask about home prices, rental properties, mortgage availability, interest rates, closing costs, and so forth. These people will be happy to help you.

If you find that a certain area "feels right," then you may want to plan a trip to the area. You will need to know what to look for and how to pick out the best properties.

HOW TO PICK THE BEST PROPERTIES

Some rules don't change. Here are a few of the most important questions to consider when you are trying to decide which piece of investment property or which personal home to buy:

- Is it close to parks, schools, shopping, library, exercise, and/or recreational facilities?
- Is there a sense of community?
- What areas must you drive through to get to the property? (Beautiful streets are a plus, industrial sites are a minus.)
- What is the size of the lot, and how does it compare to others in the area? If it is an area with pools, is there room for one? Is there privacy?
- How much light is in the home? Can it be made brighter with windows, skylights, and/or white paint?
- What is the size of the master bedroom and bath? (Some analysts believe that this area should occupy 25 to 30 percent of a house's floor plan.)
- Is the kitchen large and full of light? Is there room for conversation and entertaining? What is the view from the kitchen window? If it is poor, can it be improved?
- What do you see when you enter the front door? Do you get a feeling of spaciousness and light?
- Is there enough closet and storage space?
- Is there a home office or potential office area?
- How does the price compare with others in the area? (For investment, the smaller house in the more expensive neighborhood is a good sign. Larger homes increase the value of smaller ones by just being there.)
- Does the floor plan allow for indoor–outdoor access and entertaining?
- Would you be proud to own it? Could you live there?

Whenever you look at a home, run through a mental checklist of these questions. Add as many more questions as you like. Look at the home through the eyes of a potential homeowner and ask yourself how you *feel* about the home. If there is something about the home that just "bothers" you, try to figure out what it is. There is a chance that it could be something as simple as a wallpaper pattern, a musty smell, old paint, or dirty windows. Picture the home repainted and cleaned top to bottom, and reconsider your feelings. If you can develop your ability to do this, you'll end up buying some real gems that others have passed by.

POSITIVE INVESTMENT ENERGY DRAWS SUCCESS

One of the single biggest reasons I've been successful with real estate is that I love it. A home is more than an elaborate shelter to me. My home is a creation, an extension of myself into the material world. The same is true of my real estate investments.

Many people involved in real estate will say that you don't have to like a piece of property to profit from owning it. They might be right, but I want something more out of ownership than just profits. I want the creative energy I feel when I find a good property in a good location. I enjoy the feeling of productivity that comes from transforming a property into something better and more desirable than when I bought it.

If I find a property that has been neglected, I think of ways to give it life. I look at its potential. I do this with a very sharp pencil, for it is important to keep an eye on costs. I believe that envisioning a positive outcome with my investments helps my investment prosper.

Before you enter the world of real estate, consider your true desires. Do you really *want* to be involved with real estate, or do you want your weekends free for tennis? Place the images of what you want in your mind, and then create them in your world.

When I first started in real estate, I visualized myself with income-producing investment property that would give me financial security and freedom. I made it happen, and you can too, if that is what you want. If, like me, you like real estate, then there is a higher probability that your investments will do well. Now that you know about cycles and the trends in real estate, the opportunity is before you. *Now* is your chance. You have every reason to be optimistic about future trends in real estate. If you connect to your own intuition and combine it with solid research and information, your efforts will be profitable. Make a commitment to your financial future. You can absolutely succeed!

Chapter 14

Commodity Futures: The Fastest Game in Town

If it seems too good to be true, it usually is.

Futures trading sends out messages few can resist: "Come make a fortune with very little money!" With as little as a few thousand dollars, you can buy or sell a contract for 5,000 bushels of corn, wheat, or soybeans; 100 ounces of gold; 40,000 pounds of cattle; or 12.5 million Japanese yen. If you buy a futures contract and the price of the contract moves up even a little, you can make big profits, sometimes in just a few minutes. Sound too good to be true? It usually is. It has been estimated that only 5 percent of individual commodities futures traders make money consistently.

A futures contract is an agreement between two traders who are parties to an exchange. One trader buys and the other trader sells a specific amount of a commodity, at an agreed-on price, to be delivered in the future during a specified month. If you buy a futures contract, believing that the price will go up, then you hold a *long* position. If you sell a contract, believing the price will go down, then you hold a *short* position.

What makes the commodities futures market so attractive is that you can make trades with a tremendous amount of financial leverage.

What makes the commodities futures market so attractive is that you can make trades with a tremendous amount of financial leverage. With just a small margin (a good-faith cash deposit), sometimes less than 5 or 6 percent of the contract value, you can make returns (or accrue losses!) on a much larger underlying asset base. For example, if the March gold futures contract is selling for $360 per troy ounce (few contracts go beyond one year), then for a deposit of a few thousand dollars, you can hold a contract worth $36,000! If the price goes up to $365 per ounce, then you make $5,000 with just a few thousand dollars actually invested! The problem is, you can lose just as much money just as fast.

There are basically two kinds of participants in the futures markets: *hedgers* and *speculators.* A hedger is a person who wants to "lock-in" a profit for a commodity in the future. For example, if a wheat farmer knows his production costs and knows that the price of wheat futures will guarantee him a profit, he may sell futures contracts so he can count on certain profits. There are other, much more complicated strategies that hedgers use. A speculator, on the other hand, is concerned only with the prospects of profiting by buying and selling futures contracts, and has no intention of making or receiving delivery of the commodity. If you participate in the futures markets, it will probably be as a speculator.

Contrary to what many people think, futures contracts are an essential tool for many businesses.

Contrary to what many people think, futures contracts are an essential tool for many businesses. Consider the case of Sam Sterling, a silver manufacturer. In January, Sam receives an order to produce silver trays that will require 50,000 troy ounces of silver. Sam has a problem. He must determine what price to ask for the trays even though the order will not be delivered to the customer until July. Sam needs to know what the price of silver will be in several months, when he begins production.

He could purchase the silver right away, in January, and set his prices on that basis, but this would tie up a substantial amount of capital and would create storage and insurance expenses for the several months when the silver would sit idle. On the other hand, if he were to quote his customers a price and wait until May to purchase the silver, he would take the chance that silver prices will rise and wipe out his profit margin or, worse yet, cause him to take a loss on the order.

Sam avoids these problems and risks by making a hedge transaction. In January, Sam purchases 50 May silver contracts (1,000 troy ounces each, slated for May delivery). The price he pays for the May silver futures contracts in January will be the price he uses to establish his profit margin on the sale of his silver trays. Thus, by buying in the future, he assures himself a profit.

Speculator Sylvia Cycle, who sells Sam the contracts, has no intention of making delivery herself. Believing that silver prices will fall, she sells Sam the May silver futures contracts with the intent to buy an equivalent amount of contracts back at some later date at a lower price. If prices fall, she will make a profit. If they rise, then she will buy an equivalent amount back at a higher price and pay the difference out of her pocket.

NOT LIKE THE STOCK MARKET

In some ways, it may seem that commodity futures are like the stock market. You are long when you buy, expecting prices to rise. You are short when you sell, expecting prices to fall. You accumulate profits from correctly predicting market movements. Although these similarities are striking, the two markets are very different. Undoubtedly, the biggest difference is that successful commodities investing requires very precise timing, or a lot of good luck. Commodities are much riskier than stocks.

In the stock market, there is a margin of error, however small, in the timing of your investments. The commodities futures market is much less forgiving. If you buy a stock expecting the price to rise, you do not have to pinpoint the exact month in which the rise will occur. You can simply buy the stock and sell when the stock price goes up, even if it takes a few months longer than you anticipated. This is not possible with commodities.

As a speculator, if you buy a December futures contract, the price must increase by December or you have not made any money. Worse yet, if the price has dropped, you have lost money—in some cases, far more than your initial investment. If the price of your futures contract goes up before the contract expiration date, you can always sell and take a profit. When the expiration date arrives, everyone *must* settle up. If you own a December contract and prices go up in January, it does you absolutely no good.

THE LURE OF QUICK RICHES

In *Trading Places,* Eddie Murphy and Dan Akroyd justifiably swindle two wealthy brothers who own a commodities brokerage firm. The two eccentric brothers bet that they can turn Murphy, who was a lighthearted con man looking for street contributions, into an executive at their firm, while turning their star young executive, Akroyd, into a common thief.

The two brothers take away Akroyd's money, credit cards, home, butler, and chauffeur and have him arrested so he spends a night in jail. Murphy is taken from the street and given Akroyd's home, butler, chauffeur, and executive position at the firm. After Akroyd and Murphy discover the plot, they decide on revenge. As they put it, "The best way to get back at rich people is to turn them into poor people."

Akroyd and Murphy accomplish this by trading commodities. They devise a scheme to change an illegally obtained orange juice crop report (the brothers are illegally using inside information to make money in their own account) so that the brothers think the price of orange juice is going to rise. Thinking they have advance knowledge of a forthcoming price rise, the two brothers purchase all the orange juice contracts they can before the crop report is issued. The price of orange juice more than doubles because of their heavy buying. Dan and Eddie short the market, knowing that the price of orange juice will plummet once the *real* news breaks out. In the end, Akroyd and Murphy get rich and the brothers must use all their assets to pay for their worthless long positions.

There are technical glitches in the movie with respect to commodities trading, but the scenes on the trading floor are priceless. At the end, Dan, Eddie, and friends are enjoying life on a luxurious island beach. They had become millionaires in about an hour, with very little money. It is this "get rich quick" prospect that draws people into the spirited world of commodity trading.

MY FUTURES SPECULATING—AN EXPENSIVE LESSON

I am a risk taker. I am not a gambler. I'm not quite sure what prompted me to try my hand in the futures markets. In the fall of 1987, I took a long position in the Swiss franc. A part of me felt strongly that the value of the Swiss franc would rise, and I was absolutely right; the price appreciated substantially. But I was to find out that, no matter how good your intuitive ability, the futures market is a formidable challenge. I also learned what many people who have tried commodity futures already know: *You can be right and still lose a great deal of money!*

When trading futures, you can be right and still lose a lot of money.

I was fascinated with the appreciation of the Swiss franc. Although the Japanese yen seemed to be the most popular currency, I had a fondness for the franc. I had once lived in Europe, and I could remember when the exchange ratio was 7 francs to 1 American dollar. Now the exchange rate was almost 1.5 dollars to the franc, and I wanted to see how high the franc would go.

I assembled a number of charts and cycles from various sources. I identified what appeared to be a major upward trend in the Swiss franc. I held my breath and purchased two contracts, putting up a good faith deposit of $2,500 for each of them. My broker protected himself by having me sign a risk acknowledgment statement and telling me quite frankly, "Patricia, you can lose your a—."

After an initial drop of about 1 cent per franc, the price of the franc increased 2 cents. With each 1-cent move, my contract value moved up $1,250. My two contracts had each moved up 2 cents, so I had "made" $5,000. I was very excited, but I had a lot to learn.

The franc was still solid and moving higher each day. I was soon ahead $7,500. "Wow," I thought, "why didn't I do this years earlier?" All that painting and cleaning of rentals, all those leases and mortgages, all those phone calls from prospective tenants, and all those years to build financial security. It looked to me as though the futures market was the way to go.

I purchased two more contracts. Now, each movement of 1 cent would move my contract values $5,000. I started making several calls a day to my broker. How did the market open? Any new trend in sight? Where were the major areas of support? I felt good about the major trend, but as a novice speculator, I was not experienced enough to know how to protect my profits.

It was a heady experience; I was fascinated that I was making money "so easily." During this time, I came to recognize some important information about myself. The "excitement" of trading currencies was taking an emotional toll. I had always been a long-term investor, yet here I was playing the fastest game in town. I recognized the inconsistency between the rules of this game and my own investor personality. I was still making money, but I was beginning to wonder whether the mental energy and worry were worth it. My cherished peace of mind was being devoured by price quotes and market movements.

Late in December, the upward price trend on the Swiss franc reversed, dropping drastically as the U.S. and other governments began selling francs and buying dollars in massive quantities. I had been so busy watching my profits that I had failed to protect them with appropriate stops (placing a stop involves putting in an order to buy or sell when prices hit a certain point). By this time, I had seven contracts. Within one week, I lost all but a few thousand dollars of my "profits." Instead of getting out of the market completely and reassessing my positions, I stayed in. In retrospect, I believe I was a little bewildered.

Before it was all over, I had etched my name on the list of the 90 percent of all small investors who trade in the futures market. I lost money. My life-style was not appreciably affected by the loss, but the experience was very expensive research for this chapter. I learned several lessons, which I will now share with you.

Trouble at the Chicago Mercantile Exchange

One of the dangers in commodities trading is centered on the industry itself. "Violations Widespread at Merc, Survey Finds," announced a headline on April 18, 1989, in *The Wall Street Journal*. "Trading violations are so widespread at the Chicago Mercantile Exchange that most Merc members responding to a *Wall Street Journal* survey said they had witnessed illegal trades in the last year. Nearly half acknowledged breaking exchange rules themselves." The article went on to explain that most respondents felt brokers are honest but that archaic rules make it appear that the law is being broken. Still, everyone agreed that certain practices do hurt customers.

Prearranged trading, in which two or more traders buy and sell futures among themselves, is one such practice. Because trades are supposed to be openly auctioned in the pit, prearranged trades shut out the beneficial effects of auctioning. Front running is another technique that hurts customers. In this procedure, brokers trade ahead of large customer orders that they have been given to execute, and they profit from the market effect of the orders. Most survey respondents felt that dual trading, in which brokers trade for both their own and customers' accounts, should be banned.

SUCCESS FOR THE FEW

The futures market does have its success stories. Paul Tudor Jones II has made millions for himself and his clients. He is head of the Tudor Investment Group, and lives a life that many would envy. He entertains the important and famous at his 3,000-acre wildlife preserve on Chesapeake Bay. His vacation hideaway in

Switzerland is equipped with computers so he can keep on trading. He is frequently seen in Manhattan's more exclusive night clubs, and apparently aspires to be a member of high society. At 40, he is said to be the oldest person in his organization, and it is reported that he has signed letters to investors as the "senior camp counselor." Although Jones will consider any trading technique that makes money, he has stated that he is a believer in *cycle theory*—the notion that market trends repeat themselves!

Although there are many successful futures traders, very few of them are individual investors.

Although there are many successful futures traders, very few of them are individual investors. The fact is, it is very difficult for the individual investor to make money in futures. The swiftness and severity with which price changes can occur make fast action a must. A man like Paul Jones can watch the markets minute-by-minute, using his own market monitors, and can move in and out as swiftly as he needs to. For individual investors, this is difficult, if not impossible. If you work during the day, you can't be calling your broker every five minutes to see what is happening, or if you do, you're liable to lose your job. In addition, brokers' commissions can be high and are paid with every trade. Commissions can eat up small profits, especially if you trade frequently.

Some brokers will tell you that you can protect your profits with stops. A stop order is a buy or sell order that is to be executed if prices hit or go through a certain level. For example, if you bought a gold contract at $360 per ounce, and the price is now $365 per ounce, then you may want to put an order to sell a gold contract at a $364 stop. If prices trade at or below $364, then a broker on the floor of the exchange sells one gold contract for your account at the current trading price. The idea is that you lock-in a $4-per-ounce profit.

It sounds good in theory, and it often works, but there are never any guarantees. At the close of one business day, the price may be $365 per ounce. If some important news breaks overnight, however, the opening price could be $355 or even lower! Your stop is "hit," but because the order is to sell at the current trading price, you may lose as much as $5 per ounce, or $5000 per contract. On the other hand, if you set a stop close to your purchase price, during the day your stop may be touched and executed, putting you on the sidelines. A few minutes later, the market may go up to a new high without your benefiting from it. If you want to reestablish your position, it will cost you additional commissions, and then the same thing can happen all over again. The net effect is you can be right about the long-term trend of the prices, but the short-term volatility can cause you to lose money.

COMMODITIES FUTURES FUNDS

You can also participate in the futures market through commodity futures pools or mutual funds. Basically, all you are doing is turning over your money to professionals who will trade it in the futures market in return for a fee and/or a portion of the profits. Individual investors can sometimes purchase a share of a partnership in a pool for as little as $5,000.

Beware of these futures funds and pools, they can be very risky.

Beware of these funds and pools; they can be very risky. Over the years, stock mutual funds have developed a reputation as a relatively safe haven for investment dollars, at least over the long term. *Don't confuse commodities futures pools or mutual funds with their stock counterparts!* The commodities pools carry the same risk as futures contracts that are purchased individually. Read very carefully the risk disclosure statement that comes with your prospectus. The statement is required for a reason! Here is a typical example:

RISK DISCLOSURE STATEMENT

You should carefully consider whether your financial condition permits you to invest in the partnership (fund). You may lose a substantial portion or even all of such investment, and may be responsible for losses beyond your initial investment.

In considering whether to invest, you should be aware that trading commodity contracts can quickly lead to large losses as well as gains. Such trading losses can sharply reduce the new asset value of the partnership and consequently the value of your interest in the partnership.

Under certain market conditions, the partnership may find it difficult or impossible to liquidate a position. This can occur, for example, when the market makes a "limit move." Placing contingent orders, such as "stop-loss," or "stop-limit" orders, will not necessarily limit the partnership's losses to the intended amounts, since market conditions may make it impossible to execute such orders.

This brief statement cannot, of course, disclose all the risks and other significant aspects of investing in the partnership. You should, therefore, study this prospectus and commodity trading before you decide to invest in the partnership.

You should also know that when the sales brochures and prospectuses show spectacular gains in the 50, 60, and 70 percent range, you may not be getting the whole story. Three New York professors—Edwin Elton and Martin Gruber of New York University's Graduate School of Business, and Joel Rentzler of the Baruch College of the City University of New York—selected 77 new commodities funds and compared the manager's past performance to the performance of the new fund. Their verdict was that the funds were a disaster and as a group, earned less than one-tenth of the rates of return shown in the prospectuses. In addition to these risks, you must pay management fees and commissions whether or not the funds show a profit. In most cases, it will cost you money just to redeem your share of the pool.

Because commodities trading is such a fast-paced game, I have found it virtually impossible to apply intuitive abilities to decisions. There is little solace in being right about the direction of the trend when you have lost money. If your intuitive abilities tell you not to participate, then by all means, *DON'T.*

If you decide to play the fastest game in town, let me wish you the very best. I sincerely hope that your profits are all spendable. Whatever you decide to do, please remember the eleventh commandment: "If it seems too good to be true, it usually is."

Afterword: An End and a Beginning

What a joy it has been to share my life with you in these pages! With my passion for cycles, I didn't want to just explain them, I wanted you to experience them. I wanted you to feel what I have felt and to appreciate the courage that cycles have given me.

The natural, repeating rhythms of cycles give me a sense of constancy and security in this quickly changing world. They support my courage, hope, optimism, and success, because the future seems less intimidating, more promising, and more predictable when you are in touch with these naturally repeating patterns. Within the context of cycles, the past seems sensible, the present more purposeful, and the future more certain.

Cycles support courage, hope, optimism, and success, because the future seems less intimidating, more promising, and more predictable when you are in touch with these naturally repeating patterns.

We all have the power to create. Our mind and our view of the world have, to some extent, created what is in our lives today.

Examine carefully your thoughts, words, and passions. They are, at this minute, creating your future.

If you have not reached your personal goals in the past, perhaps it was because you could not "see" yourself reaching them. Perhaps you were not patient and demanded results in *your* time frame rather than allowing events to unfold within the natural rhythms of cycles. You do not need to repeat these experiences.

Use cycles as a technique for seeing your future success. Use them as your North Star to reach places where you have never been. Let cycles open your life to your own creativity, your own personal power, your own intuition. See your future in your mind, fill your actions with passion, surround your life with love, and you will have everything you want. May joy be with you.

Bibliography and Readings

My work with cycles has taken me down many paths. I have found small pieces of important information among the writings of both historical and contemporary authors. I share these sources with you in the following pages; an asterisk appears next to those books that I most recommend. ENJOY!

*Agor, Weston H. *Intuitive Management.* Englewood Cliffs, NJ: Prentice-Hall, 1984.

Albrecht, Karl. *Brain Power.* Englewood Cliffs, NJ: Prentice-Hall, 1980.

Allen, Frederick Lewis. *Only Yesterday: An Informal History of the Nineteen-Twenties.* New York: Harper and Bros., 1931.

Allen, Robert G. *Nothing Down.* New York: Simon & Schuster, 1980.

Allis, Sam. "Company Towns: Those Who Rate Cities as Business Sites Like Mid-Size Sun Belt Ones." *Wall Street Journal,* March 14, 1980, p. 1.

"America's New Financial Structure." *Business Week,* November 17, 1980, pp. 138–44.

Angrist, Stanley W. "Investors Can Take a Bite Out of Fraud." *Wall Street Journal,* January 24, 1989, p. C1.

Arden, Lynie. *Franchises You Can Run from Home.* New York: John Wiley & Sons, 1990.

Armstrong, Martin A. "The Empirical Nature of Cycles." *Cycles,* 40, no. 5 (1989).

Ascani, Dan. "Commodities in the Perspective of the Elliot and the Kondratieff Waves." *Cycles,* 40, no. 2 (1989).

Babson, Roger W. *Bonds and Stocks.* Wellesley Hills, MA: Babson Statistical Organization, 1913.

Bartlett, Charles M. "When the Broker Calls with a Hot New Issue." *Forbes,* June 27, 1988, pp. 290–92.

Baruch, Bernard M. *Baruch: My Own Story.* New York: Henry Holt, 1957.

Bassie, V. L. *Economic Forecasting.* New York: McGraw-Hill, 1958.

Baumol, William J., and Alan S. Blinder. *Economics.* San Diego: Harcourt Brace Jovanovich, 1985.

Becker, Gary S. "Why a Depression Isn't in the Cards." *Business Week,* November 9, 1987, p. 22.

Benderly, Beryl Lieff. "Intuition." *Psychology Today* (September 1989): 35–40.

Benner, Samuel. *Benner's Prophecies of Future Ups and Downs in Prices.* Cincinnati: Chase and Hall, 1876.

Beveridge, W. I. B. *Seeds of Discovery.* New York: W. W. Norton, 1980.

Biddinger, Janelle. "What Today's Homebuyers Want." *Realtor News,* March 27, 1989, pp. 1, 6.

"The Big Land Rush: No Slowdown in Sight." *U.S. News & World Report,* December 13, 1971, pp. 32–34.

Bladen, Ashby. *How to Cope with the Developing Financial Crisis.* New York: McGraw-Hill, 1980.

Blaug, Mark. *Economic Theory in Retrospect.* Cambridge: Cambridge University Press, 1988.

Bleiberg, Robert M. "Lean Years, Fat Years." *Barron's,* December 7, 1987, p. 11.

Blotnik, Srully. *Winning: The Psychology of Successful Investing.* New York: McGraw-Hill, 1979.

"The Boom Counties." *U.S. News & World Report,* November 9, 1987, p. 108.

Boone, Louis E., and David L. Kurtz. *Contemporary Marketing.* Chicago: Dryden Press, 1989.

Bragg, John M. *Protecting Against Inflation and Maximizing Yield.* Atlanta: Georgia State University, 1986.

*Brouwer, Kurt. *Mutual Funds.* New York: John Wiley & Sons, 1988.

Browne, Harry. *You Can Profit from a Monetary Crisis.* New York, Macmillan, 1974.

———. *New Profits from the Monetary Crisis.* New York: William Morrow, 1978.

Bryant, William C. "Productivity: Only Real Cure for Inflation." *U.S. News & World Report,* March 12, 1979, p. 80.

Buell, Barbara. "Bloody Monday Didn't Bloody the Tokyo Exchange Much." *Business Week,* November 16, 1987, pp. 82–85.

Burns, Arthur F., and Wesley C. Mitchell. *Measuring Business Cycles.* New York: National Bureau of Economic Research, 1946.

———. *The Business Cycle in a Changing World.* New York: Columbia University Press, 1969.

Byrns, Ralph T., and Gerald W. Stone. *Macroeconomics.* London: Scott, Foresman and Co., 1989.

Byron, Doris. "Home Builders Battle to Stay Alive." *San Jose Mercury News,* July 6, 1981, p. E1.

Callanan, Robert J. "Cycles, Waves, and Market Dynamics." *Cycles,* 39, no. 9 (1988).

Cameron, Juan. "I Don't Trust Any Economists Today." *Fortune,* September 11, 1978, pp. 30–32.

Canetti, Elias. *Crowds and Power.* New York: Farrar Straus Giroux, 1984.

Carey, John. "The Changing Face of a Restless Nation." *Business Week,* September 25, 1989, pp. 42–50.

"Cartoon 'Cels' Animate a Sellers' Market." *Wall Street Journal,* August 13, 1990, pp. B1, B3.

Castro, Janice. "Staying Home Is Paying Off." *Time,* October 26, 1987, pp. 112–13.

Church, George J. "Panic Grips the Globe." *Time,* November 2, 1987, pp. 22–33.

*Ciaramitaro, Andrew J. *Beat the IRS Legally.* New York: Barkley Publishing, 1987.

Clarke, William Kendall. *The Robber Baroness.* New York: St. Martin's Press, 1979.

"Cashing In with the Japanese." *Builder* (July 1989): 172, 174.

Clemence, Richard V., and Francis S. Doody. *The Schumpeterian System.* New York: Augustus M. Kelley, 1966.

Crane, Burton. *The Sophisticated Investor.* New York: Simon & Schuster, 1964.

"The Desert Song." *Time,* March 2, 1959, p. 64.

Dewey, Edward R. *Alleged Economic Cycles of About 9.2 Years and a Study in Depth of this Cycle in Copper Prices, USA, 1928–1973.* Pittsburgh: Foundation for the Study of Cycles, 1974.

———. "Cycle Synchronies." *Cycles,* 40, no. 6 (1989).

*———. *Cycles: Selected Writings.* Pittsburgh: Foundation for the Study of Cycles, 1970.

*———. *Cycles: The Mysterious Forces That Trigger Events.* New York: Manor Books, 1973.

———. *The 17.7 Year Cycle in War.* Pittsburgh: Foundation for the Study of Cycles, 1964.

*Dewey, Edward R., and Edward F. Dankin. *Cycles: The Science of Prediction.* Pittsburgh: The Foundation for the Study of Cycles, 1947.

Dewey, Edward R., and Jeffrey H. Horowitz. "The Kondratieff Wave Revisited." *Cycles,* 39, no. 3 (1988).

*Dewey, Edward R., and Og Mandino. *Cycles: The Mysterious Forces That Trigger Events.* New York: Hawthorn Books, 1971.

Dillard, Dudley. *The Economics of John Maynard Keynes.* Englewood Cliffs, NJ: Prentice-Hall, 1973.

"Dixie Zeckendorf Runs for Cover." *Business Week,* December 31, 1966, pp. 78–79.

Drake, Christopher. "Behavior Entering Downturn, Psychiatrist Believes." *San Jose Mercury News,* June 26, 1980, pp. 1–2C.

Drake, Phyllis. "Adding Livability to Compact Quarters Is 80s' Challenge." *San Jose Mercury News,* April 12, 1980, p. 9D.

Drake, Phyllis. "The Housing Slump." *San Jose Mercury News,* August 1, 1981, p. D1.

Dreman, David. *Contrarian Investment Strategy.* New York: Random House, 1979.

Duffy, Brian, and Jack Egan. "Staring into the Abyss." *U.S. News & World Report,* November 2, 1987, pp. 19–23.

Dunn, Donald H. "Buy Your North 40 While It's Dirt-Cheap." *Business Week,* April 20, 1987, pp. 92–93.

Dunnan, Nancy. *How to Invest in Real Estate.* New York: Harper & Row, 1987.

"Economic Prospects for the Year 2000." *Business Week,* September 25, 1989, pp. 94–95.

Edgerton, Jerry. "Crash of '87: How the Small Investor Got the Shaft." *Money* (January 1988): 13–22.

*Ellis, Edward Robb. *A Nation in Torment.* New York: Coward-McCann, 1970.

"Emerging Values for the 1990's." *The Chivas Regal Report on Working Americans.* New York: The House of Seagram, 1989.

Entin, Bruce. "Wall Street's Raging Bulls Push Dow Average Past 1,000 Mark." *San Jose Mercury News,* October 12, 1982, p. A1.

Flagg, Michael. "New Home Tab Up to $364,550 This Year." *Los Angeles Times,* April 22, 1989, p. 5R.

"Florida Land Sales." *Business Week,* December 27, 1958. pp. 20–22.

"Florida Loses Its Boom." *Business Week,* June 24, 1961, p. 125.

"Florida Real Estate Revives, But Wounds Heal Slowly." *U.S. News & World Report,* August 23, 1976, p. 63.

"Florida's New Land Rush." *Newsweek,* January 5, 1959, pp. 55–57.

"Florida's Zany Real Estate—Lots for Sale by Mail." *Newsweek,* January 11, 1954, p. 57.

Forrester, Jay W. "The Economy and the Kondratieff Cycle." *Cycles,* 39, no. 3 (1988).

Fox, Emmet. *Find and Use Your Inner Power.* New York: Harper & Bros., 1941.

Fremerman, Bernard. "Cycles in Consumer Sentiment—A New Clue to the 41-Month Cycle." *Cycles,* 30, no. 3 (1979).

Freud, Sigmund. *Group Psychology and the Analysis of the Ego.* New York: W. W. Norton, 1959.

Frost, Alfred John, and Robert Rougelot Prechter, Jr. *Elliot Wave Principle.* Gainesville, FL: New Classics Library, 1985.

Galbraith, John Kenneth. *The Great Crash.* Boston: Houghton Mifflin, 1955.

*Gallwey, Timothy W. *The Inner Game of Tennis.* New York: Random House, 1974.

Gann, W. D. *How to Make Profits Trading in Commodities.* Pomeroy, WA: Lambert-Gann Publishing Co., 1976.

Garvy, George. "Kondratieff's Theory of Long Cycles." *Cycles,* 34, no. 9 (1983).

Gibbs, Nancy. "How America Has Run Out of Time." *Time,* April 24, 1989, pp. 58–67.

———. "I Feel a Lot Poorer Today." *Time,* November 2, 1987, pp. 37–40.

Gibson, Thomas. *The Cycles of Speculation.* New York: The Moody Corp., 1909.

Gilbert, Bruce. "After The Meltdown of '87." *Newsweek,* November 2, 1987, pp. 14–20.

Gillies, Jerry. *Money Love.* New York: Warner Books, 1978.

Glasgall, William. "Wall Street's Wounds Have the World Bleeding." *Business Week,* November 2, 1987, p. 54.

Goldberg, Herb, and Robert Lewis. *Money Madness.* New York: William Morrow, 1977.

*Goldberg, Philip. *The Intuitive Edge.* Los Angeles: Jeremy P. Tarcher, 1983.

Goldston, Linda. "Researchers Find More Women Prefer Condominium Living." *San Jose Mercury News,* December 3, 1979, p. 3B.

Gordon, John Steele. "The Problem of Money and Time." *American Heritage* (May/June 1989): 57–66.

Gould, Bruce G. *How to Make Money in Commodities.* Seattle, WA: Bruce Gould Publications, 1982.

Granville, Joseph E. *Granville's New Strategy of Daily Stock Market Timing for Maximum Profit.* Englewood Cliffs, NJ: Prentice-Hall, 1976.

"A Greater Variety in Real Estate Deals." *Business Week,* December 22, 1973, pp. 126–30.

Grebler, Leo, David Blank, and Lewis Wimnick. *Capital Formation in Residential Real Estate.* Princeton, NJ: Princeton University Press, 1956.

Greenfield, Samuel C. *The Low-High Theory of Investment.* New York: Coward-McCann, 1968.

Guenther, Robert, and Masayoshi Kanabayashi. "Japanese Firms Boost Purchases of Real Estate in U.S." *Wall Street Journal,* October 20, 1986, p. 6.

Hald, Earl C. *Business Cycles.* Boston: Houghton Mifflin, 1954.

Hallman, Victor G., and Jerry S. Rosenbloom. *Personal Financial Planning.* New York: McGraw-Hill, 1983.

Harris, T. George, and Daniel Yankelovich. "What Good Are the Rich?" *Psychology Today* (April, 1989): 36–39.

"Has the Land Boom Crested?" *Forbes,* June 15, 1974, pp. 32–36.

Hayes, Robert Michael. *Forecasting Stock Market Cycles: An Empirical Evaluation of Existing Techniques.* Ann Arbor, MI: University Microfilms International, 1972.

Heller, Robert. *The Naked Investor.* New York: Delacorte Press, 1977.

Herbst, Anthony F. "The Kondratieff Long Cycle." *Cycles,* 39, no. 5 (1988).

Hewes, Laurance. *Boxcar in the Sand.* New York: Alfred A. Knopf, 1957.

*Hill, Napoleon. *Think and Grow Rich.* New York: Fawcett Crest Books, 1960.

*Hill, Napoleon, and Harold E. Keown. *Succeed and Grow Rich Through Persuasion.* New York: Fawcett Crest Books, 1970.

*Hill, Napoleon, and W. Clement Stone. *Success Through a Positive Mental Attitude.* New York: Pocket Books, 1960.

Hirsch, Yale. *Don't Sell Stocks on Monday.* New York: Penguin Books, 1987.

Holbrook, Stewart. *The Age of the Moguls.* New York: Doubleday, 1954.

"Homebuilding Goes Limp Again." *Business Week,* December 8, 1980, pp. 22–25.

Homer, Sidney. *A History of Interest Rates: 2000 BC to the Present.* New Brunswick, NJ: Rutgers University Press, 1963, 1977.

Hornblower, Margot. "Snapped by Their Own Suspenders." *Time,* November 2, 1987, p. 53.

"Housing's Rewards Turn Less Surefire." *Business Week,* December 28, 1981, pp. 144–47.

"Investing in Real Estate—Without Buying Property." *U.S. News & World Report,* May 17, 1971.

"Is the Bloom Coming Off Florida's Boom?" *U.S. News & World Report,* July 18, 1960, pp. 56–58.

"Is This a Good Time to Buy a House?" *U.S. News & World Report,* November 18, 1955, p. 116.

Jarman, Rufus. "New Style in Florida Booms." *The Saturday Evening Post,* February 18, 1956.

Josephson, Matthew. *The Money Lords.* New York: Weybright and Talley, 1972.

Juglar, Clement. *Brief History of Panics and Their Periodic Occurrences in the United States.* New York: G.P. Putnam's Sons, 1916.

Kessler, A. D. *A Fortune at Your Feet.* New York: Harcourt Brace Jovanovich, 1981.

Kimberly, John R., and Robert H. Miles and Associates. *The Organizational Life Cycle.* San Francisco: Jossey-Bass, 1980.

Kishel, Gregory, and Patricia Kishel. *Cashing in on the Consulting Boom.* New York: John Wiley & Sons, 1985.

———. *Dollars on your Doorstep—The Complete Guide to Home Based Businesses.* New York: John Wiley & Sons, 1984.

Kondratieff, N. D. "The Long Waves in Economic Life." Reprinted from *Review of Economic Statistics,* XVII, November 1935. New York: Foundation for the Study of Cycles, 1944.

Koten, John. "Violations Widespread at Merc, Survey Finds." *Wall Street Journal,* April 18, 1989, pp. C1, C13.

Kotkin, Joel. "Los Angeles: America's Most Influential City." *San Jose Mercury News,* December 7, 1980, p. 1C.

Kristol, Irving. "The Economics of Growth." *Wall Street Journal,* November 16, 1978.

Kutscher, Ronald E. "Overview and Implications of the Projection to 2000." *Bureau of Labor Statistics: Monthly Labor Review* (September 1987): 3–63.

Laderman, Jeffrey M. "Steady Hands for Unsteady Times." *Business Week,* February 18, 1991, pp. 76–79.

Lamott, Kenneth. *The Moneymakers.* Boston: Little Brown, 1969.

"A Land Development Wave Hits Hawaii." *Business Week,* November 25, 1972, pp. 63–64.

Landscheidt, Theodor. *Sun–Earth–Man.* London: Urania Trust, 1989.

Lavine, Alan. "The Ins and Outs: What Did Black Monday Tell Us About Market Timing?" *Financial Planning* (April 1988): 67–73.

Lebow, Joan. "The Flow of Money into Real Estate." *Wall Street Journal,* July 24, 1989, p. B1.

Lichtenstein, Grace. "Homes in the Range." *American Home* (Fall 1989): 28, 114–15.

Lochray, Paul J. *The Financial Planner's Guide to Estate Planning.* Englewood Cliffs, NJ: Prentice-Hall, 1987.

Long, Jr., Clarence D. *Building Cycles and the Theory of Investment.* Princeton, NJ: Princeton University Press, 1940.

Lowry, Albert J. *How You Can Become Financially Independent by Investing in Real Estate.* New York: Simon & Schuster, 1977.

Lundberg, Ferdinand. *The Rich and the Super Rich.* New York: Lyle Stuart, 1968.

*Lynch, Peter. *One Up on Wall Street.* New York: Penguin Books, 1990.

Magnuson, Ed. "A Shock Felt Round the World." *Time,* November 2, 1987, pp. 34–36.

Maloney, Lawrence. "Houses in the 80's: Smaller, Fewer, Costlier." *U.S. News & World Report,* April 2, 1979, pp. 54–56.

Mamis, Robert. *When to Sell.* New York: Farrar Straus & Giroux, 1977.

Mandino, Og. *Mission Success!* New York: Bantam Books, 1986.

"A Market Model with a Big Payoff." *Business Week,* June 2, 1980, pp. 92, 96.

Martin, Everett Dean, *The Behavior of Crowds.* New York: Harper & Bros., 1920.

Mayo, Herbert B. *Investments.* Chicago: The Dryden Press, 1983.

McCarthy, Michael J. "Small Businesses Blossom Near Atlanta." *Wall Street Journal,* March 28, 1989, p. B1.

McCormick, John. "America's Hot Cities." *Newsweek,* February 6, 1989, pp. 42–44.

McCullough, Keith. "Cycles in Short-term Interest Rates." *Cycles,* 41, no. 3 (1990).

McDonald, John. "The $2 Billion Building Boom." *Fortune* (February 1960): 111.

———. "Where's the Ceiling on New Houses?" *Fortune* (June 1963): 128.

McMurray, Scott, and Jeff Bailey. "The Black Hole." *Wall Street Journal,* December 2, 1987, pp. A1, A13.

McMurray, Scott, and John Koten. "Exclusive Club." *Wall Street Journal,* January 26, 1989, pp. A1, A6.

Mitchell, W. C. *Business Cycles and Their Causes.* Berkeley: University of California Press, 1959.

Mogey, Richard. "The Cyclic Outlook for Real Estate." *Cycles,* 40, no. 3 (1989).

———. "Status of the 40.68-Month Cycle in Stock Prices." *Cycles,* 39, no. 9 (1988).

———. "Using Cycles in Trading." *Cycles,* 41, no. 5 (1990).

———. "Using Cycles in Trading (Part Two)." *Cycles,* 41, no. 6 (1990).

"The Money Men." *Forbes* (November 1970): 42–44.

"Money to Be Made in Real Estate," *Business Week,* October 8, 1960, pp. 128, 131.

Murray, Alan. "Bush S & L Bailout Creates Illusion of Deficit Cut That Congress Questions but Wants to Believe." *Wall Street Journal,* February 22, 1989, p. A16.

Naisbitt, John. *Megatrends.* New York: Warner Books, 1984.

"New American Land Rush." *Time,* February 28, 1972, p. 72.

"A New Choice for Real Estate." *Business Week,* October 8, 1960, pp. 128, 131.

"The New Money Target: Profitable Real Estate." *Business Week,* August 1, 1977, pp. 53–58.

"New Tactics in Florida Land." *Business Week,* June 15, 1963, pp. 54–58.

Newbury, Frank D. *Business Forecasting Principles and Practice.* New York: McGraw-Hill, 1952.

Nickerson, William. *How I Turned $1,000 into a Million in Real Estate . . . in My Spare Time.* New York: Simon & Schuster, 1959.

Noddings, Nel, and Paul J. Shore. *Awakening the Inner Eye.* New York: Columbia University, Teachers College Press, 1984.

Norman, James R. "America's Deflation Belt." *Business Week,* June 9, 1986, pp. 52–60.

*Norvel, Anthony. *The Million Dollar Secret Hidden in Your Mind.* Englewood Cliffs, NJ: Prentice-Hall, 1963.

O'Hara, Delia. "Will the 'Price Bubble' Burst in Home Market?" *San Jose Mercury News,* September 15, 1979, p. 5E.

"One More Boom That's Running Out of Steam." *U.S. News & World Report,* April 16, 1962, pp. 68–71.

Paris, Ellen. "Massacre on the Miracle Mile." *Forbes,* April 26, 1982, pp. 40–41.

Pearson, Clifford, and Lisa Saxton. "Builder Tours The West." *Builder* (June 1989): 74–89.

Peers, Alexandra. "Auctioneers Adjust as Art Sales Slow." *Wall Street Journal,* March 1, 1991, p. C1.

Peterson, Peter G. "The Morning After." *The Atlantic Monthly* (October 1987): 43–69.

Powell, Bill. "'Looking into the Abyss.'" *Newsweek,* November 2, 1987, pp. 24–33.

"In Pursuit of the Second Home." *Newsweek,* April 17, 1972, pp. 84–85.

"Real Estate Loses a Bit of Its Zing." *Business Week,* July 21, 1962, pp. 78–81.

"Real Estate: On the Brink." *Forbes,* July 1, 1970, pp. 84–85.

"Real Estate Trusts Are a Money Magnet." *Business Week,* October 20, 1975, pp. 95–96.

"Real Estate: Why the Bad Gets Worse." *Business Week,* October 20, 1975, pp. 95–96.

"Realtors." *Business Week,* November 26, 1960, pp. 146–48.

Reese, Michael, and Jennifer Foote. "California: American Dream, American Nightmare." *Newsweek,* July 31, 1989, pp. 22–29.

Roll, Eric. *A History of Economic Thought.* Englewood Cliffs, NJ: Prentice-Hall, 1946.

Rom, Martin. *Nothing Can Replace the U.S. Dollar . . . And It Almost Has.* New York: Thomas Y. Crowell, 1975.

Rose, Frederick. "California Babel." *Wall Street Journal,* June 12, 1989, p. A1.

Rose, Robert L., and Jeff Bailey. "Traders in CBOT Soybean Pit Indicted." *Wall Street Journal,* August 3, 1989, p. A10.

Rosenthal, A. M. "Greed, Arrogance, Hollow Expertise at Bottom of Wall Street Collapse." *Lexington Herald Leader,* October 28, 1987, p. A9.

*Rowan, Roy. *The Intuitive Manager.* Boston: Little, Brown, 1986.

*Salk, Jonas. *The Anatomy of Reality.* New York: Columbia University Press, 1983.

Saltzman, Amy. "The Quest For Community." *U.S. News & World Report,* April 9, 1990, pp. 75–76.

Sandler, Linda. "Integrated Resources Scrambles To Escape Looming Crisis." *Wall Street Journal,* June 15, 1989, pp. C1, C2.

Scheinman, William Z. *Why Most Investors Are Mostly Wrong, Most of the Time.* New York: Weybright and Talley, 1970.

Schifrin, Matthew. "Busy Signals." *Forbes,* November 16, 1987, pp. 38–40.

Schubert, W. L. "The Outlook for Inflation," *Cycles,* 40, no. 1 (1989).

*Schumpeter, Joseph. *Business Cycles.* New York: McGraw-Hill, 1939.

———. *History of Economic Analysis.* New York: Oxford University Press, 1954.

Seabury, David. *The Art of Selfishness.* New York: Pocket Books, 1964.

Selby, Mary Beth. "Downcycle Strategies." *Institutional Investor* (June 1986): pp. 215–22.

Sesit, Michael R. "U.S. Must Take Steps to Trim Deficit, Meeting of Bankers, Executives Is Told." *Wall Street Journal,* June 7, 1988, p. 35.

"A $750,000 Killing in 55 Days." *Business Week,* March 12, 1960, pp. 63–64.

Shirk, Gertrude. "Cycles in Interest Rates: Part 5." *Cycles,* 30, no. 3 (1981).

———. "Long Cycles in the Price of Silver." *Cycles,* 30, no. 7 (1979).

———. "The 4.8-Year Cycle in Stock prices." *Cycles,* 30 (1979).

———. "Total Construction—1985 Calculated Line." *Cycles,* 36, no. 1 (1985).

———. "Tracking the 54-Year Cycle in Long-Term Interest Rates." *Cycles,* 32, no. 7 (1981).

Shuman, James B., and David Rosenau. *The Kondratieff Wave.* New York: World Publishing—Times Mirror, 1972.

Sichelman, Lew. "Home Building Recovery Will Be Slow in This Decade." *San Jose Mercury News,* January 12, 1980.

———. "Single-Family Home Ownership to Grow Stronger in the 80s." *San Jose Mercury News,* January 19, 1980.

Skow, John. "When The Great Developer Became Extinct." *Saturday Evening Post,* October 8, 1966, p. 29.

Slater, Karen. "Reselling Your Limited Partnership Unit." *Wall Street Journal,* February 26, 1991, p. C1.

"Smart Money Moves into Land." *Business Week,* June 9, 1973, pp. 96, 100.

Smith, Adam. *The Money Game.* New York: Random House, 1967.

Smith, Adam. *The Wealth of Nations.* New York: The Modern Library, 1965.

Solomon, Ezra. *The Anxious Economy.* San Francisco: W. H. Freeman, 1975.

"A Spurt in Shopping Centers." *Business Week,* January 15, 1979, pp. 92, 94.

Steiger, Brad. *A Roadmap of Time.* Englewood Cliffs, NJ: Prentice-Hall, 1975.

Stern, Richard L., and Allan Sloan. "The Day the Brokers Picked Their Own Pockets." *Forbes,* November 16, 1987, pp. 32–33.

Storey, Donald R. "Stock Market and Business Forecast." *The Bank Credit Analyst,* (April 1980): 31.

Tamarkin, Bob. "Condomania in Chicago." *Forbes,* November 13, 1978, pp. 54–60.

Tanner, Louise. *All the Things We Were.* New York: Doubleday, 1978.

Teweles, Richard J., Charles V. Harlow, and Herbert L. Stone. *The Commodity Futures Game.* New York: McGraw-Hill, 1974.

———. *The Commodity Futures Trading Guide.* New York: McGraw-Hill, 1969.

"Theory Deserts the Forecasters." *Business Week,* June 29, 1974, p. 50.

Thomas, Dana. *The Money Crowd.* New York: G. P. Putnam's Sons, 1972.

Thompson, Louis M. "The 18.6-Year Cycle in the General Economy." *Cycles,* 40, no. 3 (1989).

———. "The 9.2-Year and 18.5 Year Cycles in the Stock Market." *Cycles,* 40, no. 4 (1989).

Thorning, Margo. *An Empirical Investigation of Money, Real Output and Prices over the Business Cycle, 1920–1970.* Ann Arbor, MI: University Microfilms International, 1979.

Toffler, Alvin. *Future Shock.* New York: Scribner's, 1975.

"Too Cold, Too Hot, Too Dry." *Time,* January 26, 1981.

"The Tools of Timing." *Financial Planning* (April 1988): 70.

Toy, Stewart, and Ted Holden. "Japan Buys into the American Dream." *Business Week,* November 7, 1988, p. 42.

Van Duijn, J. J. *The Long Wave in Economic Life.* London: Allen & Unwin, 1983.

*Vaughan, Frances E. *Awakening Intuition.* Garden City, NY: Anchor Books, 1979.

Volcker, Paul A. *The Rediscovery of the Business Cycle.* New York: The Free Press, 1978.

Wall, P. O. "Field Analysis in History and Economics." *Cycles,* 42, no. 1 (1991).

"Wall Street Olé!" *Time,* September 6, 1982, p. 46.

Ward, R. R. "Just How Do Cycles Affect Our Life?" *Scientific Digest* (July 1977): 14, 16.

Warren, George, and Frank Pearson. *World Prices and the Building Industry.* London: Chapman and Hill/John Wiley and Sons, 1937.

Weiss, Gary. "Barren Soil: The Outlook Remains Bleak for Farmland Prices." *Barron's,* May 6, 1985, pp. 40, 42.

Westcott, Malcolm R. *Toward a Contemporary Psychology of Intuition.* New York: Holt, Rinehart and Winston, 1966.

Wheeler, Raymond H. Reprints from *The Journal of Human Ecology,* 1951. *Cycles,* 29, nos. 1, 4, 5, 8 (1978); 30, nos. 2, 5, 8 (1979).

"Why Real Estate Is a 'Hot Item' Among Investors." *U.S. News & World Report,* July 23, 1973, pp. 46–48.

Wiedemer, John P. *Real Estate Investment.* Reston, VA: Reston Publishing, 1985.

"The Wild Speculation in California Homes." *Business Week,* May 2, 1977, pp. 31–32.

Williams, David. "Gold, Oil and Inflation." *Cycles,* 35, no. 2 (1984).

———. "Historic Survey of Inflation." *Cycles,* 35, no. 7 (1984).

———. "Historical Survey—Interest Rates." *Cycles,* 35, no. 5 (1984).

Willoughby, Jack. "The Best in the Business." *Financial World,* February 5, 1991, pp. 32–36.

Wilson, Louise L. *Catalogue of Cycles.* Pittsburgh: Foundation for the Study of Cycles, 1964.

"Winners and Losers in the Real Estate Game." *Business Week,* December 23, 1972, p. 92.

Wiseman, Thomas. *The Money Motive.* New York: Random House, 1974.

Wysocki, Bernard. "The New Boom Towns." *Wall Street Journal,* March 27, 1989, pp. B1, B2.

Zahorchak, Michael. *Climate: The Key to Understanding Business Cycles.* Linden, NJ: Tide Press, 1988.

Zanker, A. "Why an Old Theory of Economic Ups and Downs Worries the West: Theory of N. D. Kondratieff." *U.S. News & World Report,* November 6, 1978.

Index

G

H

I

J

K

L

M

S